I0810286

IMAGES
of America

MONTAGUE

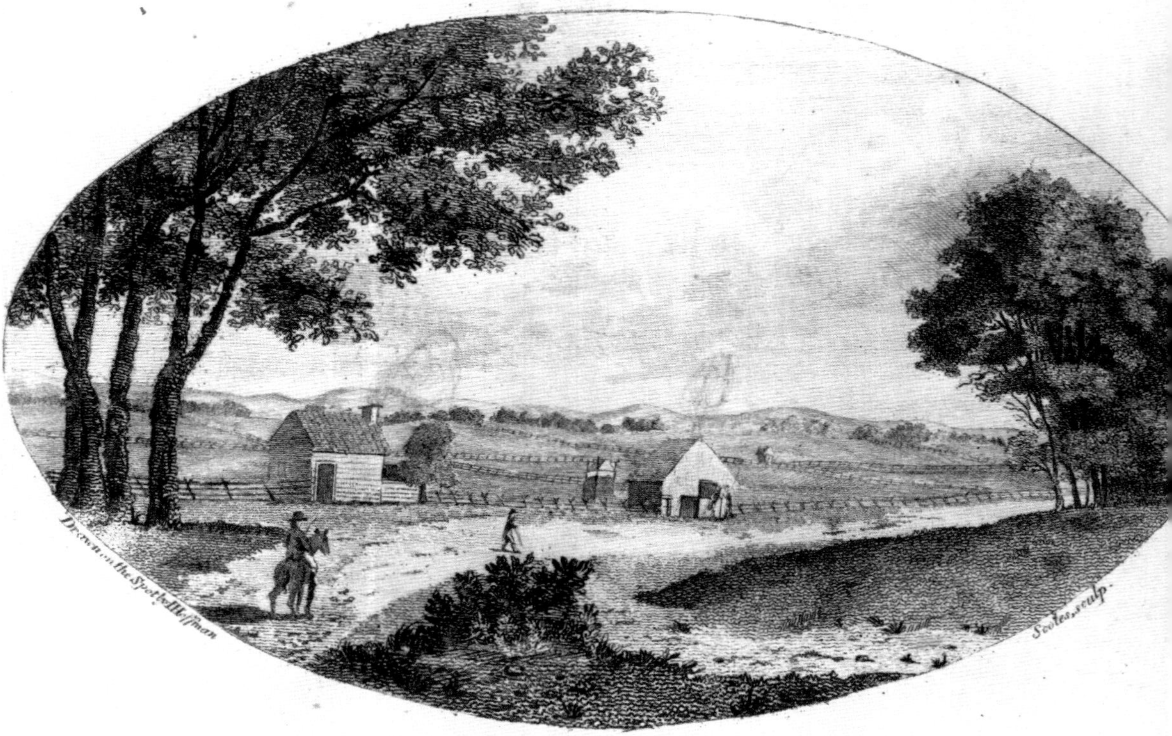

A View, at Minisink, New-Jersey.

A View, at Minisink, New-Jersey was illustrated in the June 1794 *New York Magazine*, noting, "Drawn on the spot by I. Hoffman" and "Scoles, sculp." John Scoles was known as an engraver and bookseller from New York City. While a township by that name never existed in New Jersey, the area that became Montague was identified as Minisink through Revolutionary War pension records and likely caused this identification.

On the cover: This photograph of the Clove School No. 7 was taken on May 21, 1891. It was apparently a special occasion, as evidenced by the flowers worn and the vase in the window. The young woman wearing a dark-colored dress near the doorway is identified as Ella Dutton in other Montague Association for Restoration of Community History photographs. She may have been a student or a teacher's assistant to the woman to the left of her. (Courtesy of the Montague Association for Restoration of Community History.)

IMAGES
of America

MONTAGUE

Alicia C. Batko

ARCADIA
PUBLISHING

ISBN 978-0-7385-6454-8

Published by Arcadia Publishing
Charleston, South Carolina

Printed in the United States of America

Library of Congress Control Number: 2008938841

For all general information contact Arcadia Publishing at:
Telephone 843-853-2070
Fax 843-853-0044
E-mail sales@arcadiapublishing.com
For customer service and orders:
Toll-Free 1-888-313-2665

Visit us on the Internet at www.arcadiapublishing.com

To the people of Montague, past and present.
For all that has been and for all that has yet to come.

Contents

ACKNOWLEDGMENTS

This endeavor was possible because Roman and Aurelia Szlosowski gave me life and inspiration, and my family allowed me to pursue my passion for research. I especially thank my husband, Tony, who along with Tim and Chris offered me the love and patience needed. The members of the Montague Association for Restoration of Community History (MARCH) encouraged and entrusted me with the responsibility for compiling this initial volume about Montague's heritage. Beth Jones graciously proofed the copy, while cheering me on.

Sincere thanks to those who mentored, shared, and inspired me along this journey: Robert Longcore; Mead Stapler; Peter Osborne; Minisink Valley Historical Society volunteers; Jennie Sweetman; Miriam Carpenter; Nancy Shukaitis; Richard Stevens; departed friends Roger King and Jack Decker; staff of Delaware Water Gap National Recreation Area (DEWA), Tom Solon, John Wright, and Sue Kopczynski; Dennis Bertland; Richard Veit; Ken Sandri; Pat Condrell; Fred Assmus; John Kraft; Bob Craig; Donald Montaverde; Joseph Rich; Mark Hendrickson; New Jersey Frontier Guard; 15th New Jersey Civil War reenactors; John Newcomer; the Society for Industrial Archeology and Irene Prokop of *Milford Magazine* for encouraging initial writing efforts; the inspiration of author Pali Jae Lee; my faith-filled friends; Arcadia authors Matthew Osterberg, Laura Obisco, and Brian J. Lewis for reassuring me this would be doable; and my editor, Erin Rocha, who walked me through the process.

Many residents helped provide information: Roberta and Beryle Herman, Joanna Muhlbeck, Bob and Flora Myers, Betsy Reinhardt, Cordelia Cafone, Beverly Benson, Helen Gassman, Ronald Hartrim, Duke and Loren Mortimer, Lina Scheidegger, the Thompsons, members of St. James and Minisink Reformed Churches, and members of Montague Grange and the Montague Volunteer Fire Department, along with past residents or descendants Benjamin Roberts, Marjorie Cole Shay, Tina Westbrook, Vickie Corbett, Douglas Westfall, Richard White, Janet Boernhoft, David Armstrong, Ann Croston, James Heim, Rolland Everitt, James Nelden, and others. Thank you for allowing me to tell your story.

This volume was created to help commemorate both the township's 250th and the historical society's 30th anniversaries in 2009. Unless otherwise noted, all images appear courtesy of MARCH. Image rights were released to the author. All other use is prohibited without direct permission.

INTRODUCTION

Nestled in the northwest corner of the state of New Jersey, with a current population of more than 3,000 and sandwiched between federal and state property, sits the rural township of Montague. Many residents commute to jobs nearby or at greater distances, reached by Interstate 84 or by connecting with Interstate 80. Travelers heading for the Poconos catch a passing glimpse of the town, just before crossing the bridge to enter Milford, Pennsylvania. Those stopping to refuel at the cluster of gas stations off Interstate 84, or pausing to enjoy the view from High Point, miss the central portion of town. Few people, aside from longtime area residents, have an idea of how the town became what it is today or what it was before.

As with any locale, the town holds a history that preceded its formation. The highlands of the Kittatinny/Shawungunk Range and the adjoining Delaware River valley surround Montague and hint at the region's evolution through the geology visible today. The early name given to the valley, Minisink, has been credited to an Algonquin phrase meaning "land from which water is gone." It is believed that, at one time, much of this land was covered with water until it broke through and left the existing landscape. At some stage a glacial moraine had affected the surface, leaving sandy pockets amid rock-strewn slopes. By the late 1800s, geological surveys conducted by the State of New Jersey documented the presence of significant local rock formations. Corniferous limestone was found, along with a prolific variety of lower Heidelberg limestone, which appeared in the forms of coralline, knotty, cherty, Manlius, and Pentamerus. There was also the shale of Oriskany sandstone, the red slaty rock of Medina sandstone, and Marcellus shale. Shell marl and many fossils were found. All of these, noted as being from Montague, were documented and exhibited at a centennial exhibition held in Philadelphia in 1876. Still geologically significant is the highest point in the state, aptly named High Point, and the highest body of water, Lake Marcia.

The river valley attracted both native people and the early explorers and traders who followed well-worn trails, possibly initiated by migratory animals. Hunters today continue to watch for and follow deer trails in a similar fashion. Archaeologists have found evidence of human occupation at various archaeological sites in the area that date from the prehistoric period, as early as 10,000 BC. Trails used by the Lenape people converged in Montague and linked the area by land and shallow river crossings to what later evolved as separate neighboring states. Along its western flank flows the Delaware River. It was called Lenapewihittuck, or river of the Lenape. The Dutch knew it as the Zuydt or South River, being thus named to mark the southernmost reach of the New Netherland colony. It would be renamed by the British for Lord de la Warr, for whom the current title is based upon. The river also ties the town closely to Pennsylvania and New York, where it originates. Prior to defined Colonial and state boundaries, the river was a uniting element in the Minisink valley and served as a means of transportation. The Trade Path or Old Esopus Road, a Native American trail that took on the legendary name of Old Mine Road, came from Kingston, New York, and paralleled the river. Along it arose a succession of early Colonial settlements starting by the Hudson River in New York, moving into New Jersey through the town, and ending at its southern terminus in Pahaquarra.

The Dutch, as the earliest known settlers, established the first churches, schools, and burial grounds. A village, named Minisink, overlapped southern Montague and northern Sandyston Townships. It adjoined Minisink Island, near which sat the chief council point of the Minsi tribe of the Lenape. In these early Colonial settlements, rustic local schools produced those who would shape the community and the nation. The local Dutch Reformed congregation formed in 1737. Prior to that, itinerant ministers from Kingston, New York, had attended to local settlers' needs, as reflected in church records since 1695. The Minisink church was one of four buildings erected by that denomination in neighborhoods throughout the Delaware valley. As the population increased and new emigrant groups came, other churches and denominations developed. Following the example of native burial grounds, land was set aside for such purpose by the colonists. Large property owners also dedicated family plots for that use on their land.

Along the river, settlers utilized the shore along both sides for farming and grazing. Ferries would transport both people and goods across the Delaware, while rafters floated logs and commercial products downstream toward Trenton and Philadelphia. From lush forests, pine and hemlock were shipped to naval shipyards. The supply of virgin timber fueled the development of towns and cities—both locally and downstream.

The territory of Montague was caught in many a tug-of-war, as the issue of setting boundaries and borders developed when colonies and state governments sought to define areas of jurisdiction. East and West Jersey's border fluctuated, and a contested legal dispute arose in defining the boundary line with New York. Its citizens withstood raids during the French and Indian War and a constant threat to the frontier during the Revolutionary War. Once the new nation's freedom was secured, wooden frame dwellings quickly replaced the earliest log and stone houses. Taverns and hostelries emerged, such as the Brick House Hotel that dated from the mid-1700s. Local tradesmen and small shops thrived around this hub of activity, as well as at Tappentown by the New York state border, and at Millville. A succession of grist- and sawmills serviced residents through the early 1900s, with many located along Shimer's or Chamber's Mill Brook, giving that particular section its Millville name.

Montague is in a tristate corner, abutting Pennsylvania and New York. Geographically, the township was long considered an "over the mountain" town, set off from the rest of New Jersey by its location beyond Culver's Gap and being sheltered by the Appalachian chain. The greater ease of travel to its adjoining states favored a development of trade and commerce connections. As the emerging nation grew and roads were promoted for ease of travel, turnpikes were chartered and bridges built. The Morris, the Union, the Paterson-Hamburg, and the Colesville-Carpenter's Point Turnpikes crisscrossed the town. Stagecoaches shuttled businessmen and travelers in from the larger cities. Up until 1841, the main route between New York City and western New York State's lake country went right past the Brick House Hotel. Nearby, stages crossed the Delaware River to continue on the Milford-Owego Turnpike, a Pennsylvania route in which New Jersey held stock at the time. Two prominent local men, Jacob Hornbeck and Isaac Bonnell, would become officers to the Delaware Bridge Company and further served as state legislators. Another native son, William Bross, became lieutenant governor in Illinois and participated as a pallbearer at Abraham Lincoln's funeral.

The national push for expansion and industrial development brought the Delaware and Hudson Canal to nearby Port Jervis by 1828, followed by the Erie Railroad in 1851. There was even some consideration given to having a railroad line run through Montague. To take advantage of transportation routes nearby, local businessmen relocated to those areas of commercial growth, thus leaving the township a predominantly agricultural community. Townspeople remained resourceful and utilized what the locale offered. Limestone was quarried and burned in stone kilns and its product used in tanning, for making plaster, and to improve the soil. Railroad ties were cut from area timber and used on the Erie line. Streams were dammed, creating ponds where ice could be harvested and even fish farming attempted. The highest location in the state quickly became a popular tourist destination, when High Point Inn opened. Other hotels and boardinghouses sprang up along the riverfront, and people came to enjoy nature's vistas and partake of a locally harvested bounty. Pine Cliff Lodge overlooked the river, as did the Rock View Hotel. Both attracted guests from New York City. The Rock View Hotel would expand and offer seasonal recreation and attract skiers, along with High Point Park.

From the Civil War era through to the middle of the 20th century, Montague remained a farming community where crops were grown, and poultry and dairy farms dotted the landscape. The Montague Grange, which formed in 1904, became a central place where residents gathered for functions in addition to serving as a forum for the farmers. Large farmhouses became boarding homes to handle the overflow of the hotel guests during the summer and helped the small community sustain itself. It was not uncommon for those more affluent to visit. Some who enjoyed the area's serenity would acquire property as country retreats. City dwellers were enticed toward rural escapes such as Mashipacong Club. Heiress Doris Duke would purchase that property and in 1939 through her foundation welcomed Life Magazine Camp to expand its outdoor education work on her nearly 1,000-acre tract. A National Camp training center would open there and evolve into Trail Blazers Camp by 1953. It continues to serve disadvantaged city children in a decentralized camp setting in a partnership with Nature Conservancy.

The 20th century brought further change. River Road was surveyed for the possibility of becoming Delaware Drive, linking Trenton and Port Jervis. In 1929, High Point Monument was built on land dedicated in 1923 for a state park. Clove Road realigned at its northern end, bringing the removal of the Duttonville Hotel and homes near it. Following both world wars, infrastructure changes further affected the community. A replacement of the old Milford-Montague Bridge in 1953 forced the removal of the Brick House Hotel and the relocation of an adjoining farm. The town's remnant one-room schoolhouses were consolidated into a new three-room school building on State Route 31, now U.S. Route 206. The men of the volunteer fire company undertook the building of a firehouse. Numerous gas stations arose with the advent of increasing automobile traffic, and, as the popularity of farming declined, large parcels were sold off for newer uses. Holiday Lake was created, and a vacation- and recreation-based community grew around a golf course.

The introduction of Interstate 84 by the New York border, after the modification of Route 23, impacted further change. Judd's Ice House closed, and that section witnessed the opening of the Tri-State Mall with a Jamesway department store and a Shoprite supermarket. Plans began to evolve for creating a dammed reservoir at Tocks Island on the Delaware River, and land acquisitions were initiated under the Army Corps of Engineers in the 1960s. As a result, many of the oldest homes were acquired and long-established families uprooted. The project stalled when the Vietnam War diverted government funds, and mounting opposition found the dam unsuitable. The townspeople witnessed the vacated homes being bulldozed, vandalized, or subject to arson. What remained was transferred to the National Park Service and became the Delaware Water Gap National Recreation Area, which had been originally planned to surround the reservoir, providing varied opportunities to enjoy the outdoors.

Montague lost its village of Brick House, and Duttonville was transformed into a commercial strip as a result of the changes imposed. The Holiday Lake community evolved into a growing development dotted with condominiums and homes. What resulted throughout was an eclectic mix of old and new. To help preserve surviving aspects of the township's heritage a historical society, known as the Montague Association for Restoration of Community History (MARCH), formed in 1979. It is largely through the efforts of that group, and the work initiated by its charter members, that the information presented in this book is possible.

One

In the Beginning

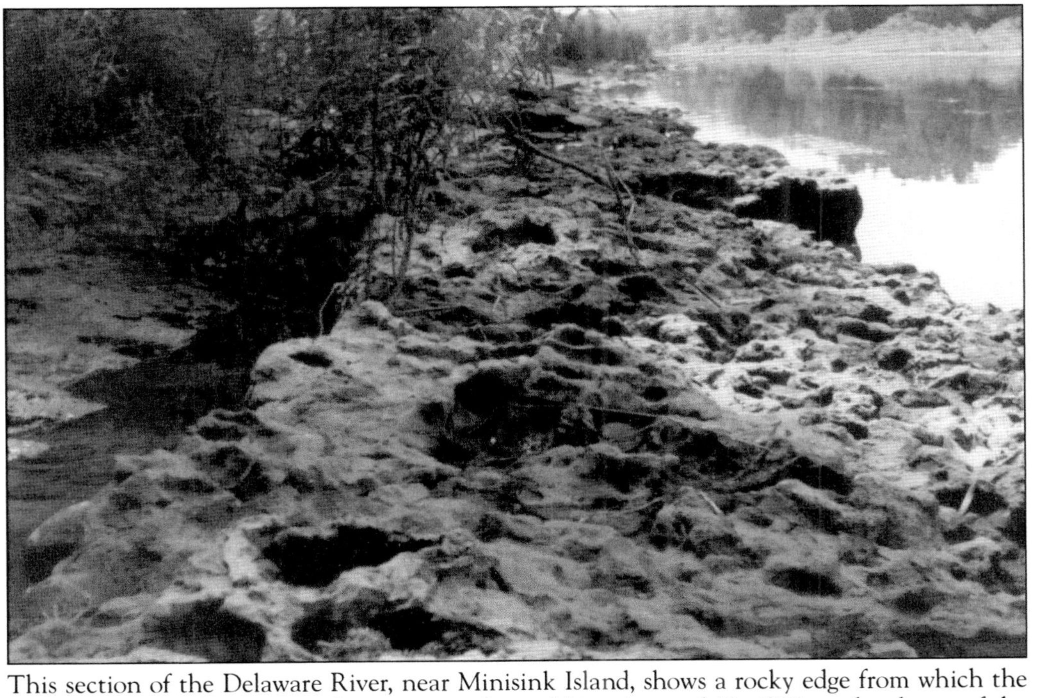

This section of the Delaware River, near Minisink Island, shows a rocky edge from which the river currents or the passage of canoes or rafts could be observed. By 1719, settlers knew of the area just above this as Shippekunk and would identify it as two miles or so northward of Great Minisink Island, according to the papers of John Jay held by the New-York Historical Society. (Courtesy of Joan Forster Erb.)

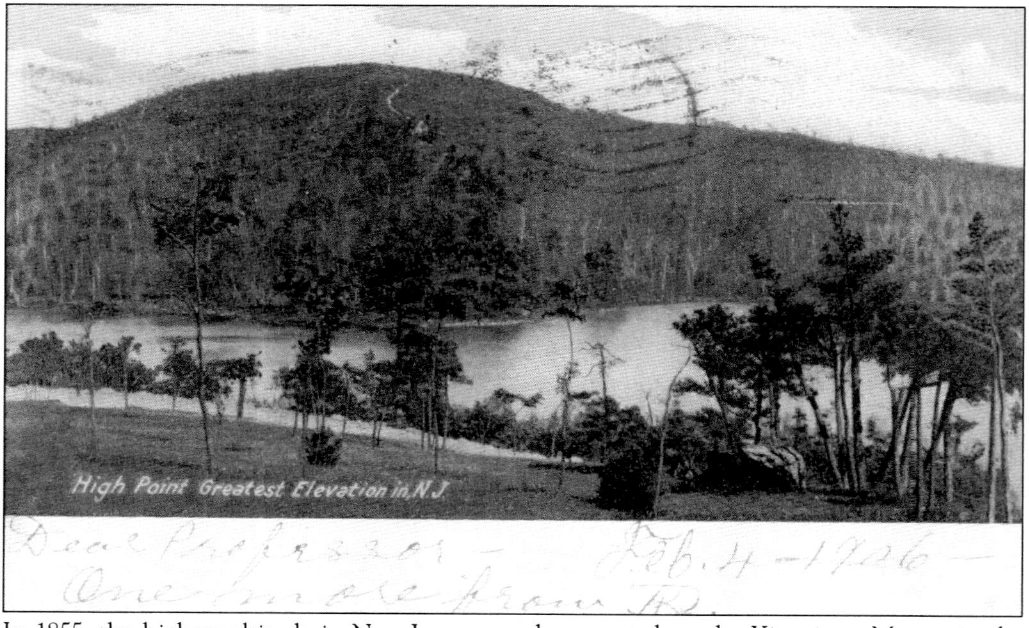

In 1855, the highest altitude in New Jersey was documented on the Kittatinny Mountains by Dr. William Kitchell, who labeled it High Point—a name associated with it since. Kittatinny is a word derived from the Lenape native language meaning "endless hill" or "great mountain." It signifies the range that is part of the Ridge and Valley Province of the Appalachian Mountains, which span from New York to Maryland. (Courtesy of Alicia C. Batko.)

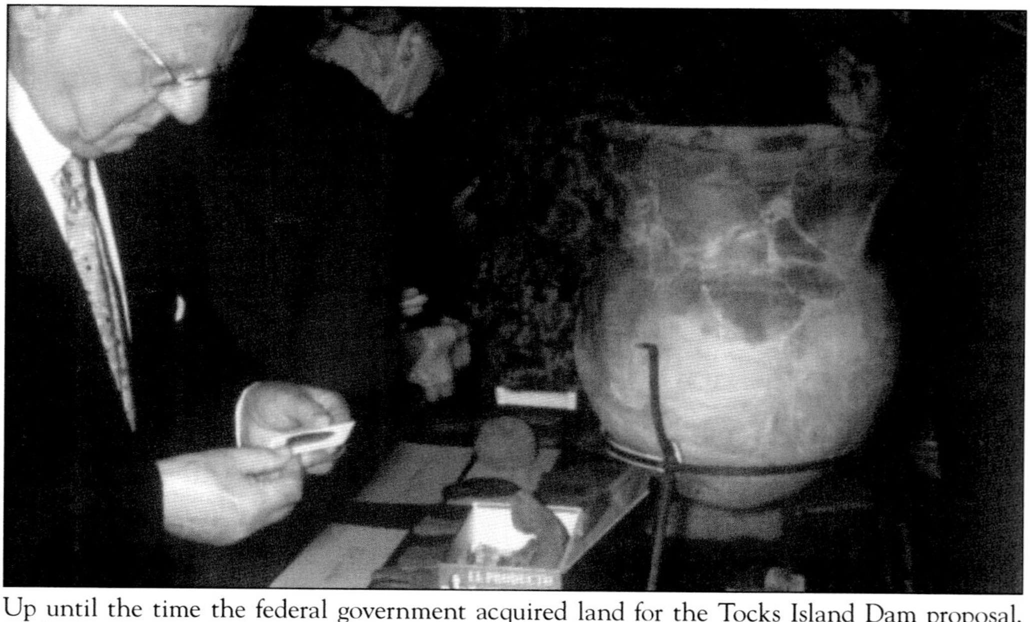

Up until the time the federal government acquired land for the Tocks Island Dam proposal, evidence was sought about the Munsee tribe of the Lenape nation. Archaeological investigations were conducted and artifacts recovered by George Heye, William Ritchie, Vernon Leslie, Herbert Kraft, and others. Native pottery was reassembled from the broken fragments found, and those items were put on display.

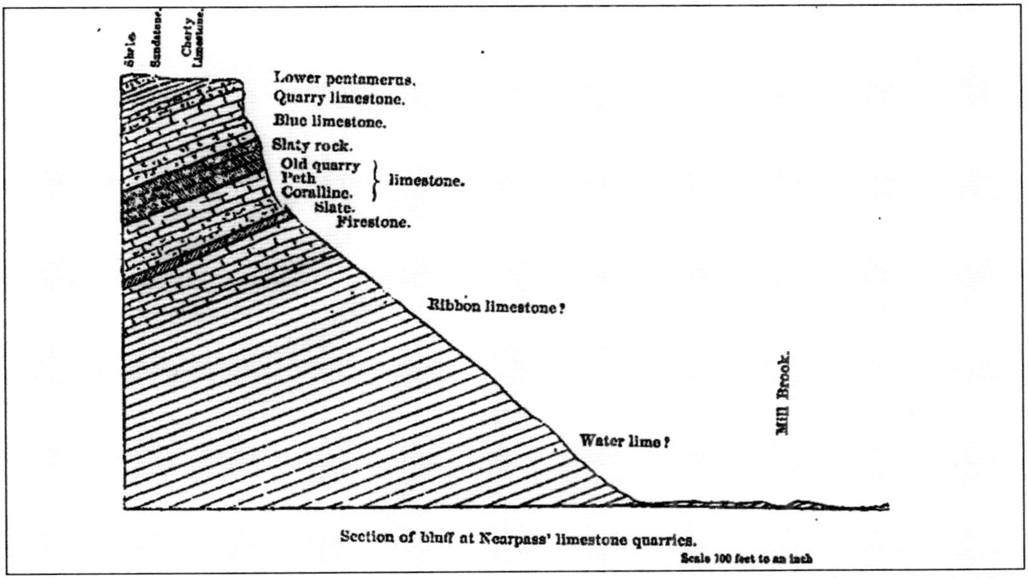

Limestone is very prominent throughout Montague Township. This diagram from an 1868 New Jersey Geological Survey study identifies the layers of strata within the Nearpass quarry bluff located between Clove and River Roads. It was an area of much study and analysis and was written up extensively in geological reports. Varied fossils were also found to be abundant throughout the township. Both Sanford and William Nearpass ran quarries that bordered the bluff. (Courtesy of New Jersey Department of Environmental Protection, New Jersey Geological Survey.)

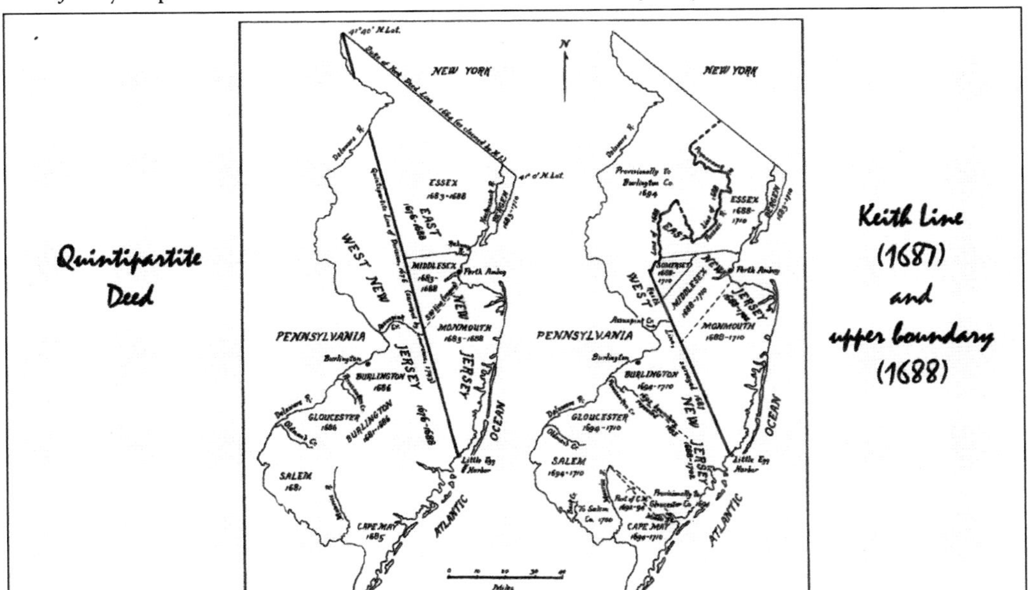

New Jersey was established in 1664 and soon after was divided into East and West Jersey. The Quintpartite Deed placed the northwest corner of the colony under East Jersey jurisdiction in 1676 and within Essex County until 1688. When the line shifted, all the territory of Montague fell into West Jersey and was placed under Burlington County in 1694. (Courtesy of New Jersey State Archives, Department of State.)

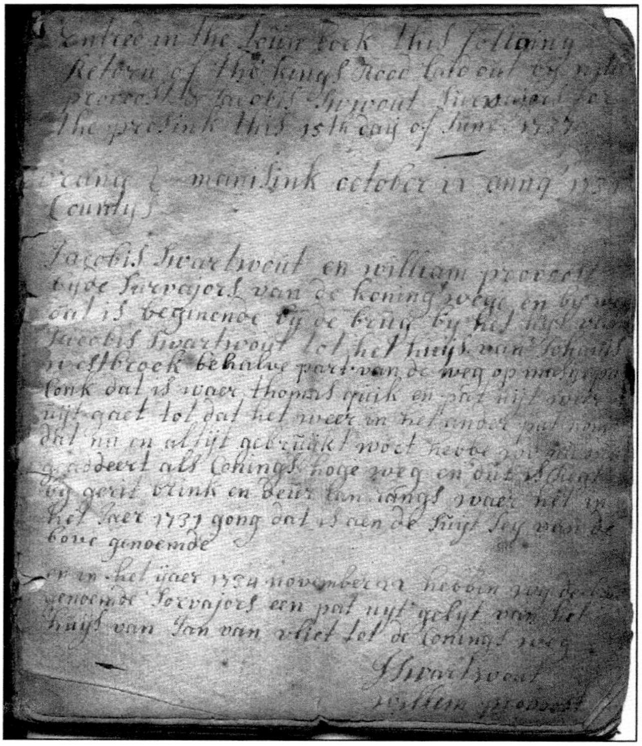

A road return appears in the Minisink/Montague town book for the Kings Road. The description is written in Dutch as surveyed by Jacobis Swartwout and William Provoost in June 1737. Thomas Quik, Johanis Westbrcek, and Gerit Brink, who settled along the river, are named, and a mention is made of the road passing through Masyepacunk. (Courtesy of Minisink Valley Historical Society.)

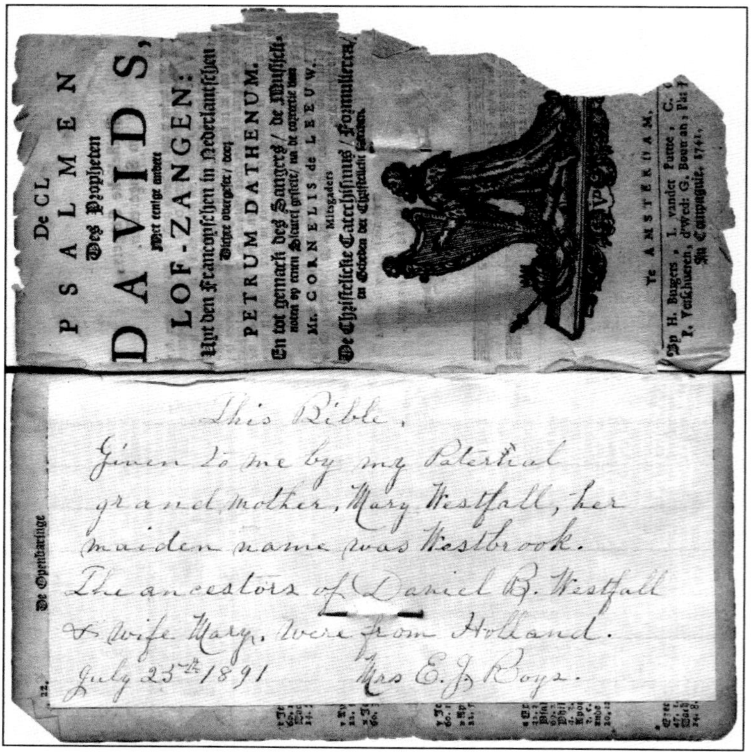

The image is of a page from a Dutch Bible, printed in 1741, that belonged to the family of Daniel B. Westfall. The note accompanying it reads, "This Bible. Given to me by my Paternal grandmother, Mary Westfall, her maiden name was Westbrook. The ancestors of Daniel B. Westfall & wife, Mary, were from Holland." His home was situated on the southwestern end of the township. (Courtesy of Douglas Westfall.)

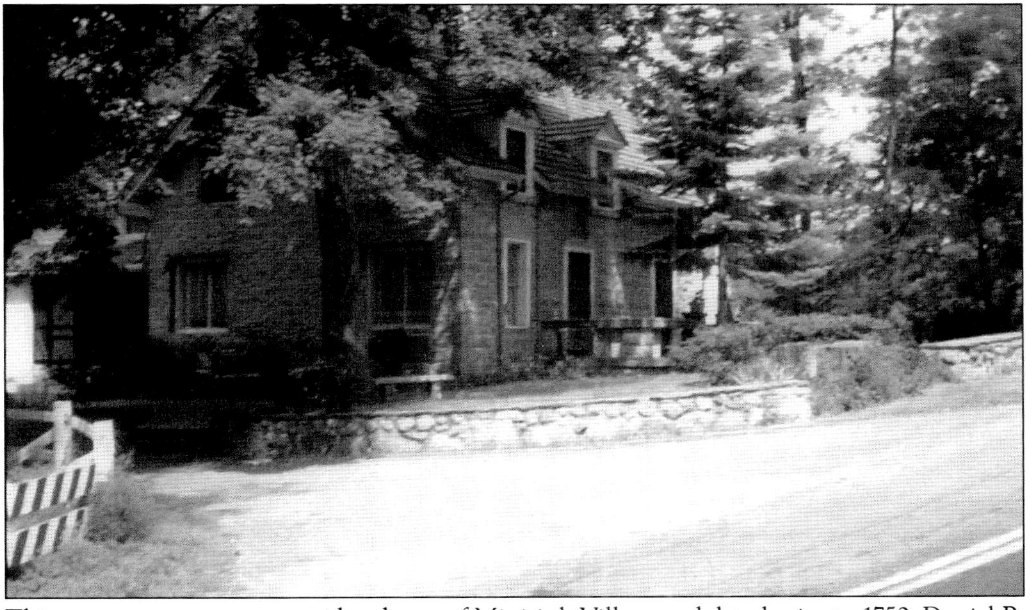

This stone structure was considered part of Minisink Village and dated prior to 1750. Daniel B. Westfall resided here, as did the Everitt family, some of whom are buried nearby along with members from the DePue and Westbrook families. It was alleged to contain a tunnel connection to the nearby stream. Aspects of the house had been remodeled, and it was demolished during the Tocks Island Dam period. (Courtesy of Jane Brace.)

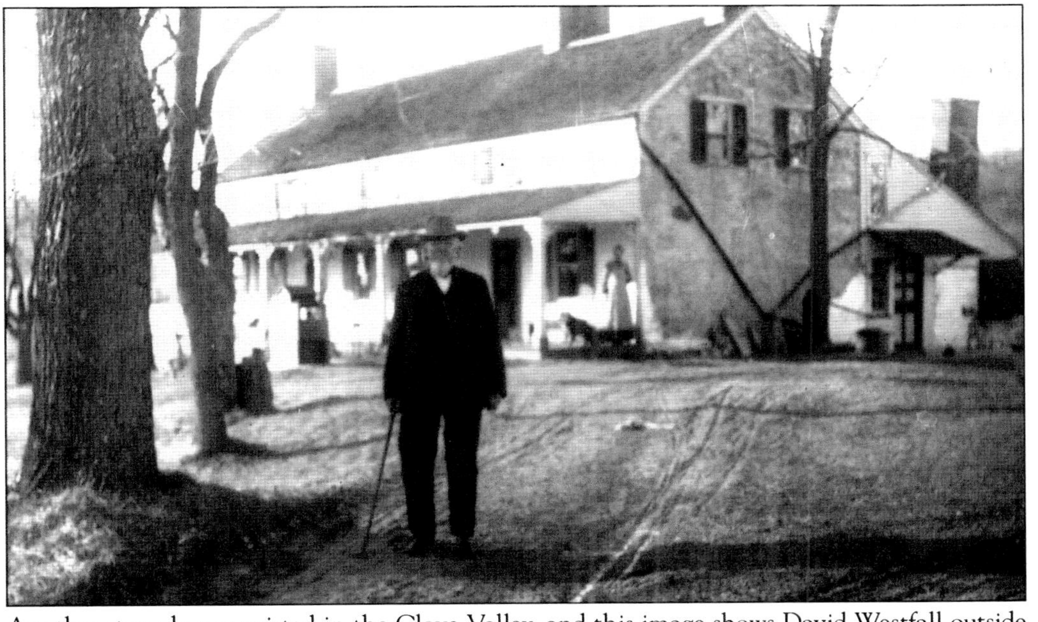

Another stone house existed in the Clove Valley, and this image shows David Westfall outside it. The original portion of his home is shown, which is believed to have been built before the Revolutionary War. The house has since been added on to, but the property still proudly bears the family name and is the current site of Westfall Winery. (Courtesy of Minisink Valley Historical Society.)

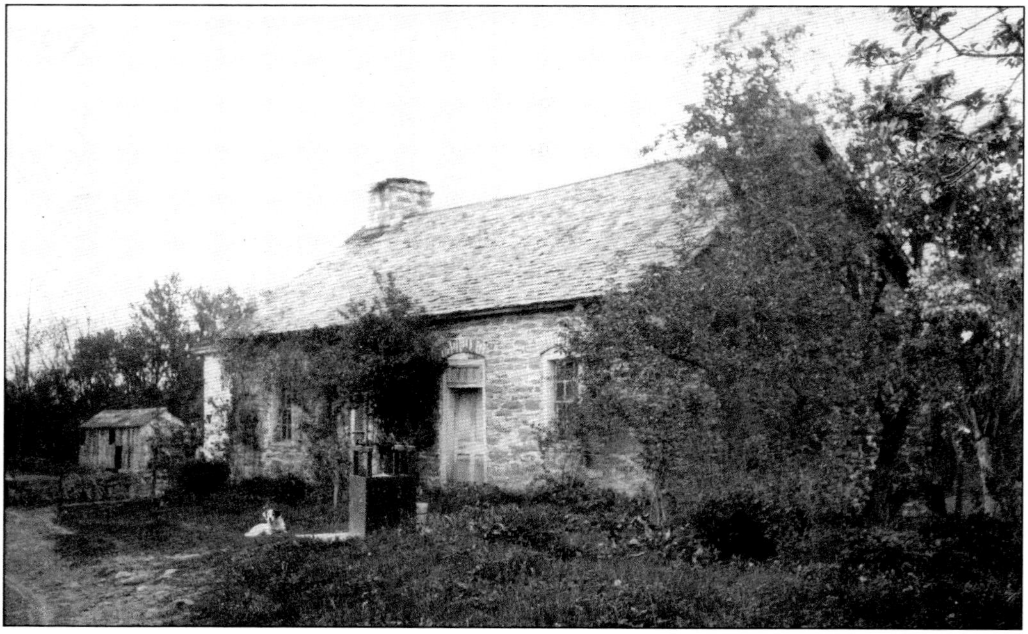

This stone house sat near the Bennekill and belonged to Isaac Van Auken, whose brothers had settled along both sides of the Delaware River. Isaac's son, Jacobus (James), and his wife lived here and along with their slaves were buried in a graveyard lot on a sand hill nearby. The white clapboard portion, visible on the left side, survives, although hidden under a cedar shake–shingled home. (Courtesy of Minisink Valley Historical Society.)

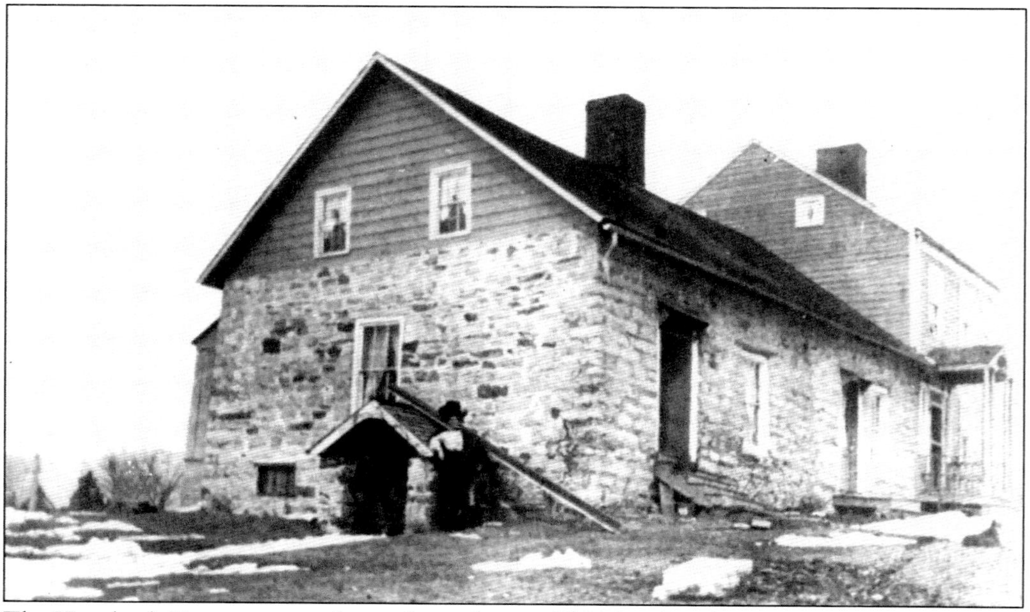

The Hornbeck Tavern once welcomed travelers on Old Mine Road. It was here that Tom Quick allegedly escaped his captors and crossed the river farther downstream to reach Pennsylvania. The original stone portion was removed in the 1900s, and the rest of the home was demolished due to the Tocks Island proposal. (Courtesy of Minisink Valley Historical Society.)

Dated to the mid-18th century, this chair is credited as having been made by Jacob Nearpass of Montague. Jacob resided on upper Clove Road. He went to Germany to attend to family estate matters, expecting to get gold and silver, but returned only with two guns. His son, Baltus, used one in the battle of Minisink. Jacob is buried at the Machackemeck Burying Ground in Port Jervis. (Courtesy of Chipstone Foundation.)

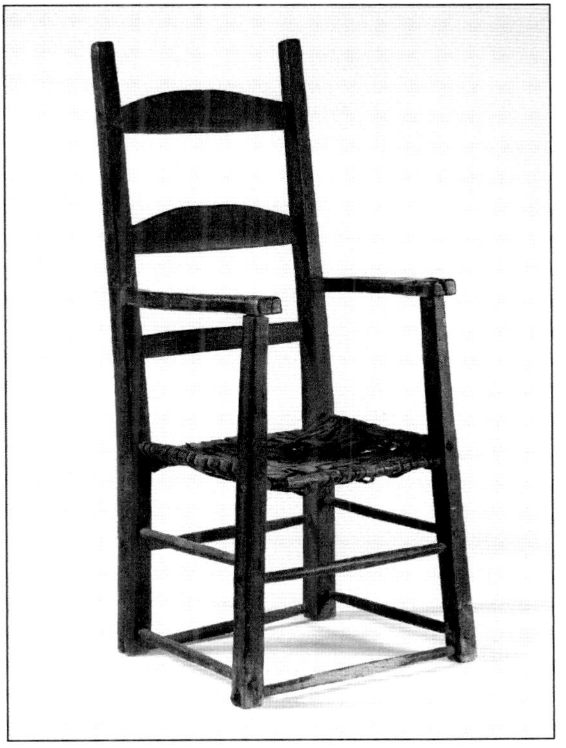

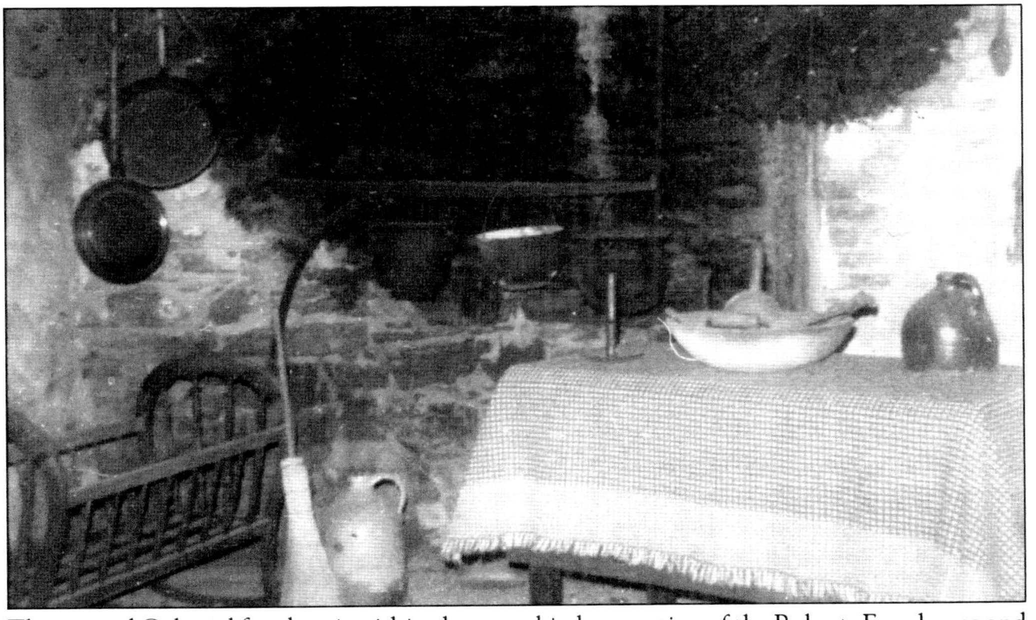

This typical Colonial fireplace is within the stone kitchen portion of the Roberts Farmhouse and was photographed for a Christmas mailing created for Robert, Ruth Ann, and Hobart Roberts. Members of the Roberts family were the last residents at Hickory Hill Farm on U.S. Route 206, before it was bought out by the government for the Tocks Island Dam project. The farm is on the New Jersey Register of Historic Places. (Courtesy of Richard Jones.)

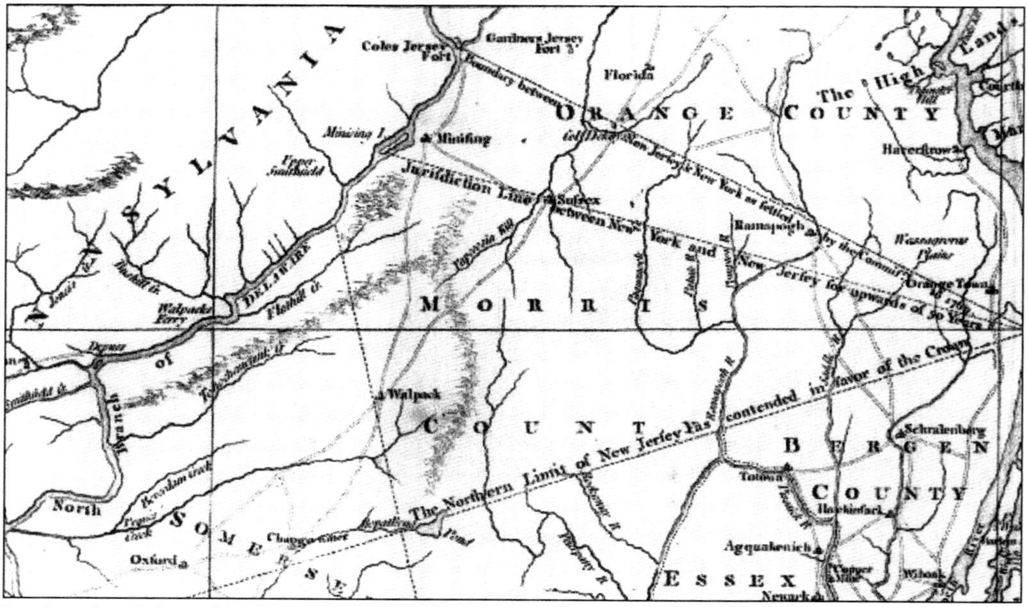

In this detail from "A New and Accurate Map of the Present Seat of War in North America" from London's 1777 *Universal* magazine, New York's attempted boundary lines are indicated. Montague's territory was once within Morris County, New Jersey. New York held control over the area labeled as Minising, although Cole's Fort and Gardner's were established through the Jersey Colony. (Courtesy of Library of Congress, Geography and Map Division.)

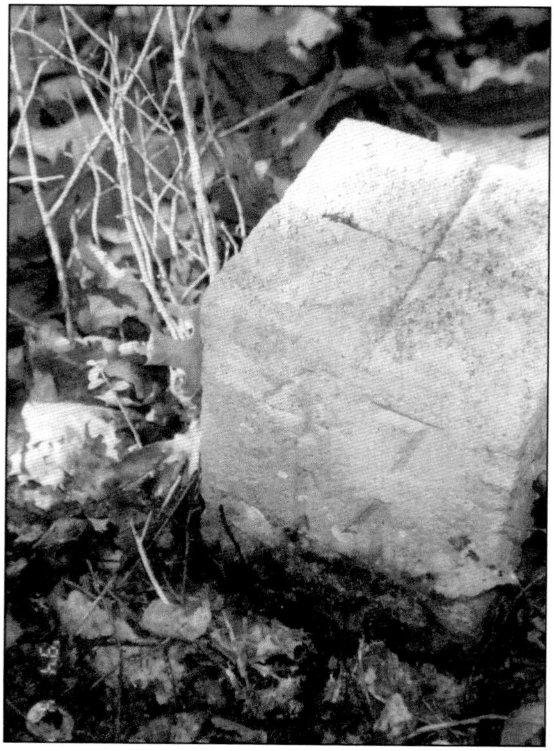

Interspersed along the state border, after the boundary dispute was resolved in 1769, are 48 stone monuments engraved with "NJ" on one side and "NY" on the other. The original markers were set in 1774 to memorialize the boundary and their positions later reconfirmed. This one is milestone 47 and was set in 1882. (Photograph by Alicia C. Batko.)

Tri-State Rock indicates the place where the three states of New Jersey, New York, and Pennsylvania unite. This granite slab was placed in 1882 and located at the extreme southern tip of Carpenter's Point north of the physical boundary. This is the junction where the Neversink or Machockemack and the Delaware or Fishkill Rivers converge. (Courtesy of Alicia C. Batko.)

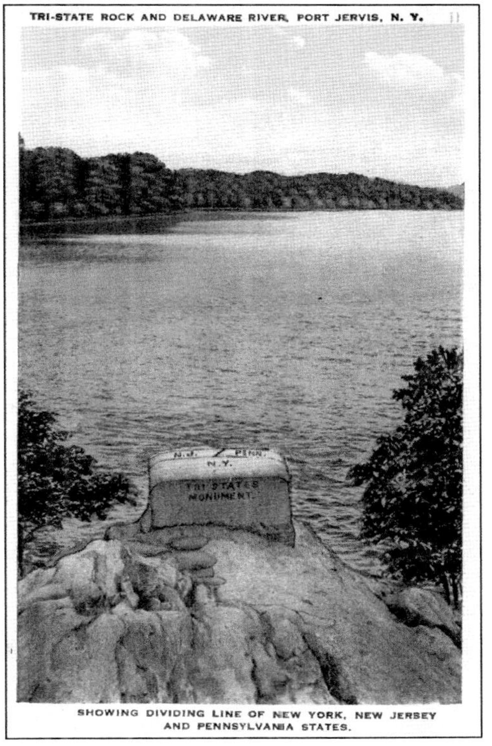

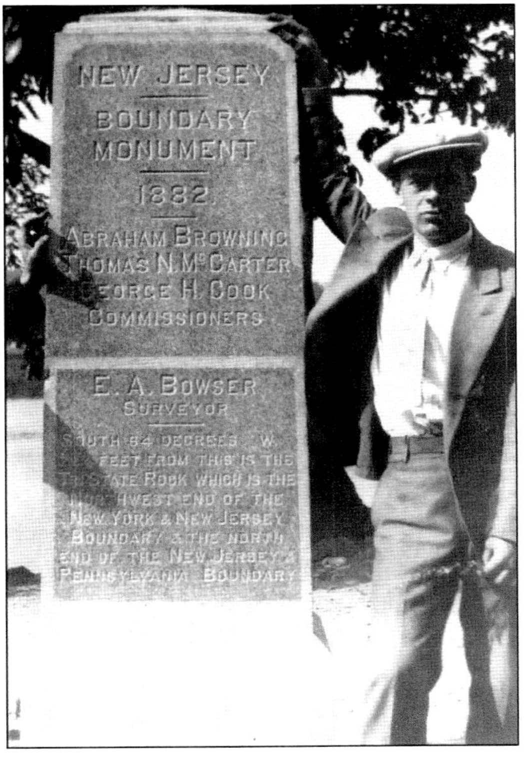

The polished granite Western State Line Monument is considered a witness monument to the marker for the actual border. It was placed in 1882 and sits 72.25 feet north of the actual boundary and in New York State. Interstate 84 currently spans the Delaware River over this location.

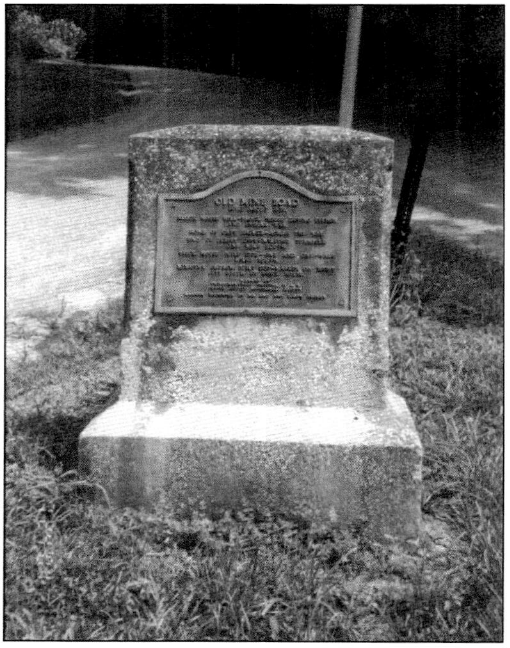

Through the efforts of Amelia Stickney Decker and her husband, markers were placed along Old Mine Road to preserve in memory for future generations the known places of historic interest. The marker, located at the intersection of Millville and River Roads, indicates, "Block House Hill—Block House during French and Indian War." (Photograph by Alicia C. Batko.)

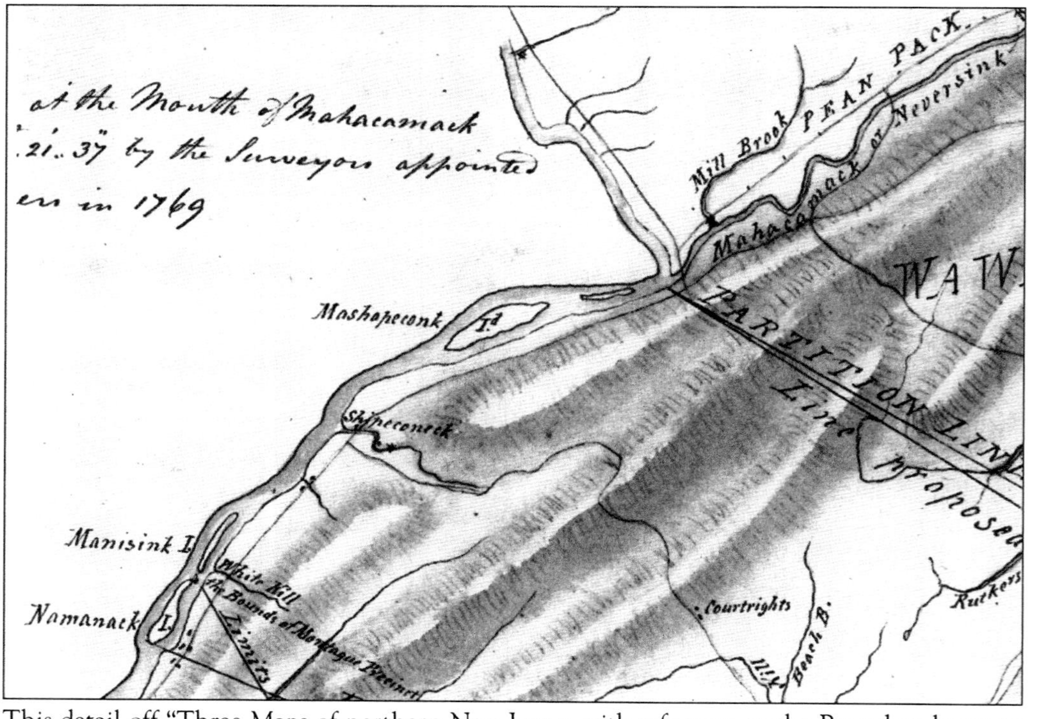

This detail off "Three Maps of northern New Jersey, with reference to the Boundary between New York and New Jersey" was created after Montague Precinct was created in 1759, with the Neversink River identified as the Mahacamack. Shipeconeck is shown near Shimer's Brook. It was also recorded on other maps of the era as Masheepycunk or by spelling variations thereof. (Courtesy of Library of Congress, Geography and Map Division.)

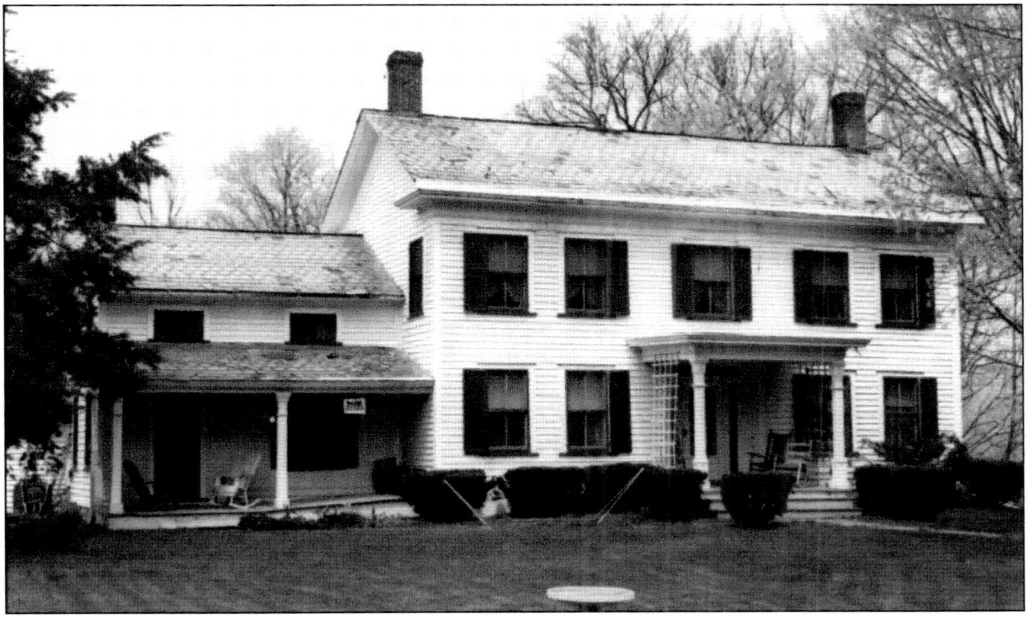

In 1872, Joseph Shimer built this on the foundation of a former structure where an infamous massacre had occurred. A Revolutionary War–era raiding party scalped members of the Jobs family here. This was a boardinghouse known as Millbrook Farm, after Irvine DeRemer acquired it in 1945. The house sits within the Millville Historic and Archaeological District of the Delaware Water Gap National Recreation Area. (Courtesy of National Park Service/DEWA.)

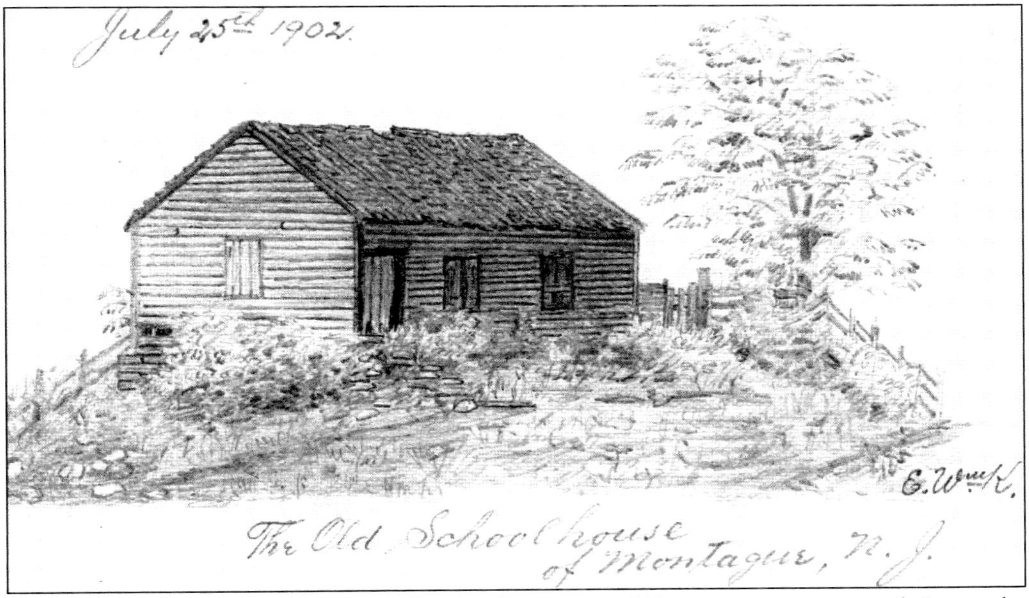

"E. Wm. K." penciled *The Old Schoolhouse of Montague, N.J.* on a penny postcard. It may be the structure that some referred to as the little red schoolhouse or another one that sat among the laurels in Millville. Those were abandoned when only the Church and the Clove Schools on Clove Road and the River and the Brick House Schools on River Road remained in use. (Courtesy of Alicia C. Batko.)

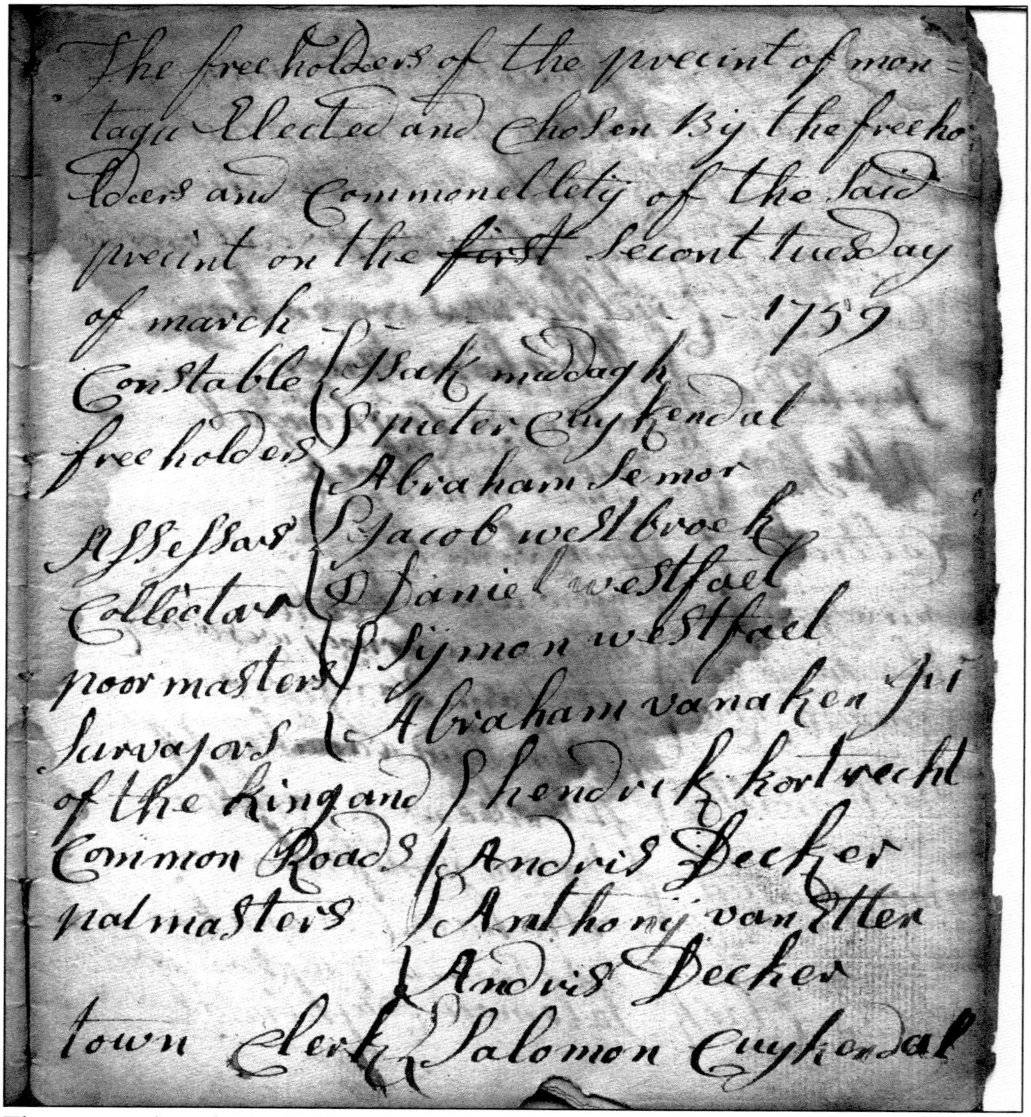
The freeholders of the precint of mon-
tague Elected and Chosen By the freeho-
lders and Commonellety of the said
precint on the ~~first~~ Second tuesday
of march — 1759
Constable { Isack middagh
freeholders { pieter Cuykendal
{ Abraham Semor
Assessars { Jacob westbroek
Collectar { Daniel westfael
poor masters { Symon westfael
{ Abraham vanaken Jr
Survayors of the king and Common Roads { hendrick kortrecht
{ Andris Decker
palmasters { Anthony van Etten
{ Andris Decker
town Clerk { Salomon Cuykendal

This memorializes the freeholders who served the newly formed precinct of Montague. The page is from the record book of Minisink Precinct and Montague Township, spanning the period from 1734 to 1782. Some early settlers named are Middagh, Cuykendal, Semor, Westbroek, Westfael, VanAken, Kortrecht, Decker, and Van Etten. In March 1759, Abraham VanCampen and other citizens of Sussex County petitioned for the formation of a new township beginning "at the mouth of a brook near the lower end of the little Minisink island, run up to its source and thence in a direct line to Jeremiah Kettle's house, thence on the same source to top of Pahoqualin mountain, thence northeasterly along the top of that mountain to the York line, thence along that line to the Mingaupack river, thence down the same to the Delaware river, and thence down the same to the beginning." The wording was revised to "the York line where it first touches it, until the same comes to the station point at the river Delaware, thence down that river to the beginning." (Courtesy of Minisink Valley Historical Society.)

Two

TRISTATE CONNECTIONS

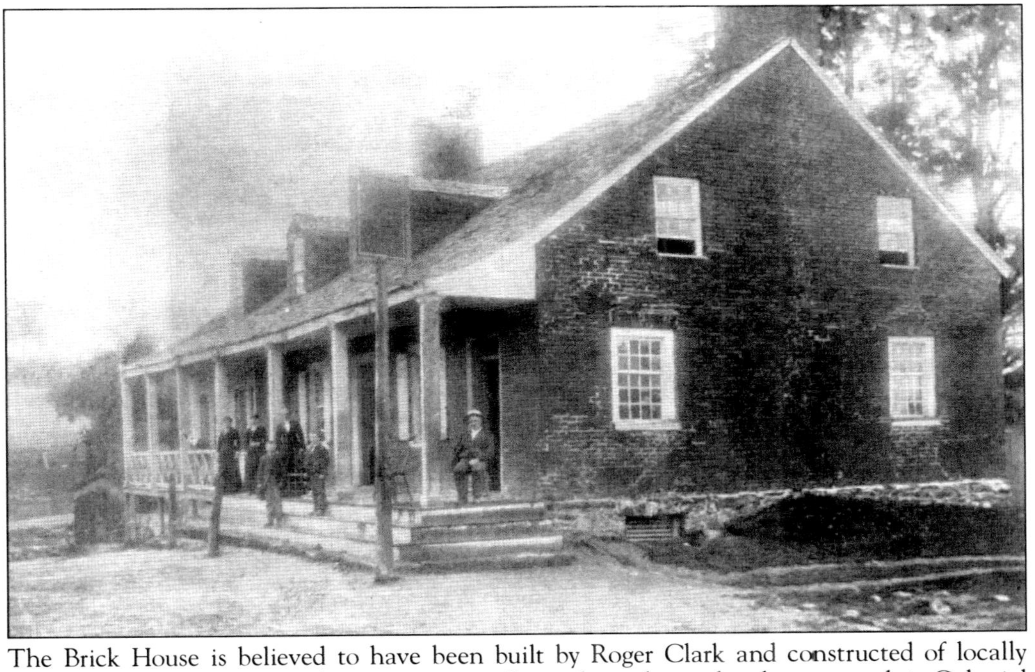

The Brick House is believed to have been built by Roger Clark and constructed of locally fashioned bricks, giving it its descriptive name. Due to being located at the crossroads in Colonial days, the inn quickly became a landmark. It is believed George Stoll owned the structure when this photograph was taken. Frame extensions would be added in 1833 and 1844.

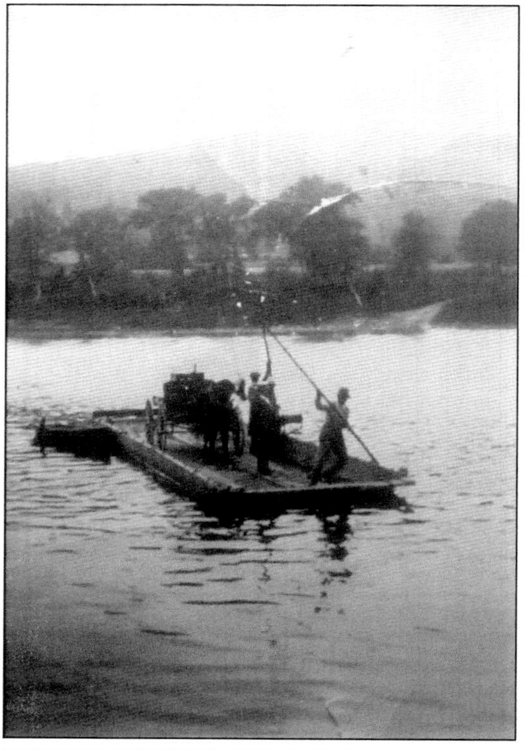

One of the earliest ways to cross the river was by ferry, and these were often cabled to withstand strong river currents. It was a convenient way for wagons, coaches, tractors, and cars to cross to the opposite shore or to access an island. After area bridges were built in the early 1800s, these were again pressed into service whenever those spans were damaged by floods or ice jams.

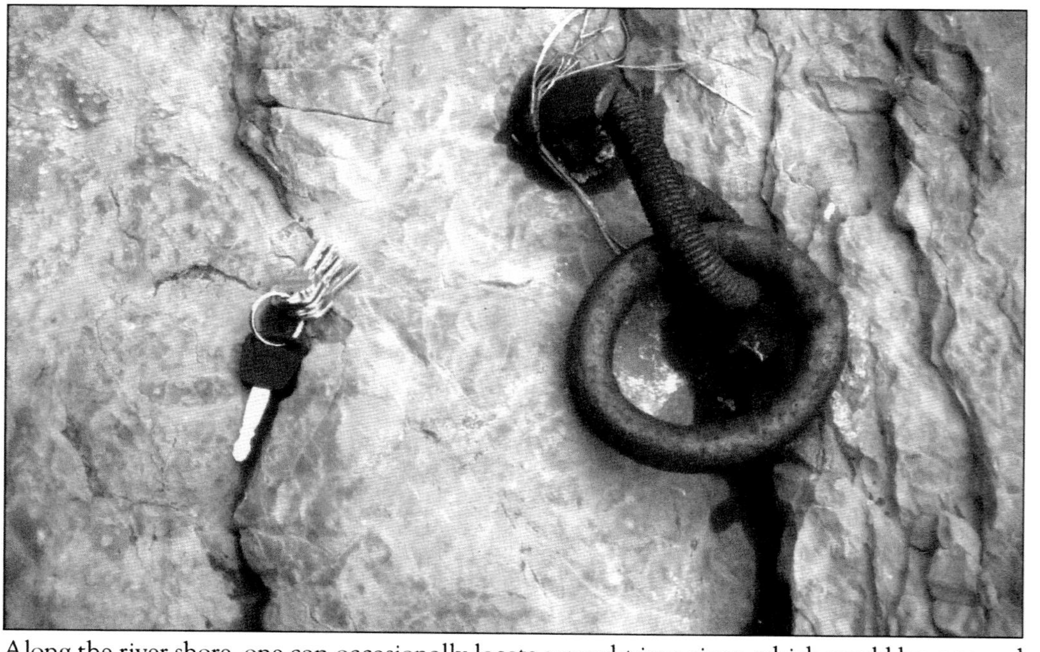

Along the river shore, one can occasionally locate wrought-iron rings, which would have served as raft tie-up locations. The scale of these rings is indicated by comparison to the set of car keys laid nearby. These rings were most likely used to secure large wooden log rafts steered downstream during spring freshets. (Photograph by Robert Longcore.)

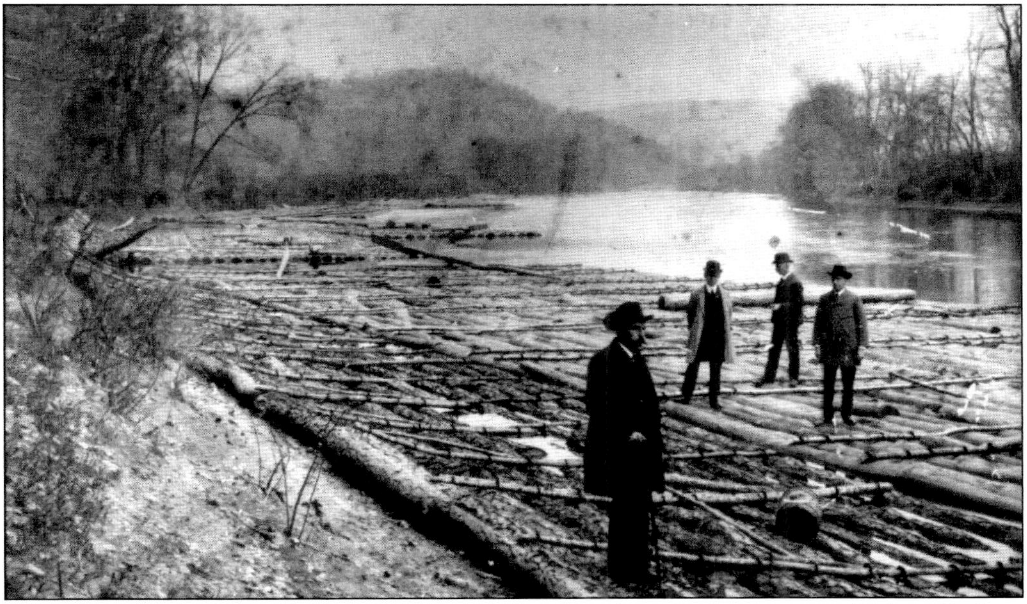

A typical sight in Colonial days was of log rafts heading downstream in spring freshets. Rafting began about 1764 and sent timber toward Easton, Trenton, or Philadelphia. The rafts measured 100 to 200 feet long by 16 to 36 feet wide. As canal aqueducts and bridge abutments impeded the open river and alternative modes of transportation developed, rafting ended in the early 1900s. (Courtesy of National Park Service/DEWA.)

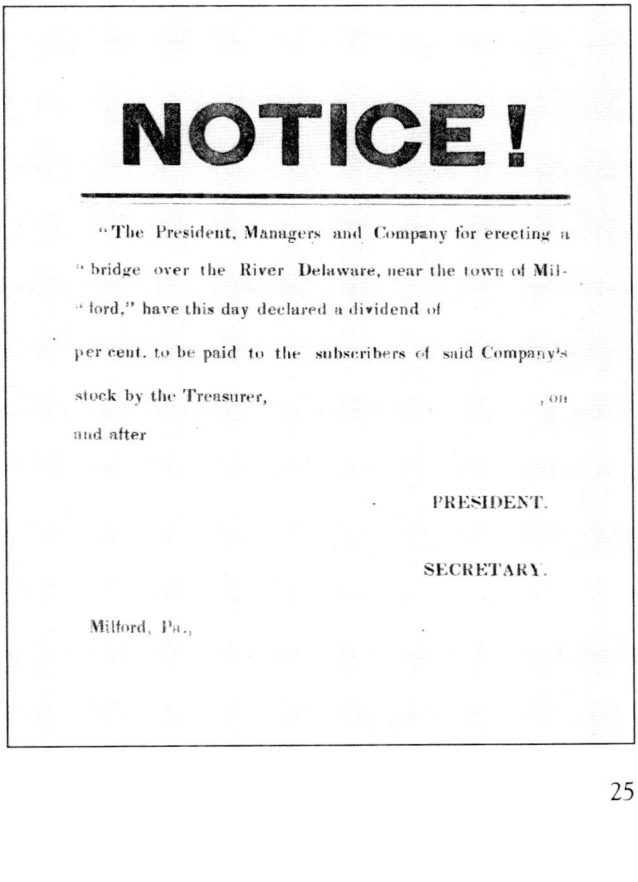

NOTICE!

"The President, Managers and Company for erecting a "bridge over the River Delaware, near the town of Mil- "ford," have this day declared a dividend of per cent. to be paid to the subscribers of said Company's stock by the Treasurer, , on and after

PRESIDENT.

SECRETARY.

Milford, Pa.,

The commissioners for the bridge company at Milford initially issued stock and paid dividends to subscribers, as this document states. During that period, the State of New Jersey held shares in the stock of Pennsylvania's Milford-Owego Turnpike Road and through a lottery mechanism became proprietor of the Union and the Paterson-Hamburg Turnpike Companies. This road network linked Jersey towns on the Hudson River to New York State's "Lake Country."

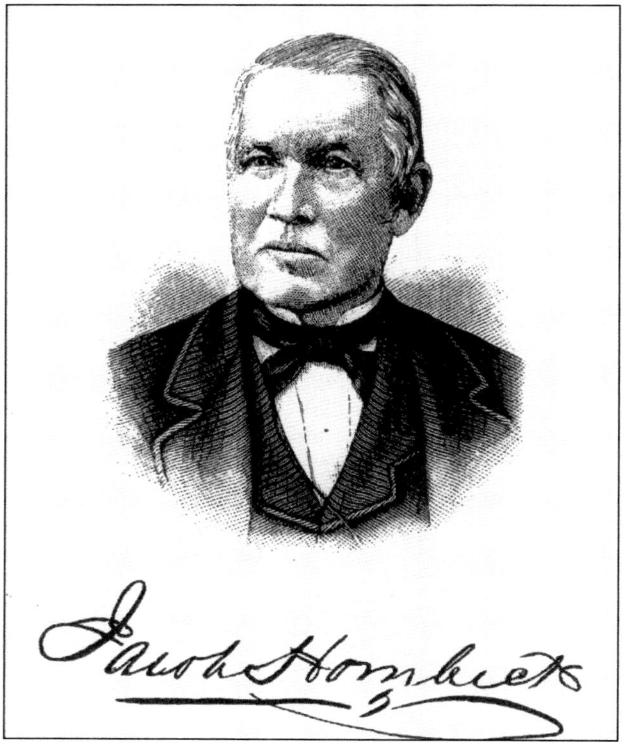

Jacob Hornbeck, son of Capt. Benjamin Hornbeck, worked at their gristmill and ran the store in the hamlet of Millville. He later established his business in Port Jervis as Hornbeck and Bonnell, partnering with his son-in-law, Thomas Bonnell. A founder of the Farmers National Bank and president of the First National Bank of Port Jervis, he served in the state legislature and on the Delaware Bridge Company. (Courtesy of Minisink Valley Historical Society.)

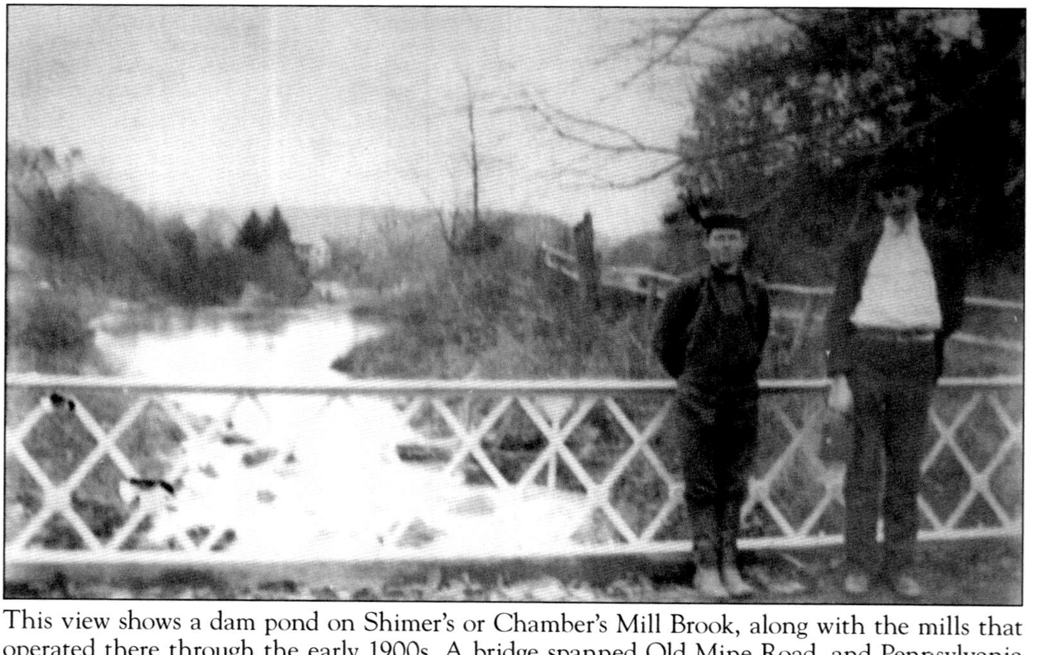

This view shows a dam pond on Shimer's or Chamber's Mill Brook, along with the mills that operated there through the early 1900s. A bridge spanned Old Mine Road, and Pennsylvania is visible in the background. Gershom Bennett's Revolutionary War pension record relates, "A Block house was built at Chamber's on the opposite side of the River from Milford . . . to protect two Grist mills from the Indians."

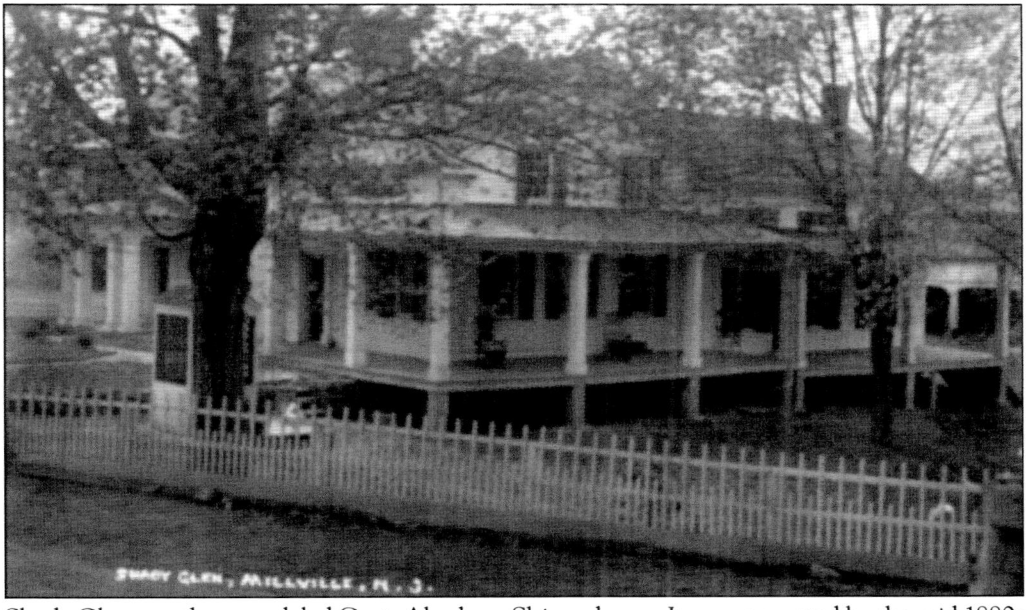

Shady Glen was the remodeled Capt. Abraham Shimer home. It was renovated by the mid-1880s to reflect the affluence of Jacob Hornbeck, who resided there at that time. In March 1893, the *Middletown Press* reported the sale of the homestead by Hornbeck to a Charles E. North of Brooklyn, New York, along with the mill and accompanying water privileges. (Courtesy of Patricia Haggerty Frato.)

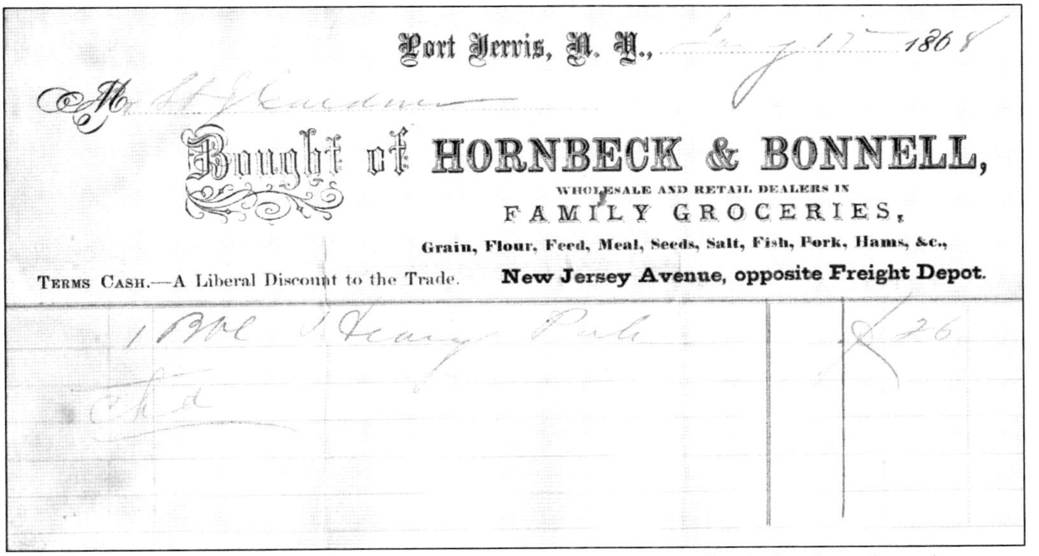

Port Jervis, N. Y., 186

Mr

Bought of HORNBECK & BONNELL,

WHOLESALE AND RETAIL DEALERS IN

FAMILY GROCERIES,

Grain, Flour, Feed, Meal, Seeds, Salt, Fish, Pork, Hams, &c.,

TERMS CASH.—A Liberal Discount to the Trade. New Jersey Avenue, opposite Freight Depot.

An 1878–1879 Orange County directory lists "Hornbeck & Bonnell, wholesale and retail grocers, flour, seed, etc., corner of Jersey Avenue and Fowler." After the canal and railroad entered Port Jervis, businesses relocated to be closer to transportation. A receipt from Hornbeck's old Millville store, archived at Rutgers, states, "miller and dealer in flour, feed grain, etc.—rye and buckwheat flour a specialty." (Courtesy of Minisink Valley Historical Society.)

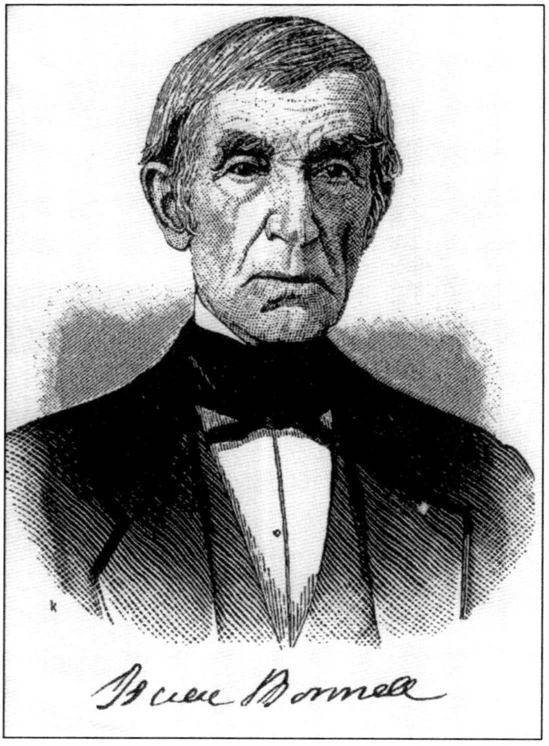

Thomas Bonnell's father, Isaac, learned the sawmill trade at an early age and built over 100 sawmills in the lumbering regions of New York and Pennsylvania. In 1832, he fabricated a large mill frame for Easton at Montague and floated it there by raft. After serving as state legislator, he became president of the bridge company and owned a limestone quarry in town. (Courtesy of Minisink Valley Historical Society.)

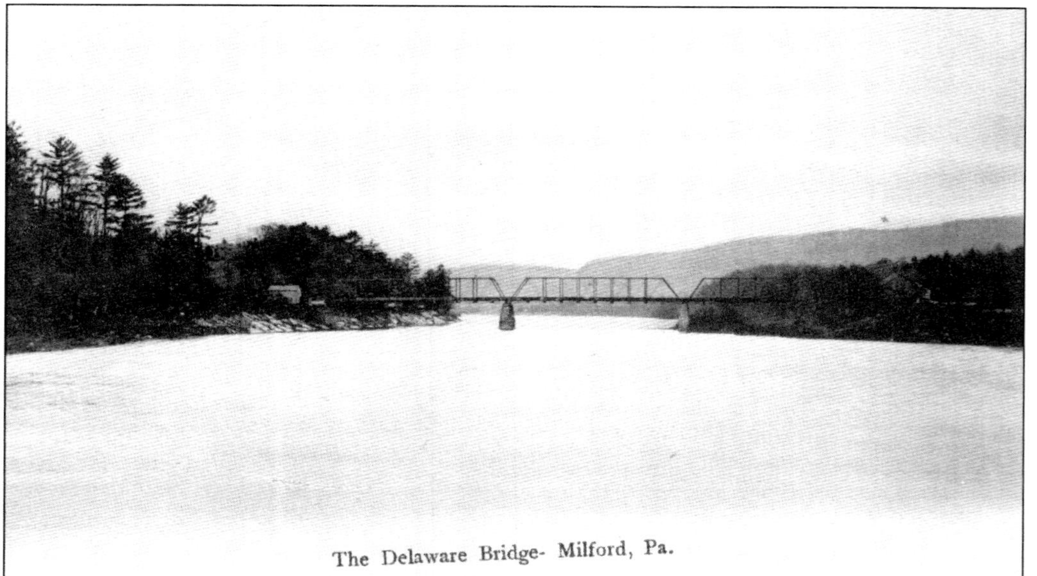

The Delaware Bridge- Milford, Pa.

This was the fifth known span to connect New Jersey to Pennsylvania. The first bridge of 1826 and its successive spans were damaged through ice jams or floods. This bridge, built in 1889, was at times crossed free or was subject to a toll. The area that became Bob's Beach, or Milford Beach, is shown to the right. The toll keeper's house, visible on left, was on the New Jersey side. (Courtesy of John Newcomer collection.)

This toll sign, exhibited at the Montague Association for Restoration of Community History (MARCH), once hung on the former Milford Bridge, which spanned the Delaware River and connected the towns of Milford, Pennsylvania, and Montague, New Jersey. The rates reflect the importance that agriculture and livestock held locally, showing a fee for passage of animals across the river in addition to people. (Photograph by Alicia C. Batko.)

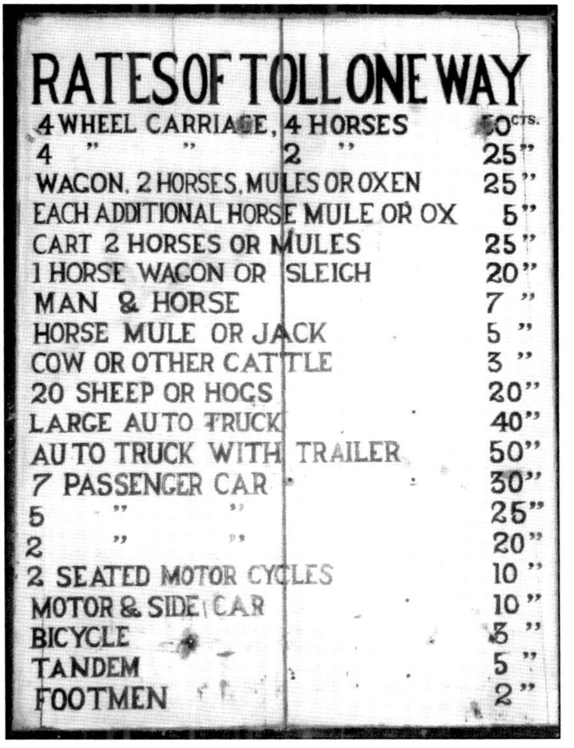

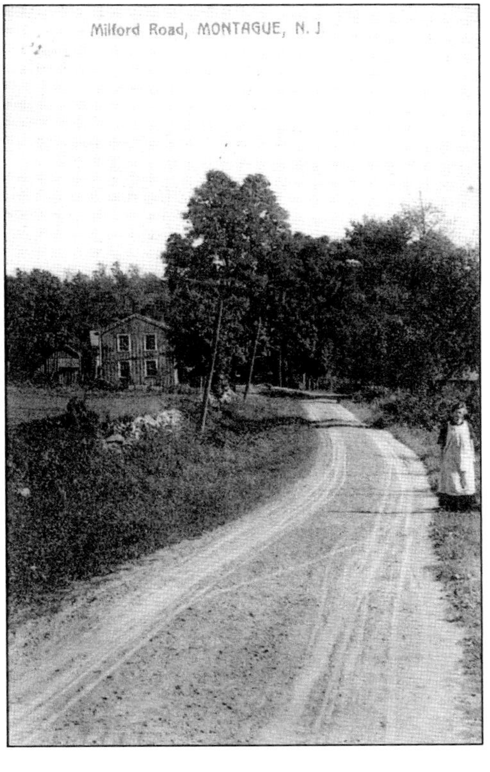

Milford Road, also referred to as Old Bridge Road, connected with River Road. This road connected with the old bridge and was sometimes referred to in that manner. It came out across from Rubin Hill Road and had homes and shops located along it. Only the stone row remains along part of the original roadway, which was covered with macadam when automobiles replaced wagons. (Courtesy of Alicia C. Batko.)

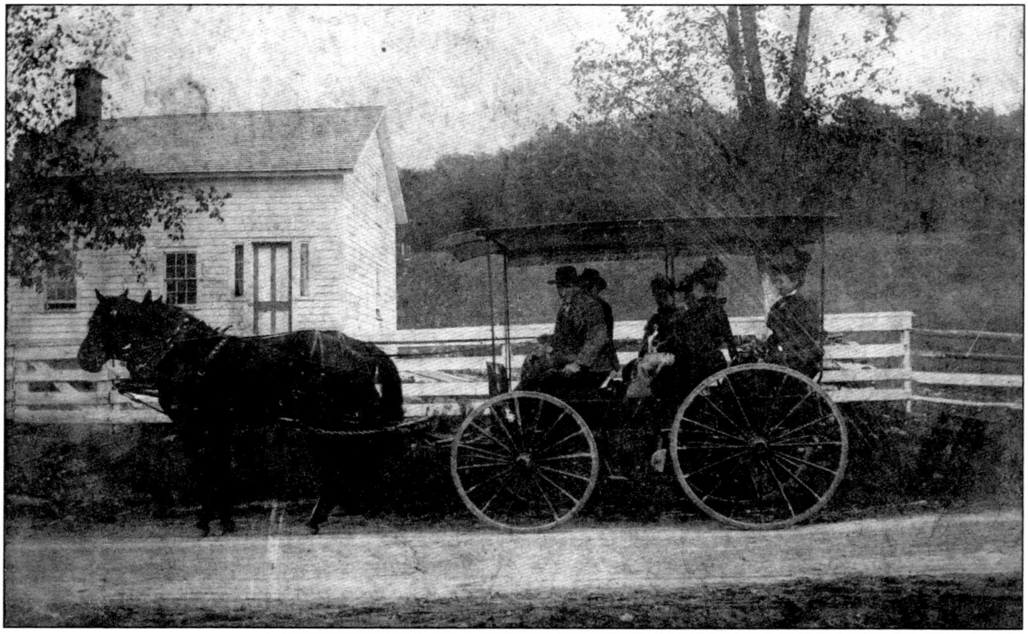

From early settlement until the advent of the automobile, travel on horseback and by horse-drawn transportation was typical. This surrey would have been used for travel from around 1880 to about 1912, when the horseless carriage was introduced. Model T automobiles became more popular by the 1920s but were not as numerous locally.

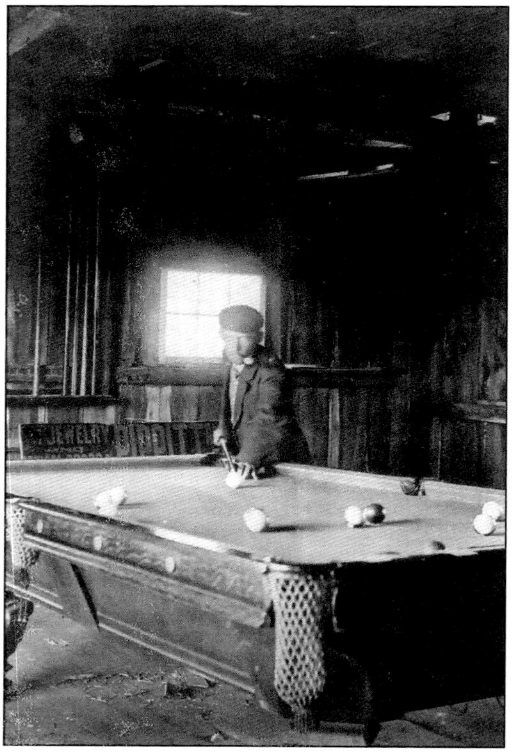

A general store was built by Judge Martin Cole and run by his son, Thomas Van Etten Cole. The store served as a local post office until that service closed in 1908 and all mail was delivered under rural free delivery through Port Jervis, New York. It was a place for townspeople to gather and had a pool hall on the upper floor. (Courtesy of Marjorie Cole Shay.)

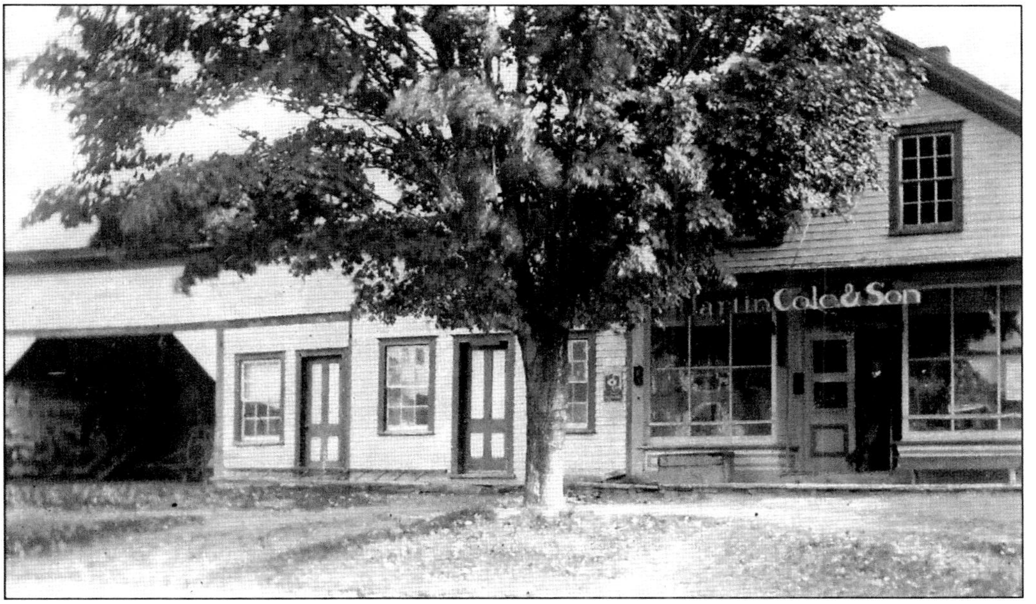

The Martin Cole and Son store first opened in the 1800s. It served as a central location for the lower section of town and where customers could get feed and dry goods, bartering for them with homegrown produce if necessary. It was last run as the Montague Inn, and that structure, the cider mill, a barn, and a garage were lost to fire in 1944. (Courtesy of Marjorie Cole Shay.)

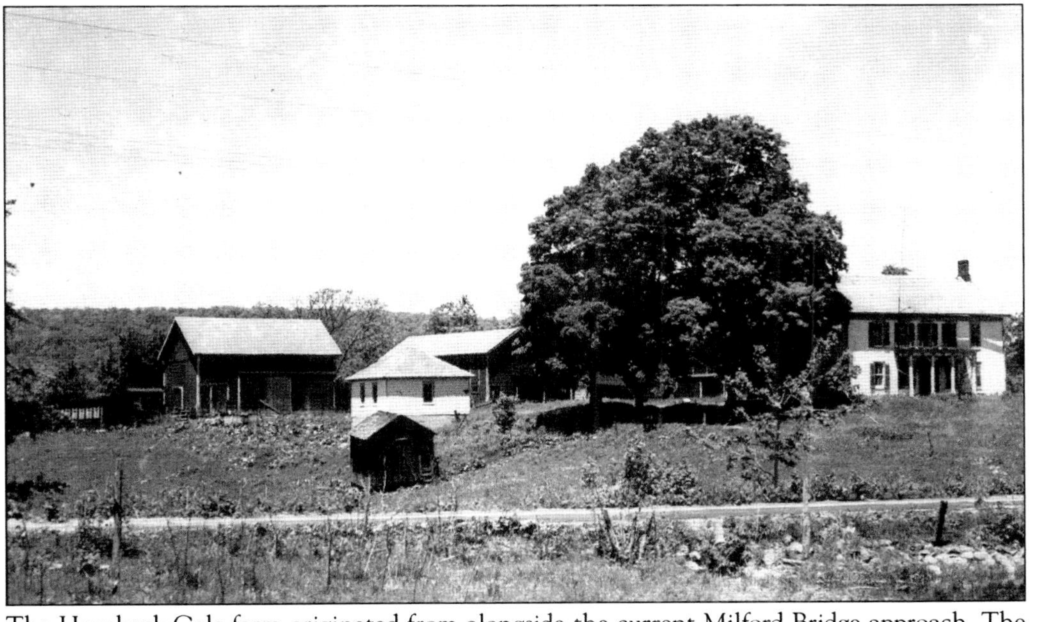

The Hornbeck-Cole farm originated from alongside the current Milford Bridge approach. The house passed from Roger Clark to his nephew, Sanford, whose daughter married Dr. Jacob Van Deusen. It was acquired by Joseph S. Hornbeck and lastly owned by Bertha Cole and her daughter, Mabel Roberts. The 1953 bridge access realignment caused its relocation to Rubin Hill Road where it came under the Tocks Island acquisitions. (Courtesy of Benjamin Roberts.)

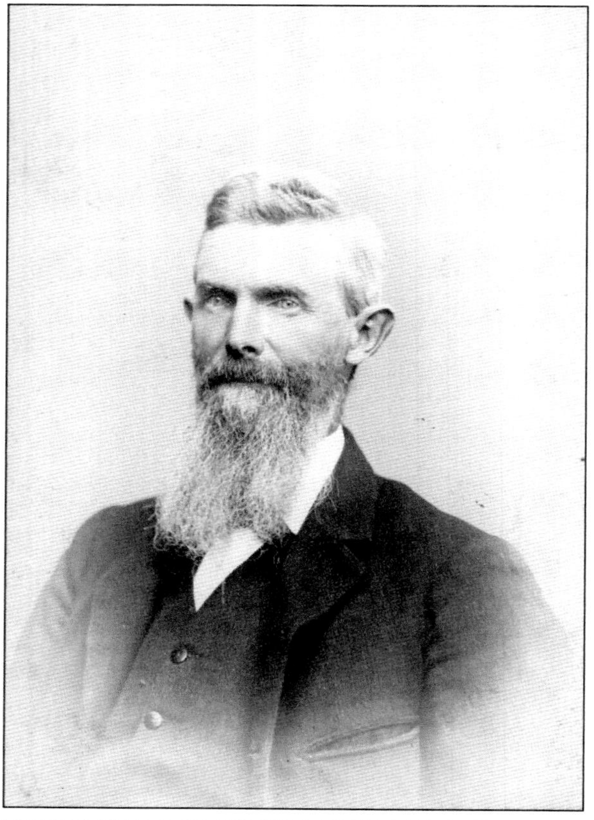

George Hornbeck was the son of Joseph Hornbeck, who purchased the John H. Nelden farm when he married. He later moved to Port Jervis. His youngest brother, Joseph S. Hornbeck, acquired the former Van Deusen farm near the Brick House and added his brother's farm in 1903. His milk and butter production brought him financial prosperity, fostered by the ability to transport goods via the Erie Railroad.

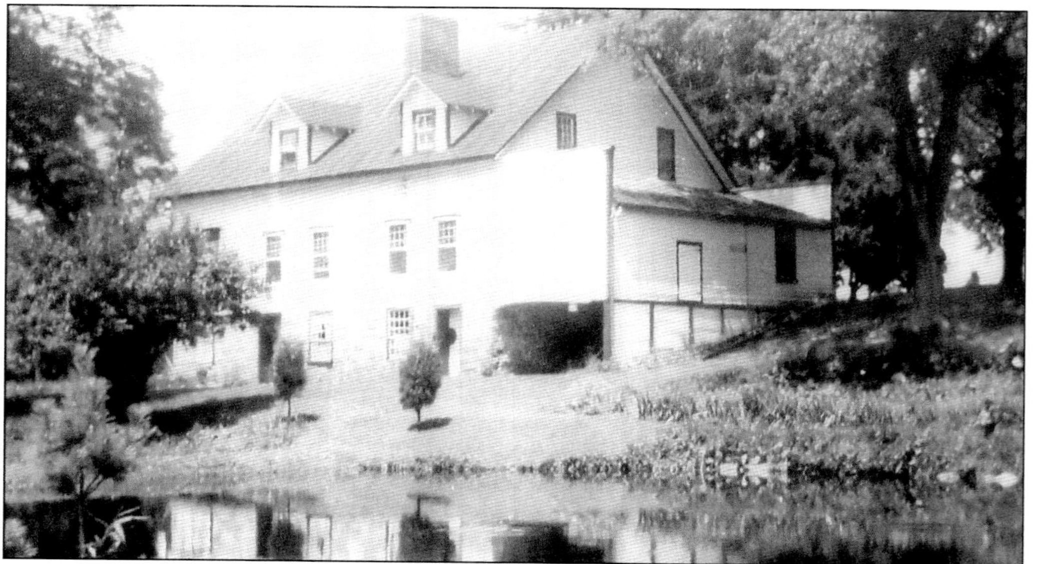

The Martin Cole house sat off Deckertown Turnpike until it was demolished by fire. Judge Martin Cole had served as a surveyor and justice of the peace and represented Sussex County in the state legislature in the 1858–1859 term. His son, Thomas Van Etten Cole, became a town merchant and postmaster. (Courtesy of Marjorie Cole Shay.)

This Sussex County Courts pamphlet names Judge Martin Cole and clerk George H. Nelden, both from the Brick House village area, as court personnel. Judge Cole had served in the legislature, and Nelden became sheriff and moved to Newton. Judge Cole's home was located off Deckertown Turnpike, and the Neldens owned the large tract on present-day Route 206. (Courtesy of Alicia C. Batko.)

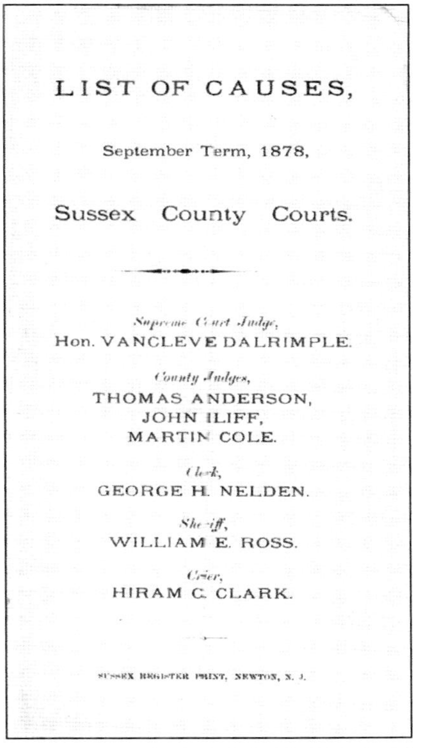

LIST OF CAUSES,

September Term, 1878,

Sussex County Courts.

Supreme Court Judge,
Hon. VANCLEVE DALRIMPLE.

County Judges,
THOMAS ANDERSON,
JOHN ILIFF,
MARTIN COLE.

Clerk,
GEORGE H. NELDEN.

Sheriff,
WILLIAM E. ROSS.

Crier,
HIRAM C. CLARK.

SUSSEX REGISTER PRINT, NEWTON, N. J.

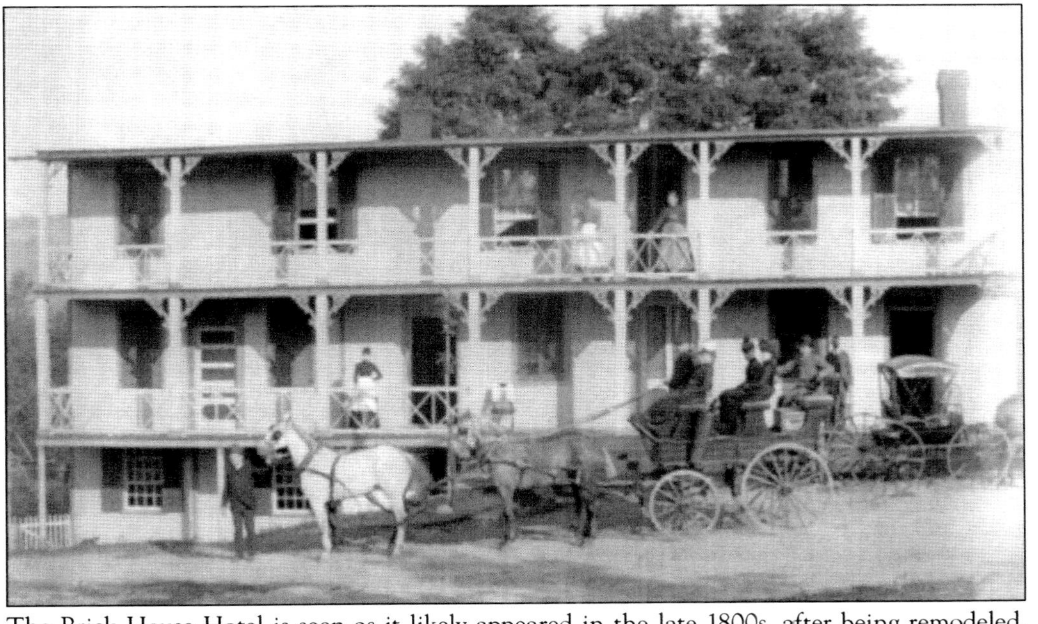

The Brick House Hotel is seen as it likely appeared in the late 1800s, after being remodeled. Stagecoaches and wagons were the primary mode of travel on the local Deckertown and Morris-Essex-Union Turnpikes that converged here. Orra Eugene Monnette, during his research, had discovered that the man pictured holding the reins was Carrie Wieland's father and that the coach and four had arrived from the Hoffman House of New York City.

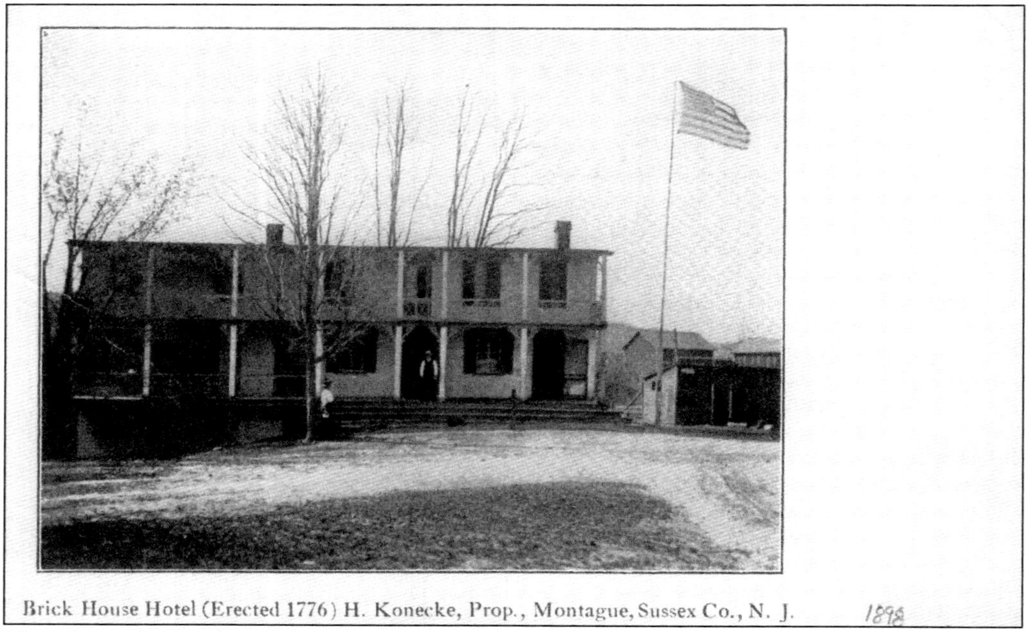

This shows the Brick House Hotel around 1920. The barns seen off to the side belonged to the Hornbeck farm. With growing competition from large establishments in Port Jervis and Milford, and farther up on River Road in Montague, the hotel continued to welcome travelers but saw greater use as a central meeting place.

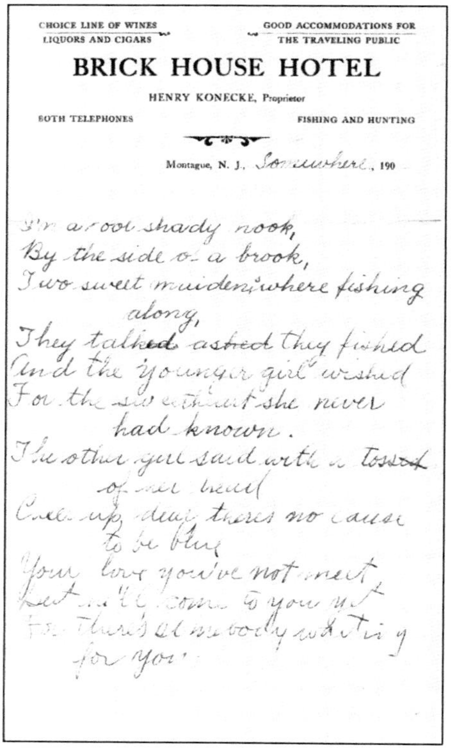

CHOICE LINE OF WINES LIQUORS AND CIGARS — GOOD ACCOMMODATIONS FOR THE TRAVELING PUBLIC

BRICK HOUSE HOTEL

HENRY KONECKE, Proprietor

BOTH TELEPHONES — FISHING AND HUNTING

Montague, N. J., Somewhere, 190

In a cool shady nook,
By the side of a brook,
Two sweet maidens where fishing along,
They talked as they fished
And the younger girl wished
For the sweetheart she never had known.
The other girl said with a toss of her head
Cheer up, dear, theres no cause to be blue
Your love you've not met
But he'll come to you yet
For there's somebody waiting for you.

Very often paper ephemera survived not because of its own significance but for the sentimental value of the letter or poem written on it. Such is the case on this Brick House Hotel letter or bill head from the time Henry Konecke was its proprietor in the early 1900s. A curious mention is made of "both telephones." It is known that Montague used a Milford exchange at the time. (Courtesy of Ronald Hartrim.)

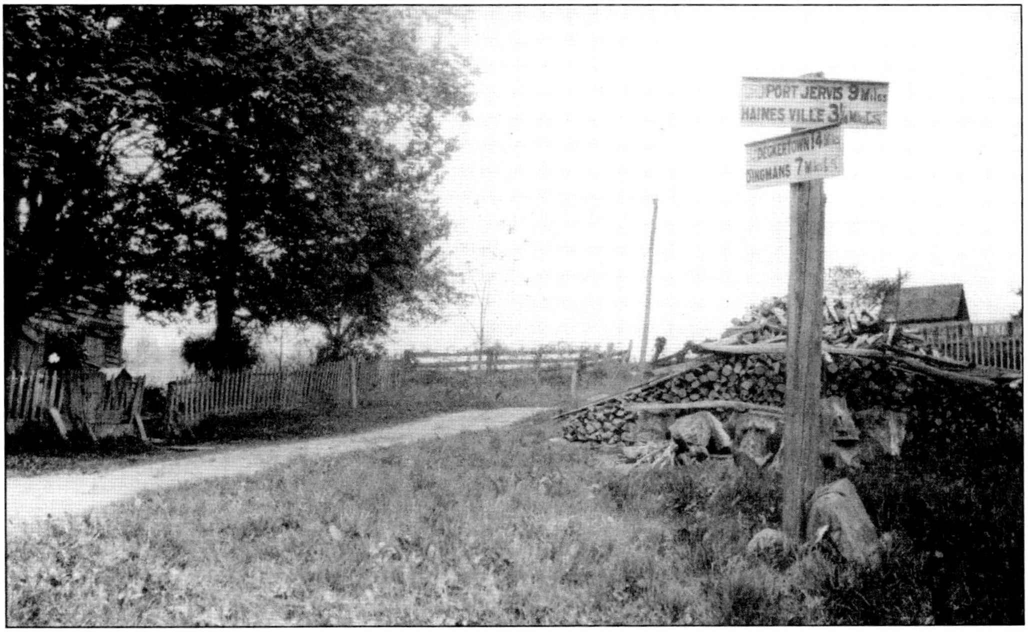

Guideposts were installed by the township in 1896 to mark major intersections. The placards seen here show the distances from the Brick House to nearby Port Jervis (9 miles), Hainesville (3¼ miles), Deckertown (14 miles), and Dingman's (7 miles). Property deeds often reflected local public roads being named by their destinations, for example, Hainesville Road.

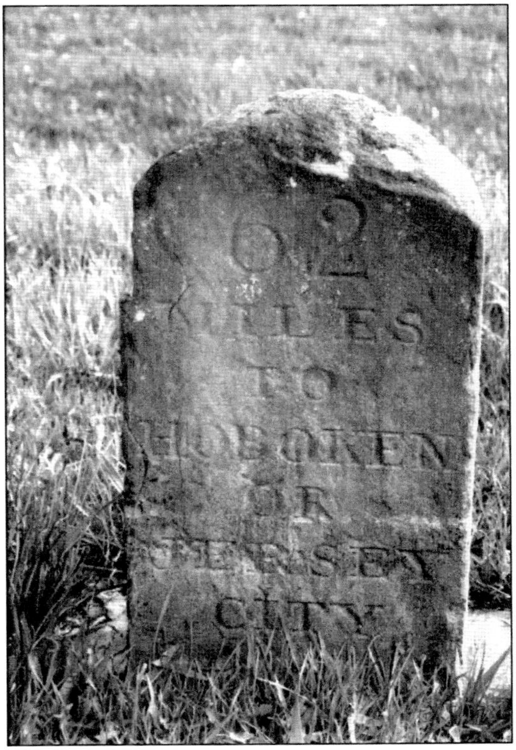

Before it was known as Deckertown Turnpike, the Paterson-Hamburg Turnpike and its Milford extension had sandstone markers placed along its original route. This one sits near a former Cole farmhouse and indicates a distance of 62 miles to Hoboken or Jersey City. This marker was relocated to its current location when the turnpike road was widened. (Courtesy of Alicia C. Batko.)

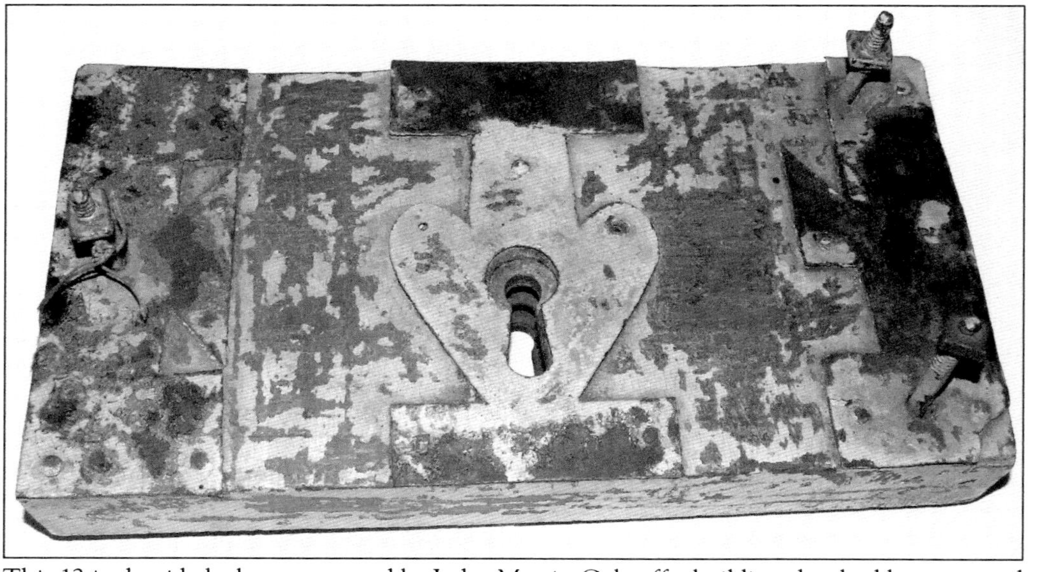

This 12-inch-wide lock was removed by Judge Martin Cole off a building that had been erected as a store by James Stoll in 1802. The structure had at the time passed into the judge's possession and was remodeled for use as a tenement house. His daughter, Eleanor Cole, was the building's owner when the lock was presented to the Minisink Valley Historical Society in 1911. The building fronted the road and is believed to have served as a store, possibly initiated by John Hull and later owned by James Stoll, as it was remembered as the Stoll House after it was transferred into use as living quarters. (Above, courtesy of Minisink Valley Historical Society; below, courtesy of National Park Service/DEWA.)

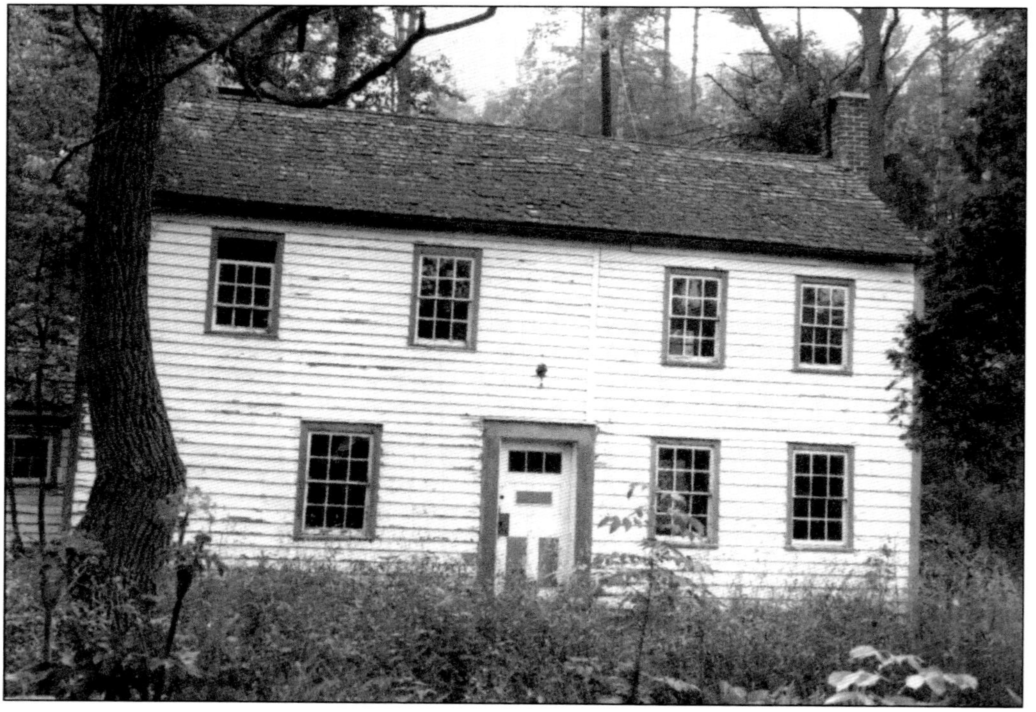

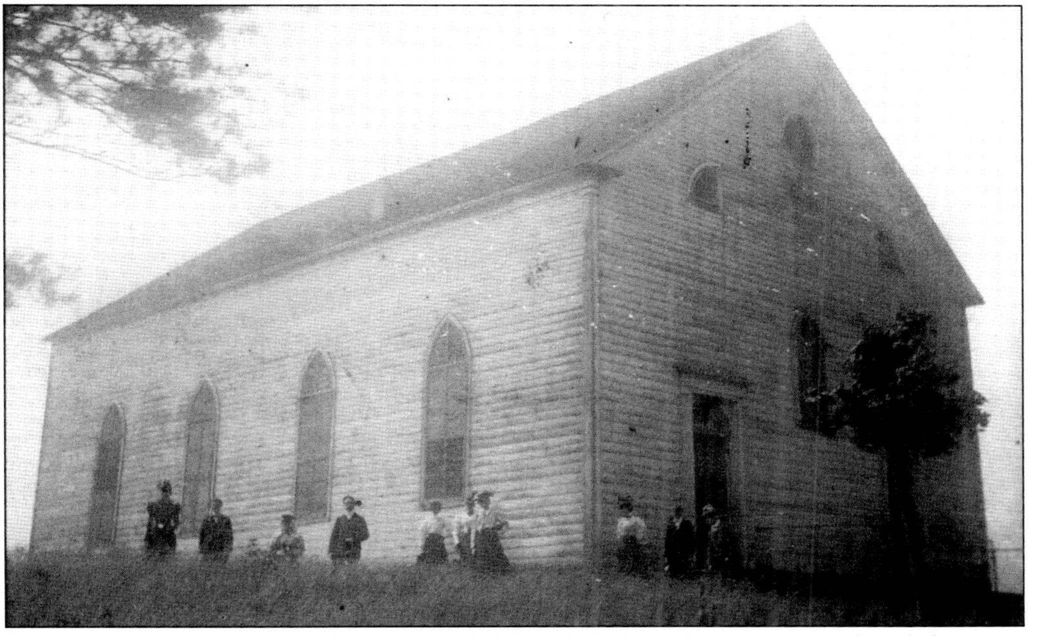

This was the second structure for the Minisink Dutch Reformed congregation, founded in 1737. It was erected on land given by John Rutherford, about a mile north of the first church site. It had a balcony where church suppers were held. The structure stood until 1898, when it was removed and a new church building constructed.

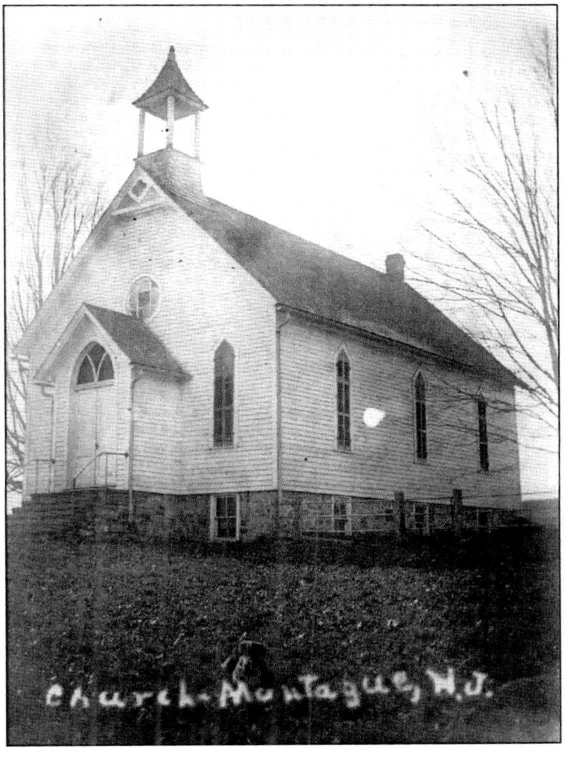

This image shows the existing church building, shortly after its construction, as viewed from its northern side. The prior building had sat on the knoll to the rear of where this is situated. The adjoining burial ground has been used since 1827 on land given by Rutherford and later added on to by the Cole family. (Courtesy of Alicia C. Batko.)

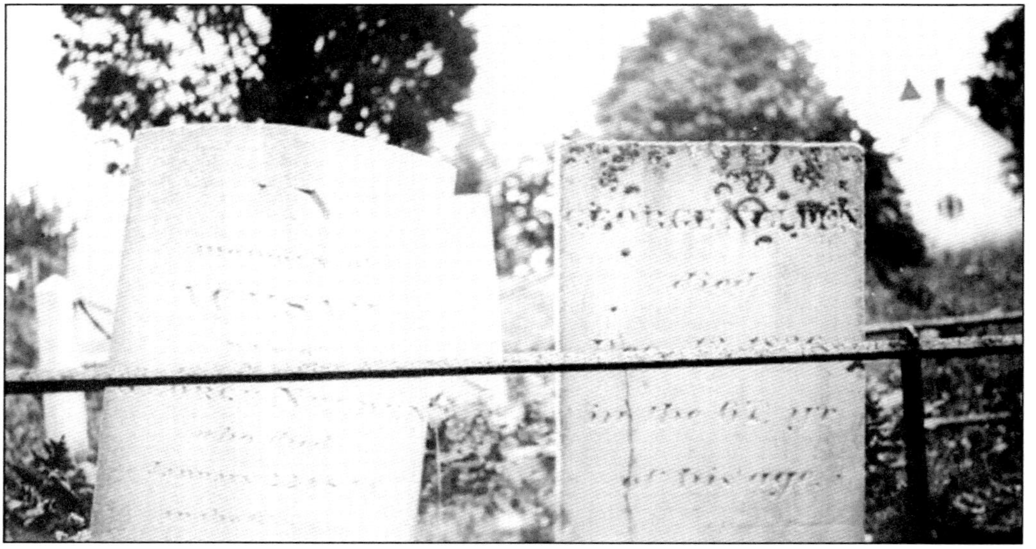

Achsah Nelden's gravestone sits alongside her husband's, to the rear of the Minisink Reformed Church, with their plot showing a railing in this 1931 photograph. George Biddis, John Brink, James Wallace, and James Barton of the commonwealth of Pennsylvania and James Stoll, John Gustin, George Nelden, and Abraham Bray of the state of New Jersey were appointed commissioners to build a bridge over the Delaware River in 1824–1825. (Courtesy of James Nelden.)

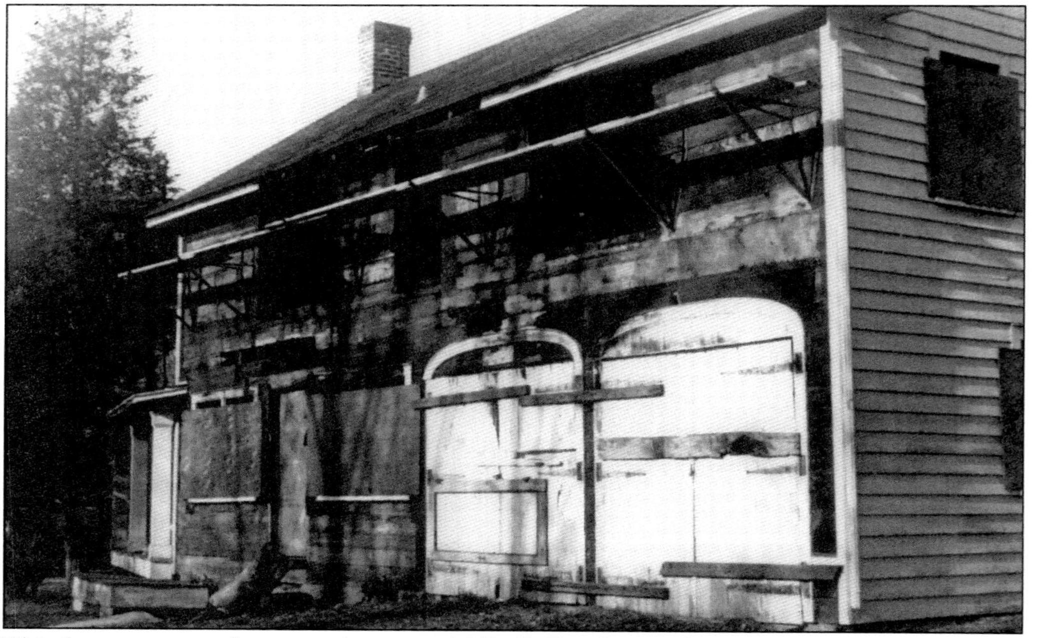

This former store and carriage house on Millville Road, remodeled in the 1900s, was adapted for residential use. Along with the DeRemer (page 21) and the Shimer houses (page 27), it represents the Millville Historic and Archaeological District. A restored Shimer home on Clove Road awaits inclusion. Other properties on the New Jersey and National Registers of Historic Places are Nelden-Hornbeck House, Foster-Armstrong House, and small Stone House (page 41). (Courtesy of Dorothy Hartman.)

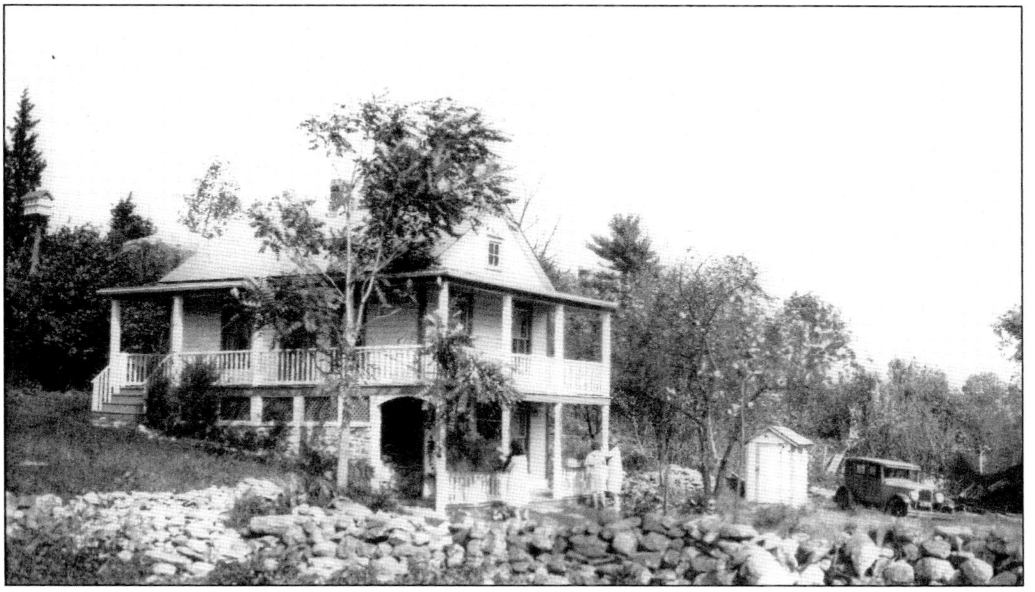

This home was constructed in the 1800s and owned by William Hankins in 1914. It was also known as the Westervelt house and was acquired by its last owner, the Trovatos, in 1948. It had not had running water, aside from an outdoor hand pump, and was heated by a woodstove and made use of an outhouse.

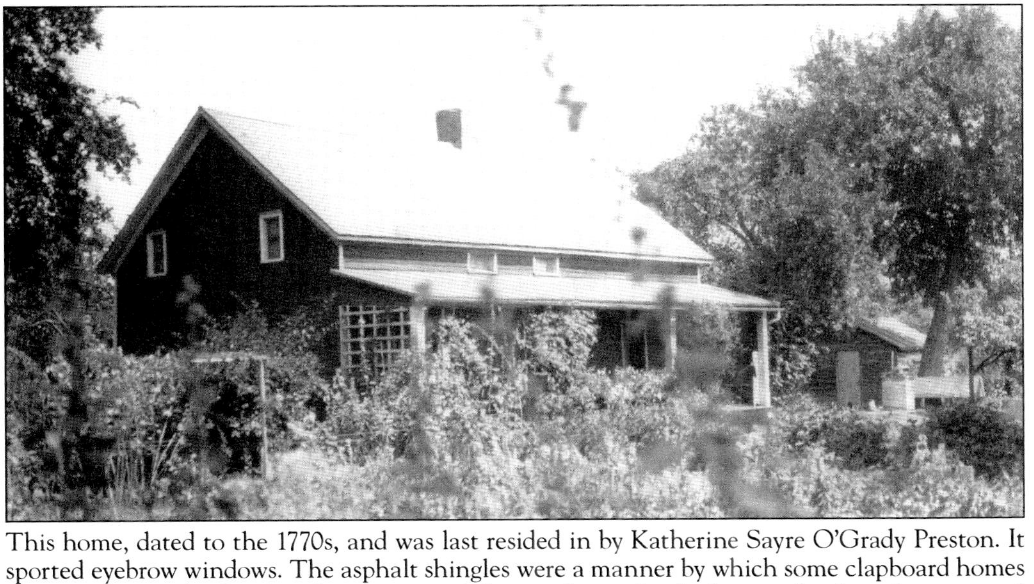

This home, dated to the 1770s, and was last resided in by Katherine Sayre O'Grady Preston. It sported eyebrow windows. The asphalt shingles were a manner by which some clapboard homes were modernized. The shingles eliminated the need to refinish the wooden boards, protected them from the elements, and offered some insulation to buffer that which was lacking between the wooden exteriors and the plaster walls. (Courtesy of National Park Service/DEWA.)

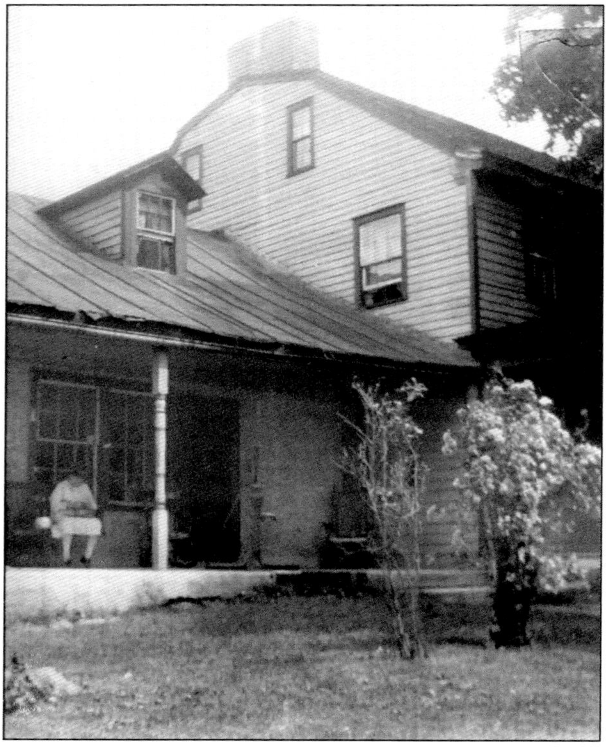

Mary Armstrong rests on the porch of the Dutch gambrel-roofed Foster-Armstrong House. The construction of its clapboard portion is credited to Julius Foster in 1790. He ran a sawmill with Abraham Shimer and also had a ferry. After James B. Armstrong married Foster's daughter, the house remained under that family's ownership until acquired by the federal government. The site is on the National Register of Historic Places and is currently run as a museum by MARCH.

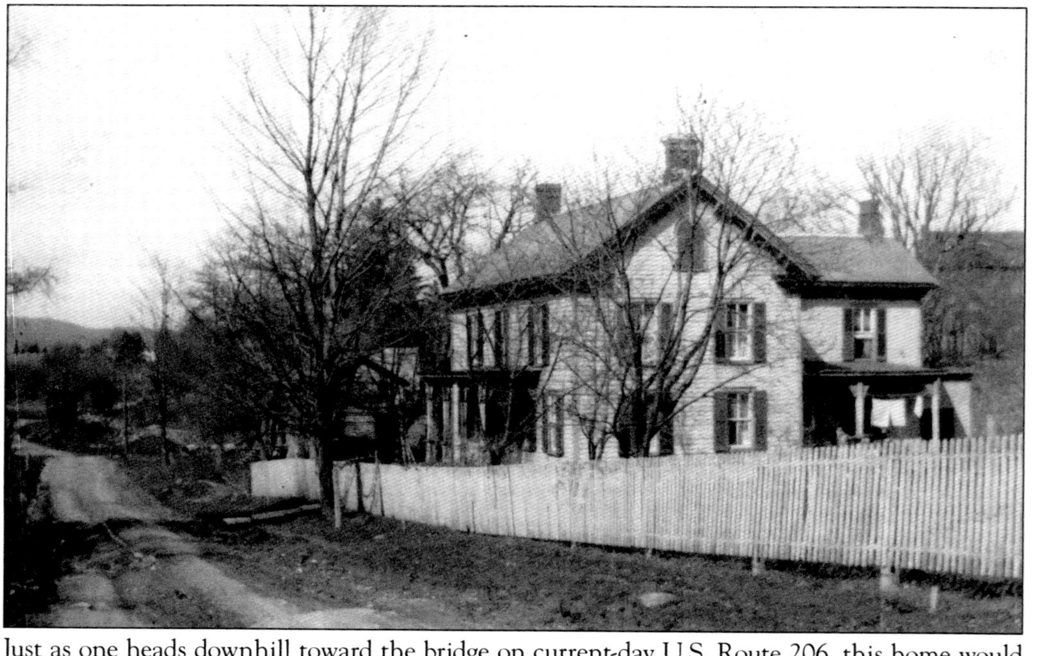

Just as one heads downhill toward the bridge on current-day U.S. Route 206, this home would have been on the right-hand side, situated below the stone house. It became the Bell home in 1903 and was sold to the Happ family in 1921. Its front porch was removed when the road widened. It was moved a bit farther from the road by a Mr. Whitesell. (Courtesy of Robert Myers.)

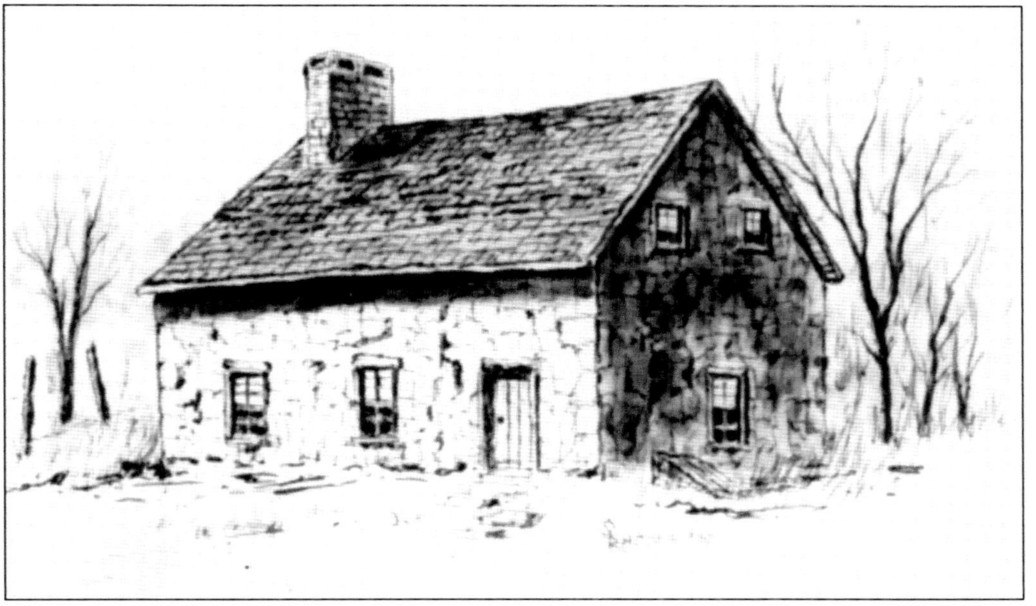

This New Jersey Register of Historic Places site on U.S. Route 206 dates from the early 1800s. It was the stone schoolhouse near George Nelden's, where John D. Everitt taught a three-month-long English day school in 1827 and 1828. After a larger and more modern school was constructed in nearby Brick House village, it was modified for use as a residence. S. Rhodes did this sketch for a 1976 MARCH coloring book.

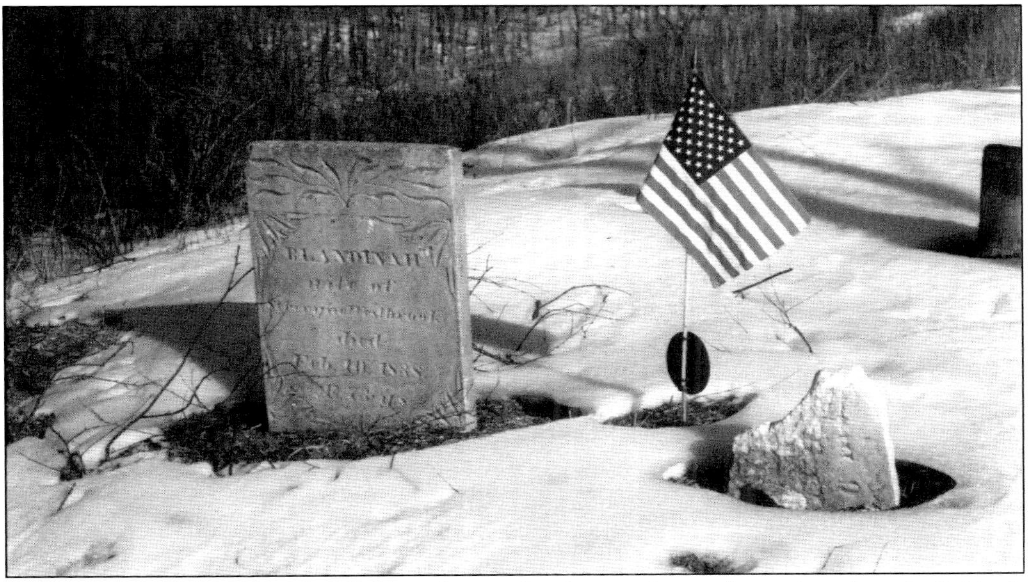

Information on gravestones reads like a history book, providing information about individuals and offering a sense about the community. This plot was restabilized after resident Robert Myers drew a map that allowed Robert Longcore and the author to locate two moss-covered footstones. With the assistance of Sussex County's Sheriff's Work Assistance Program, headstones for Soveryne and Blandina Westbrook and Saveryne Hornbeck were found and reset. (Photograph by Alicia C. Batko.)

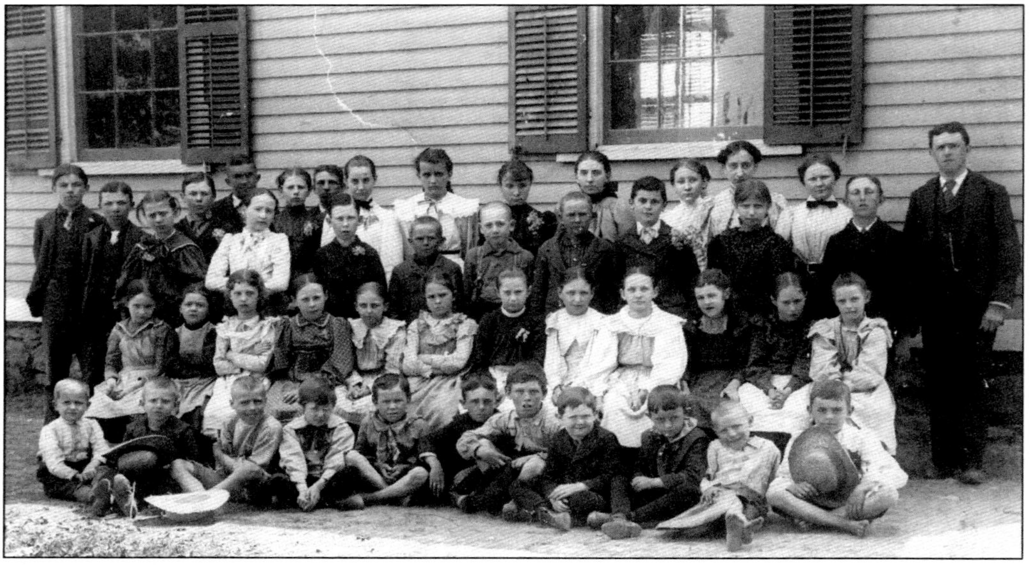

This *c.* 1900 photograph shows a large group of students with its teacher, Chester Smith, standing on the right in the back row. The students in the front row reflect the barefoot days. Smith taught at Brick House School from 1896 until he left for Washington, D.C. He had served as the Montague correspondent for the *New Jersey Herald*.

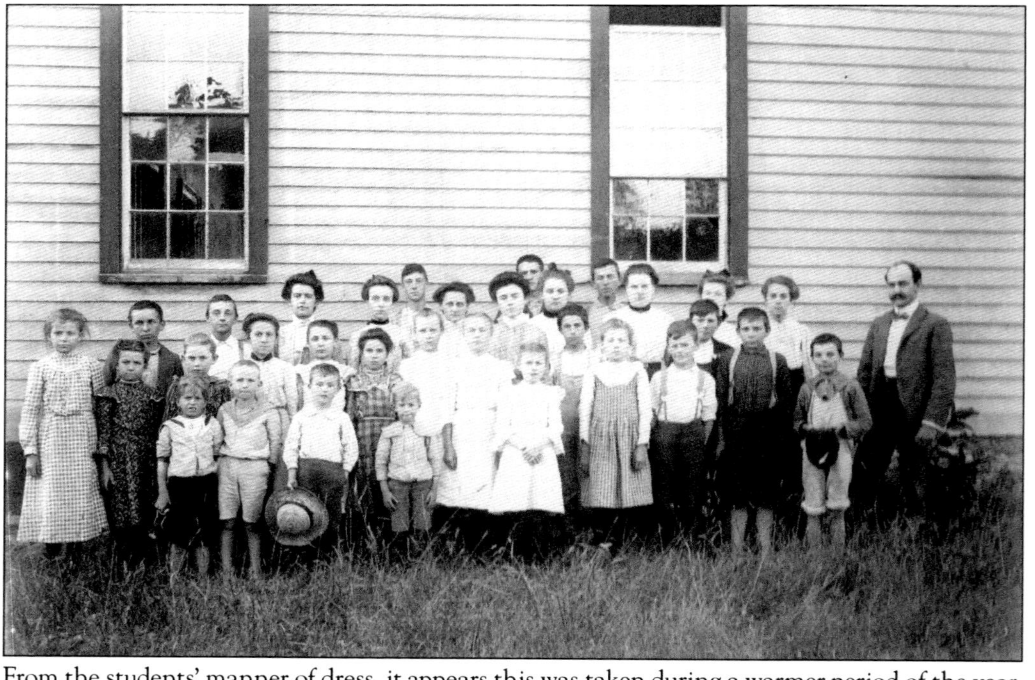

From the students' manner of dress, it appears this was taken during a warmer period of the year, as the boys wearing knickers do not appear to have kneesocks. It seems there was a large group of younger students attending. Sheep were raised on the farms immediately surrounding the school, which sat across the road from the Minisink Reformed Church.

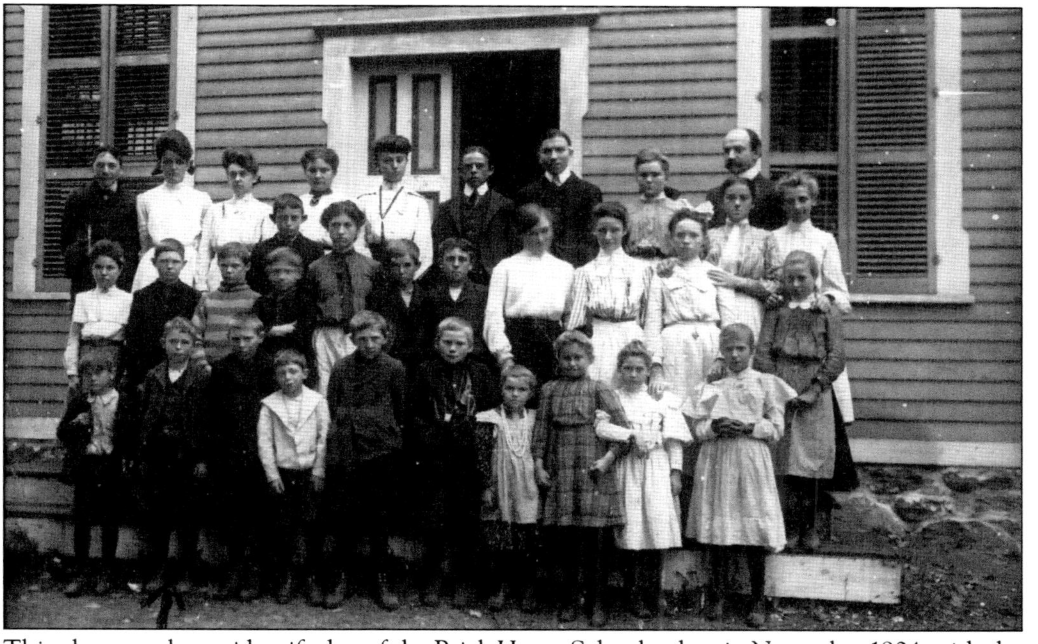

This photograph was identified as of the Brick House School, taken in November 1904, with the schoolchildren shown assembled by the entrance. The back row shows, from left to right, Elias Merrill, Donie Cortright, Kate Rundle, Anna Shay, Lillie Cole (teacher), Dayton Westbrook, Walter McKeeby, Mae Cole, and Samuel Hazelton (second teacher).

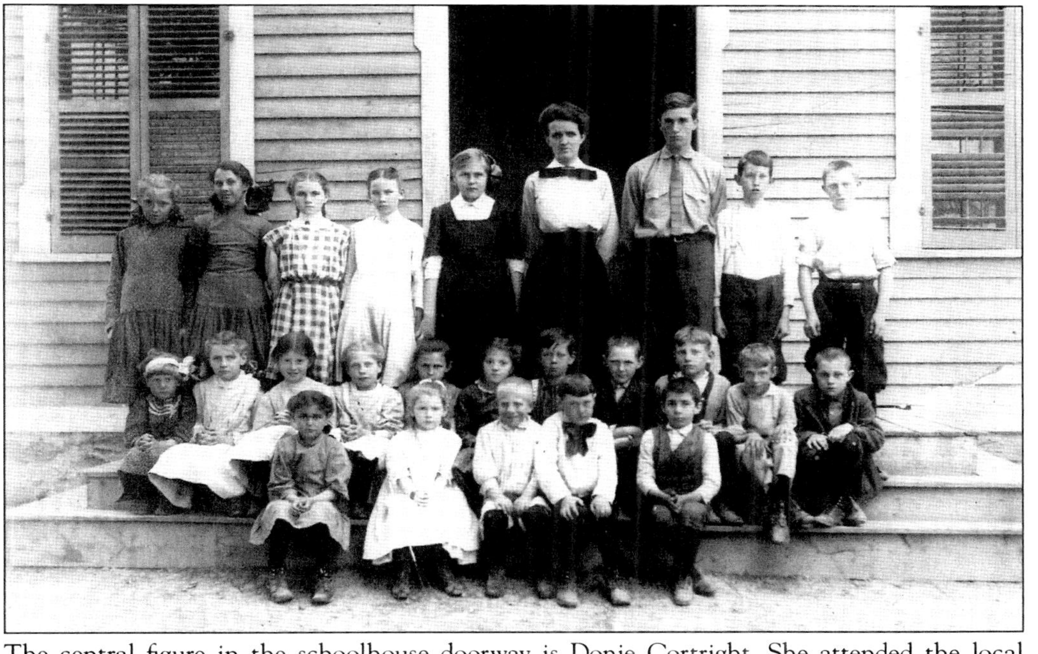

The central figure in the schoolhouse doorway is Donie Cortright. She attended the local township school, as shown by the previous image, and returned to it as a teacher. Cortright also served as a Montague correspondent for the *New Jersey Herald*, just as Chester Smith had done earlier. It seems the teachers knew all that was occurring in the area.

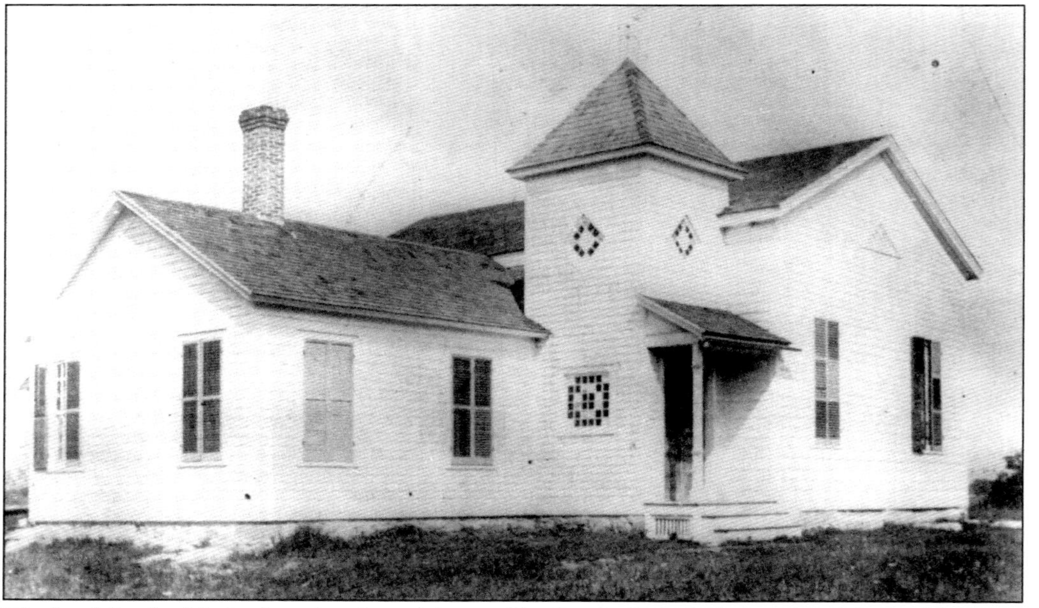

The land for the Methodist church was donated by Sanford McKeeby in 1841. The building was dedicated in 1850 by Rev. James Ayers. No known records exist from this small congregation, and it is suspected the church was rarely used from 1865 until 1905. The church was originally tied to one in Milford, Pennsylvania, but later became linked with another at Sandyston, New Jersey. It formally disbanded in 1924, when its members united with the congregation in neighboring Hainesville. Passersby on Clove Road may not realize that the building still exists, located just south of Rubin Hill Road, as it no longer has its bell tower and is now a residence. Another Methodist congregation served the Montague community on upper Clove Road. It is believed they met at the Church School.

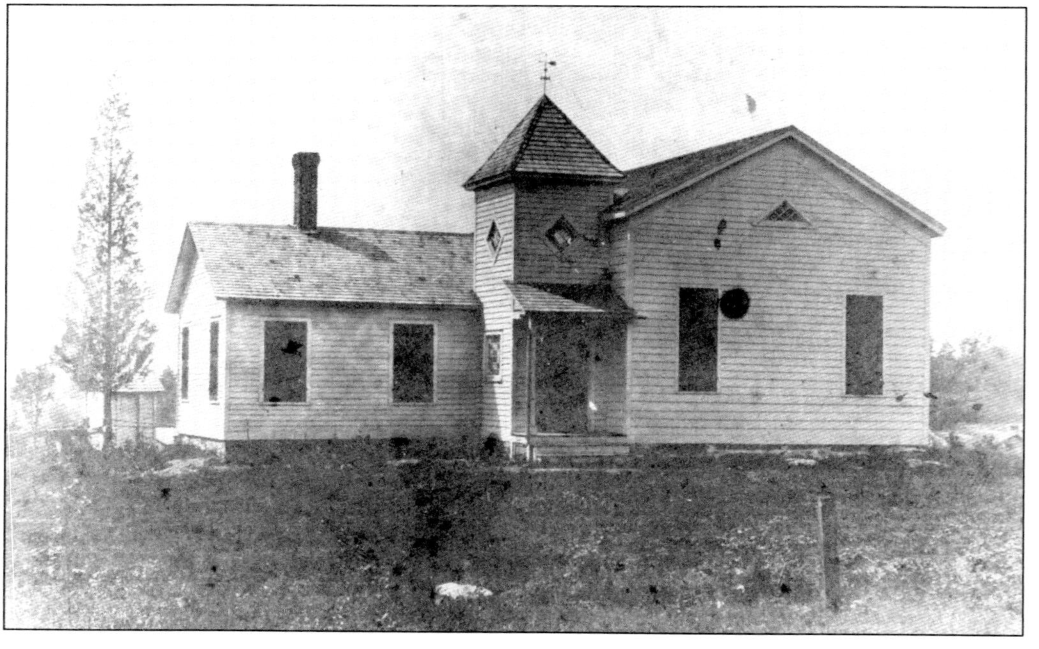

A small family plot exists, just diagonally across the road from the former Methodist church, where members of the McKeeby family are interred. This stone is for Sanford McKeeby, whose family home was nearby. He died as a farmer at the age of 41 and is known to be buried alongside three relatives who had died earlier. (Photograph by Alicia C. Batko.)

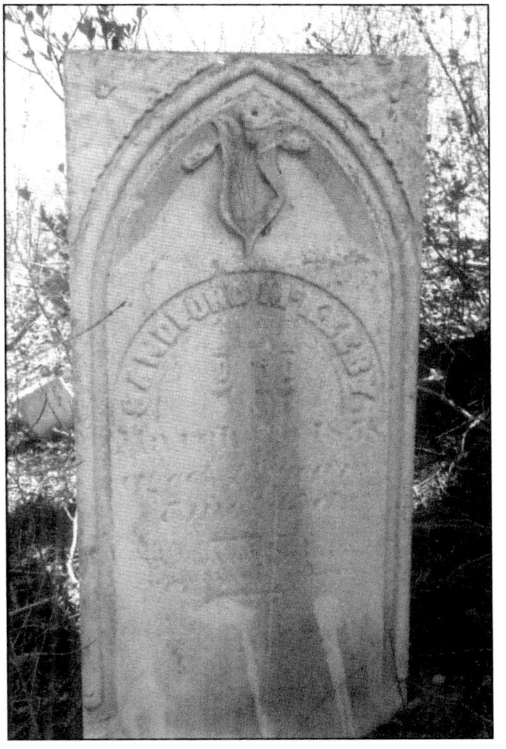

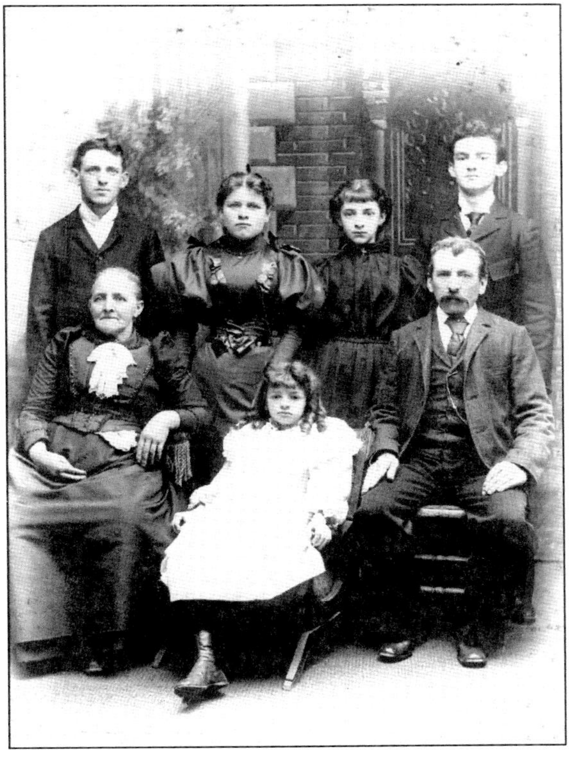

The Rundles lived in the house on the southwestern corner of Deckertown Turnpike and Clove Road. They acquired the property that had previously been owned by the McKeebys and Bennetts. The stained-glass bordered windows, which also appear in the Methodist church (page 44), were added when the home was remodeled and expanded about 1890. Their horses frequently raced on the Milford racetrack.

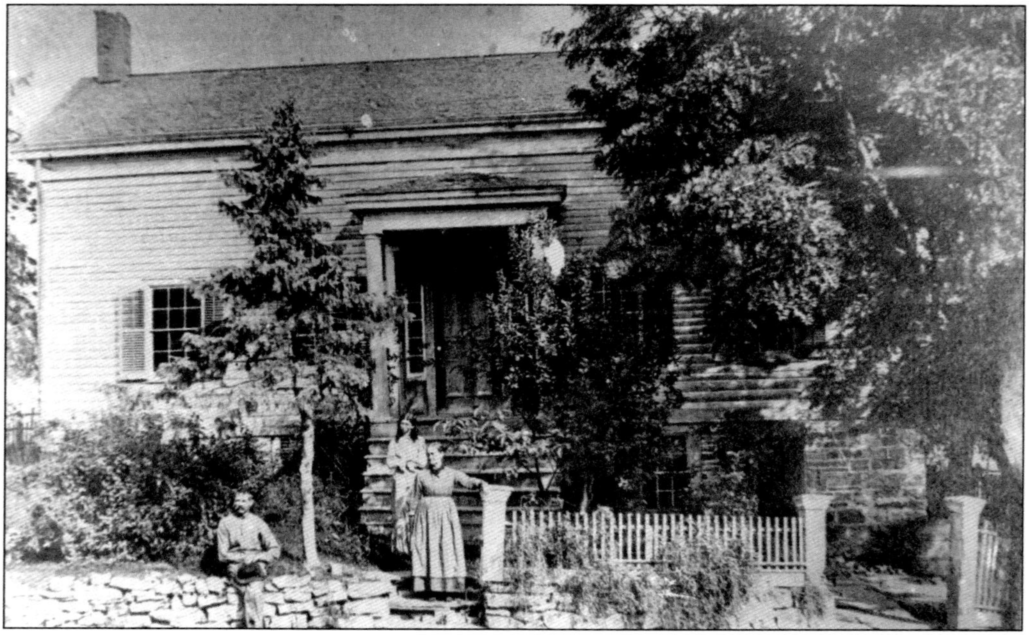

This Nearpass-Bigart home stood on Clove Road near its intersection with Reinhardt Road. Much of the property along this section was held by the Nearpasses since the mid-1700s and was later divided among brothers. John Bigart married into the family, hence the dual name. William Nearpass had run a quarry, extracting limestone from the cliffs, and Sanford Nearpass and John Bigart also farmed the area. Bigart was also a lime burner and tended to the limekilns. The home had been constructed in 1830 and was destroyed by fire in 1956. The upper photograph shows it in 1890, and the lower photograph captures the house in the winter of 1906.

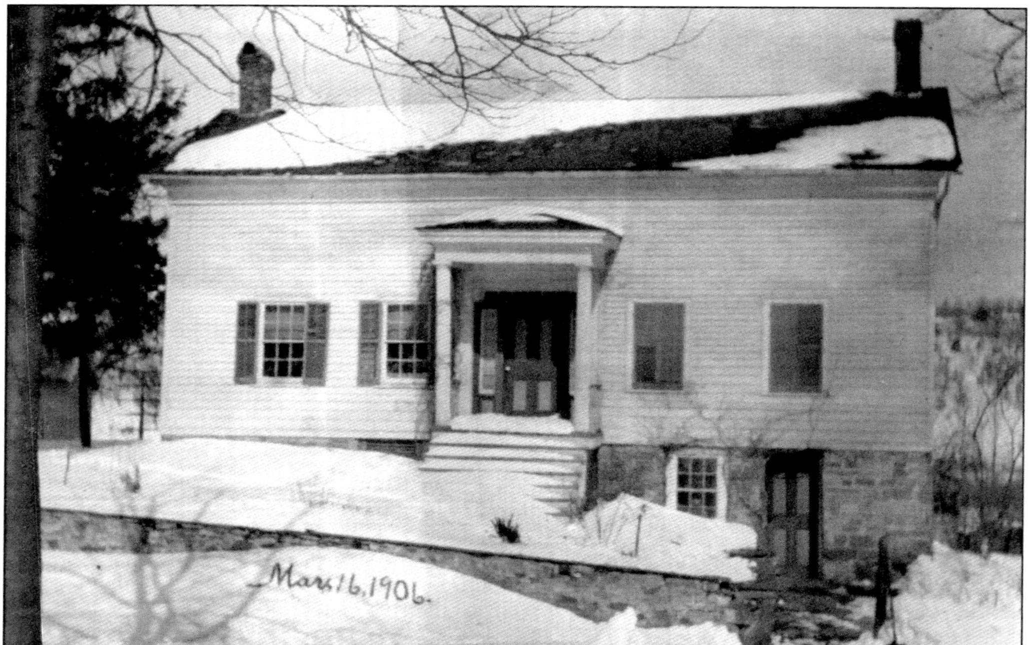

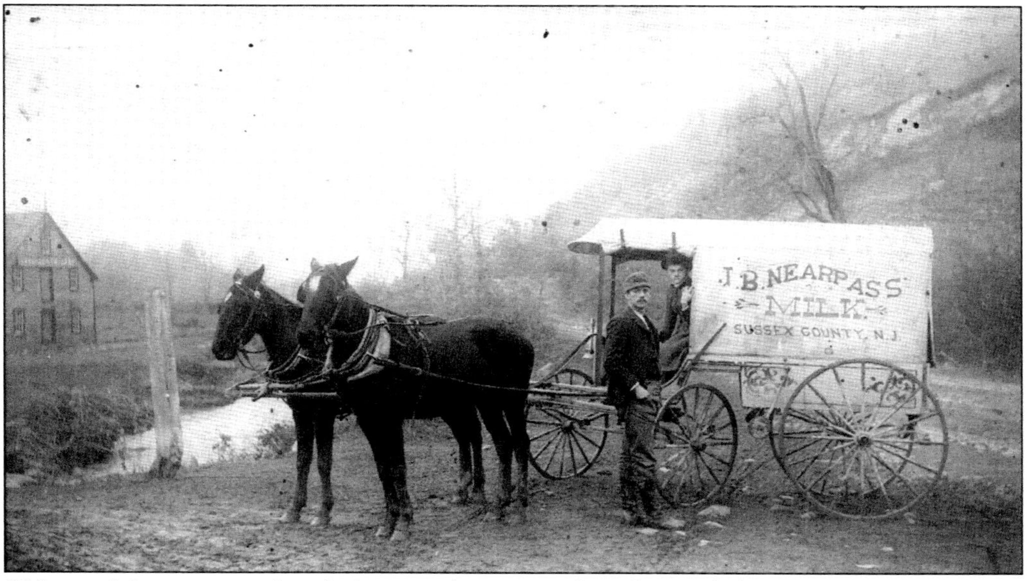

Old-time deliveries were done by horse and wagon, such as the one belonging to Nearpass' Dairy. A 1910 town census shows that Jacob B. Nearpass managed a dairy farm. In 1900, his occupation was listed as a lime burner. His son, Dalton, inherited the farm within the area of the old family quarry. That location's features were written about in an article published in a 1956 *Journal of Paleontology*.

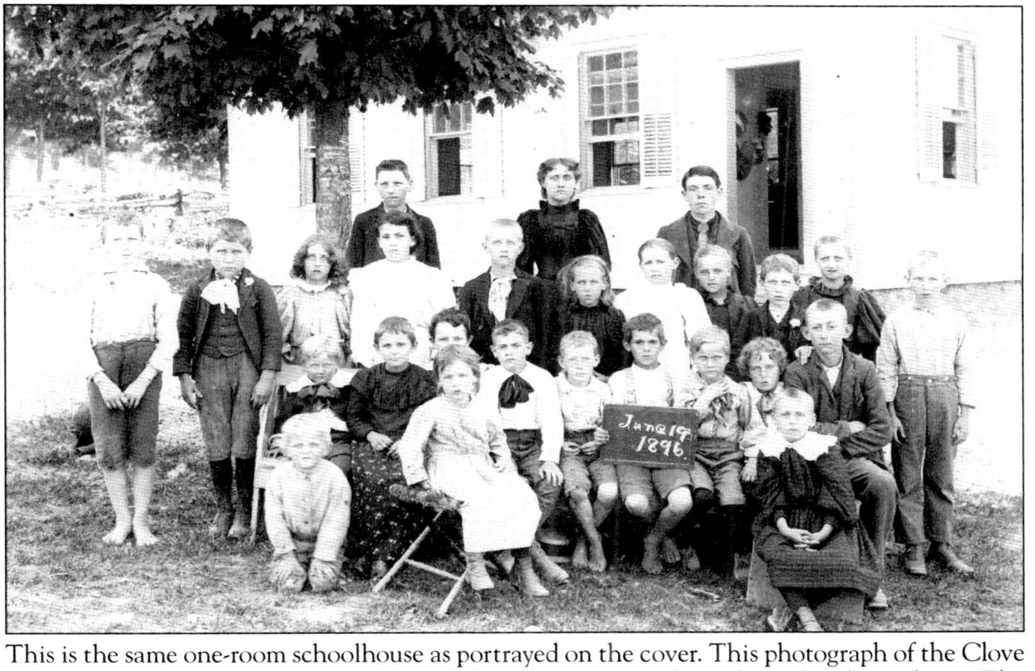

This is the same one-room schoolhouse as portrayed on the cover. This photograph of the Clove School was taken on June 19, 1896, and shows an increased number of male students. The structure stood along Clove Road, just below Steenykill Road, and was considered part of the Nearpass district. Arctic explorer Dr. Frederick Cook once visited with his cousin and her pupils while she taught there in 1906.

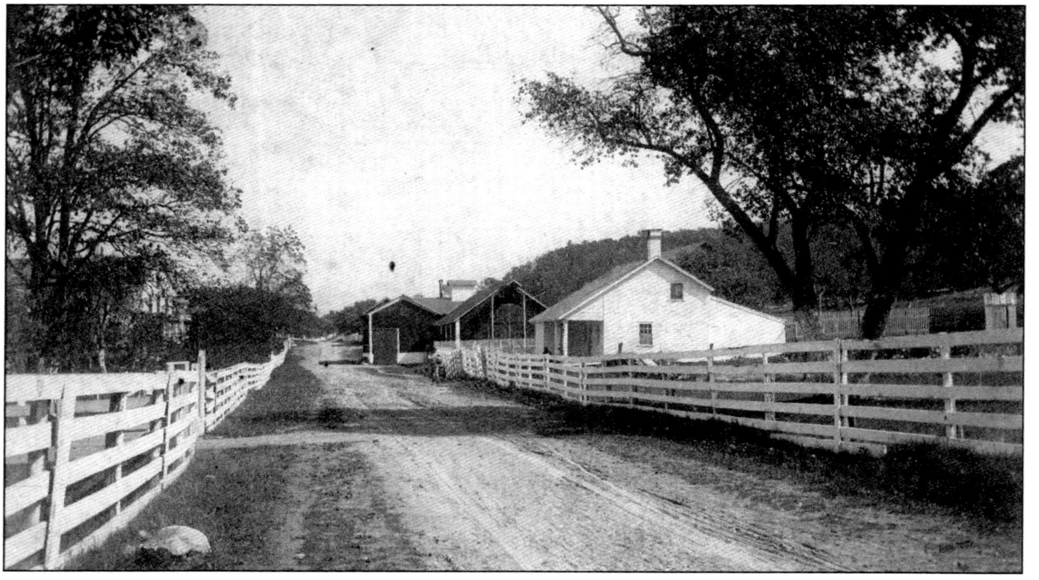

This straightaway section of road remains on Clove Road. The farm pictured here once belonged to John W. Worden, with his large farmhouse visible off to the left-hand side and the dirt road reflecting that it was traveled by wagons. Martha Price was presented this farm in gratitude for the care and kindness she extended to John W. Worden during his illness. As with many of the farms, when times were prosperous, the buildings were cared for and white picket fences abounded. The farm property was included in a later development built around a dammed portion of Mill Brook called Montague Lake or Fawn Haven Estates, although the home no longer exists.

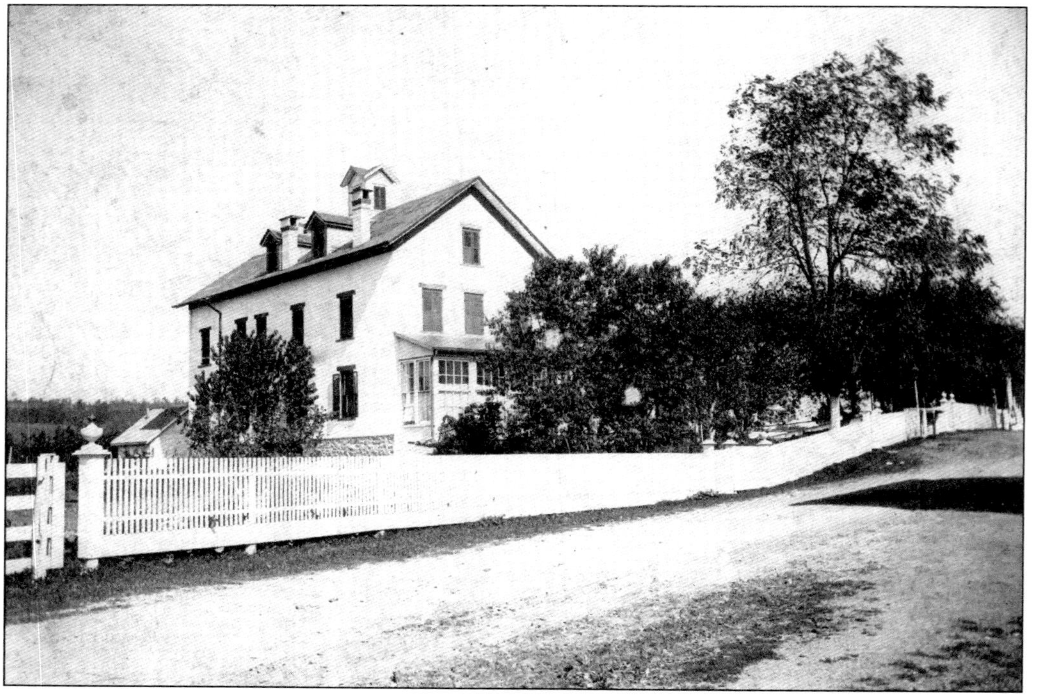

David Westfall, a dignified gentleman, is resting in his easy chair. His father, Wilhelmus, acquired the tract (page 15) that had been owned by Simon Westfall since 1774. David was a farmer and oversaw the management of the dairy and lumbering. Upon his death in 1916, the property passed to his grandson, Dr. Wilhelmus D. Westfall. He was a renowned mathematician who got his degree in Germany and afterward taught at the University of Missouri. David Westfall's dairy wagon was photographed by a building that once served as a hotel and meeting place nestled against the cliffs in the Tappentown/ Duttonville section. It and other structures were removed by the time the north end of Clove Road was realigned.

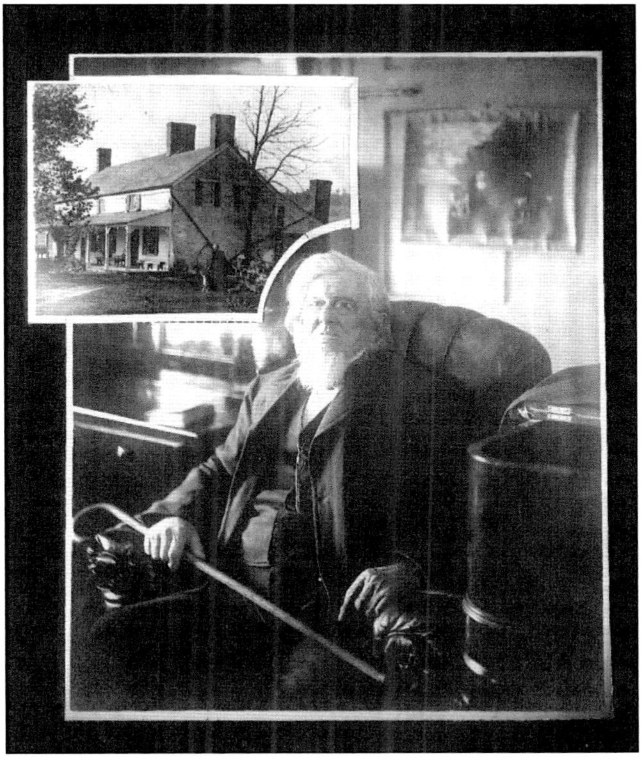

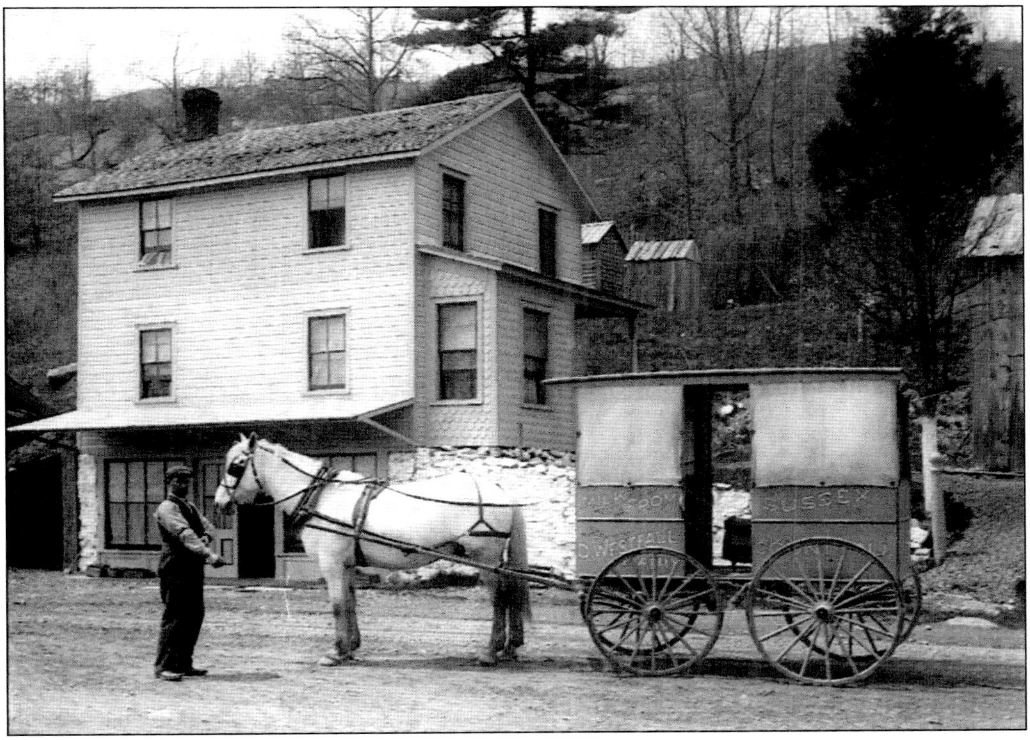

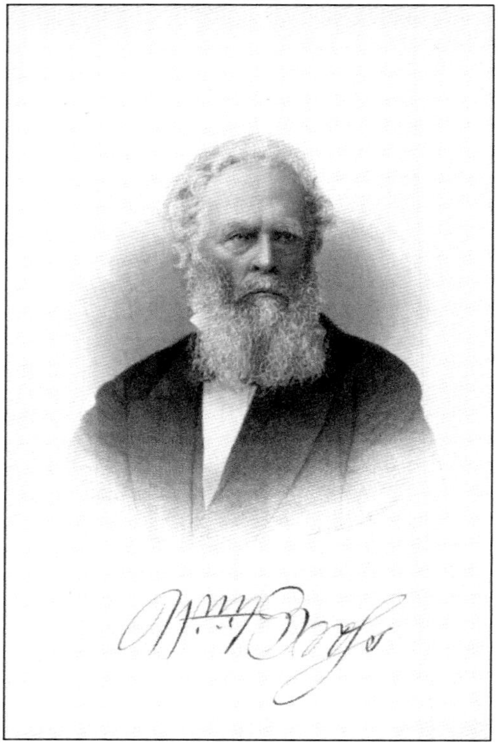

William Bross was lieutenant governor of Illinois and president of the Chicago Tribune Company. He did his first apprenticeship in a printing office at Milford, Pennsylvania, after his parents moved there from Montague. Governor Bross's name sits at the head of all the signers to the Emancipation Proclamation for Illinois, the first state to ratify the document. He was a pallbearer at Abraham Lincoln's funeral. (Courtesy of Minisink Valley Historical Society.)

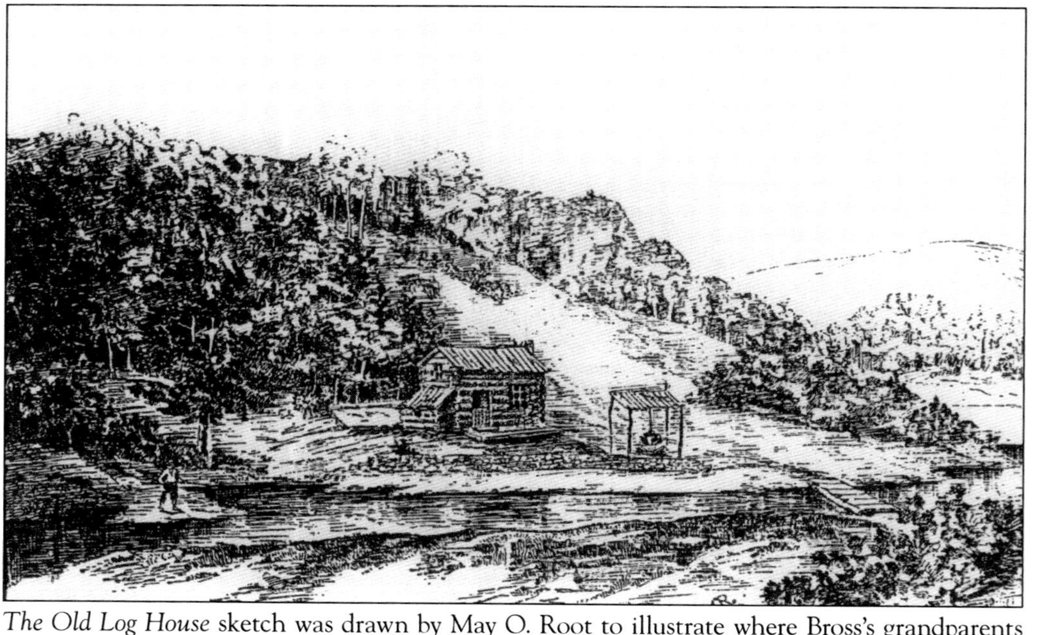

The Old Log House sketch was drawn by May O. Root to illustrate where Bross's grandparents Abraham and Margaret Winfield had lived. The home was located in "the Clove," about two miles southeast of Port Jervis, New York. The print appeared in a book William Bross authored in 1887, *Legend of the Delaware*, telling about the famed uncle of his grandmother—Tom Quick. (Courtesy of Minisink Valley Historical Society.)

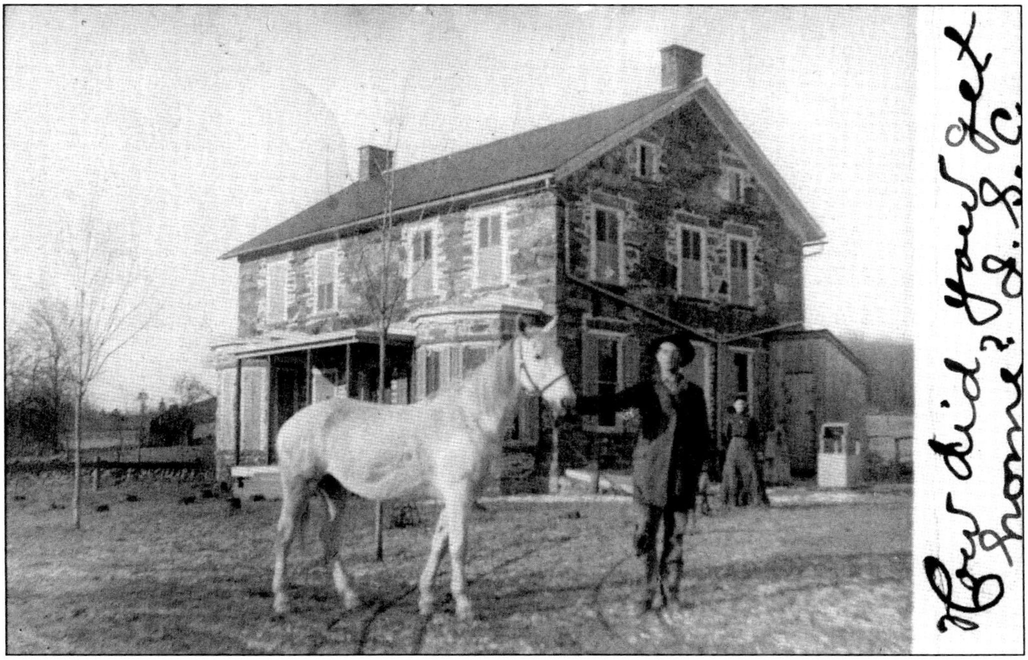

This home sits on Birch Tree Road and dates from the 1800s, having replaced a prior frame building that was destroyed in a fire. This was the farm of George N. and Emma Kyte Cole. The stones for the structure came from the back of the property. In 1933, the Williamses added a porch and a fireplace. (Courtesy of Brian J. Lewis collection.)

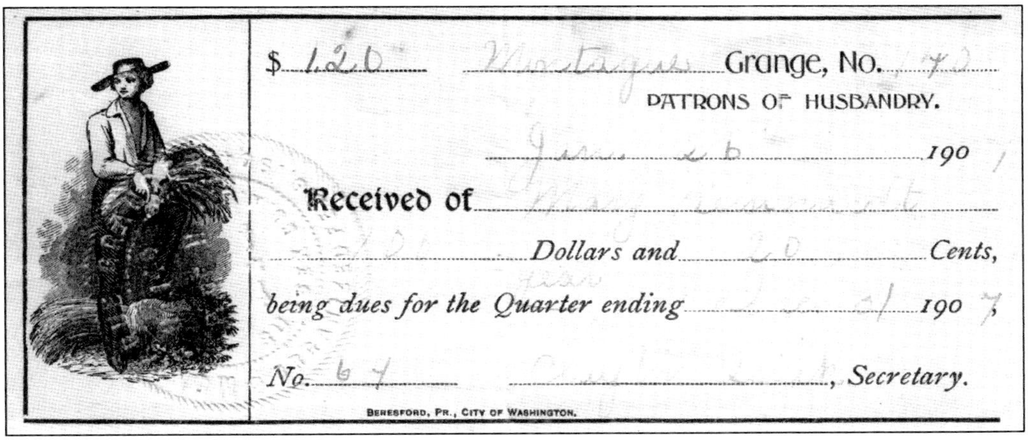

$ 1.20 .... Grange, No. ....

PATRONS OF HUSBANDRY.

.... 190

Received of ....

.... *Dollars and* .... *Cents,*

being dues for the Quarter ending *190*

No. 67 ...., *Secretary.*

BERESFORD, PR., CITY OF WASHINGTON.

This receipt dating from 1907 was for Mary Reinhardt, one of the initial members of the local Montague Grange, No. 140, Patrons of Husbandry. It is signed by Clayton Quick, as secretary. The National Grange of the Order of Patrons of Husbandry is a fraternal organization that formed in 1867. It encouraged rural families to band together for their common economic and political good. (Courtesy of the Montague Grange.)

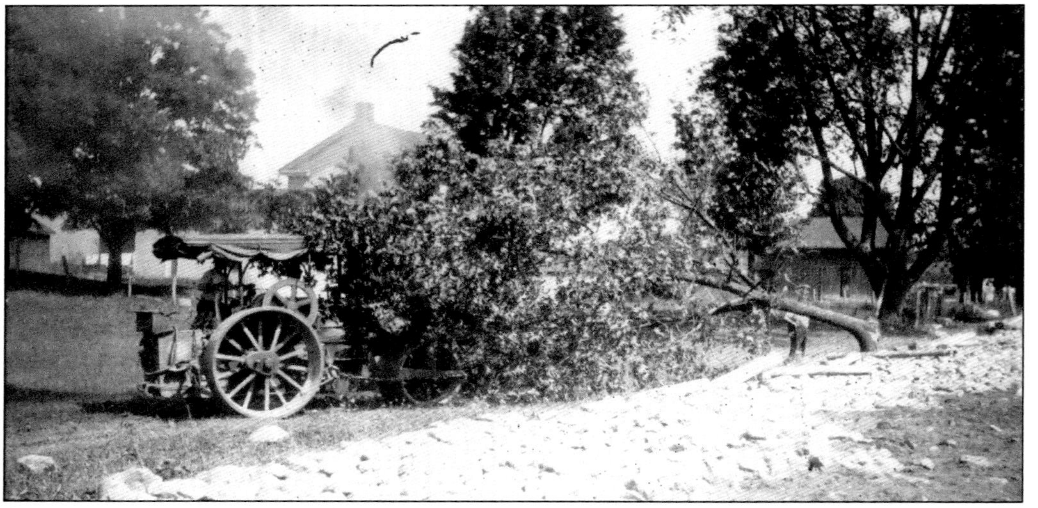

Once equipment became mechanized, horses, mules, and oxen were replaced by power. This photograph appears to show a steam-powered roller or tractor, which could be used for plowing or hauling. It enabled someone to tackle more work with less man power. It would be replaced in 1924 by gas-powered equipment.

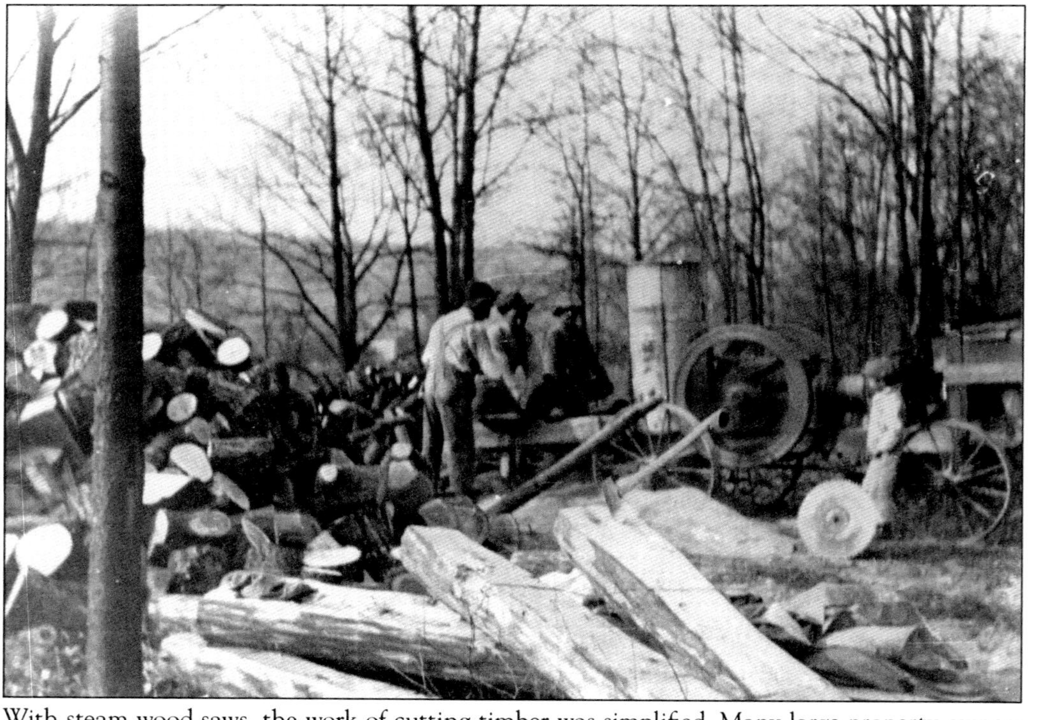

With steam wood saws, the work of cutting timber was simplified. Many large property owners owned woodlots as those parcels were more inland and up along the ridges and not suitable for farming. The timber taken off these built many homes, fueled fireplaces and stoves, and also was cut as railroad ties for the Erie Railroad.

Three

On the Mountain and Other Highlights

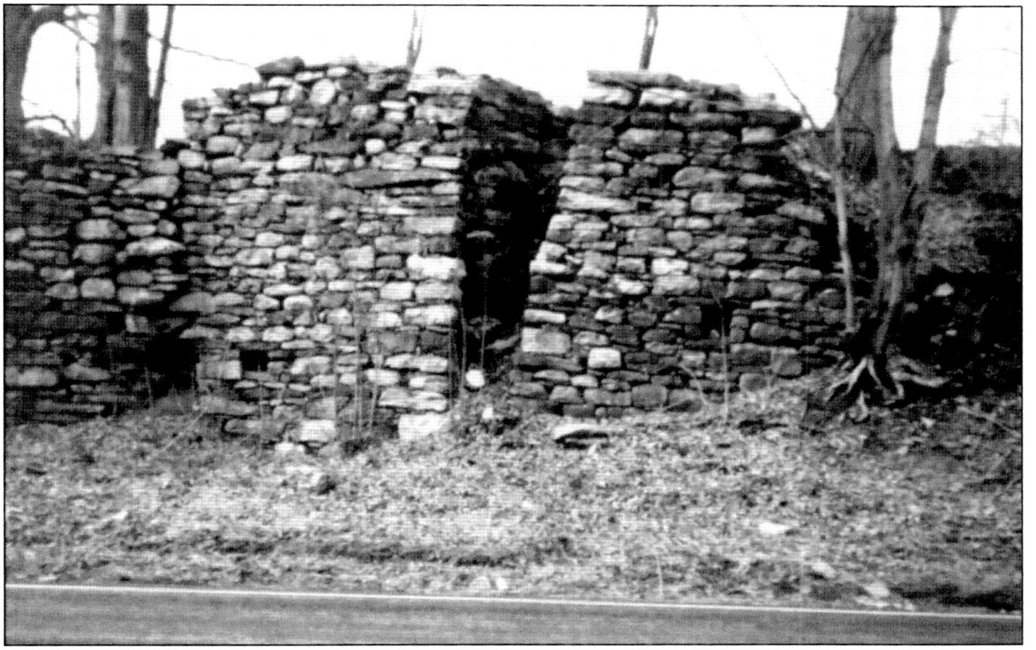

Along Clove Road, few limekilns remain as evidence of the lime burning that occurred here. The limestone was quarried nearby and the stone stacked within and burned, until the end product was what was known as quicklime. Its predominant use was as an important ingredient in plaster, whitewash, and mortar and was also used in the tanning process. It was later used in agriculture. (Courtesy of Darrin L. Brooks.)

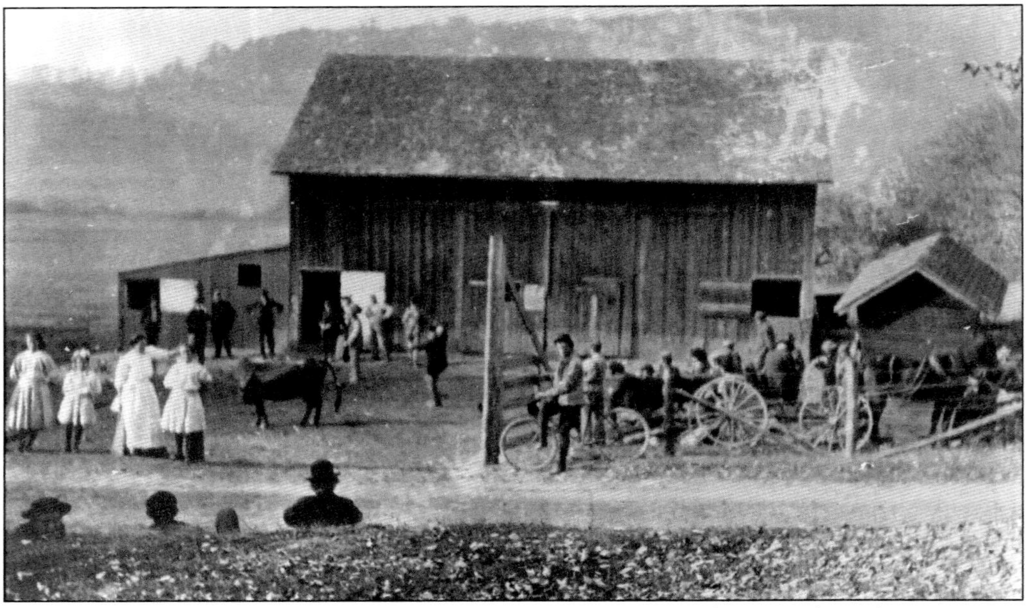

In 1912, there was a large auction held at the Granger farm on Clove Road. Such events were often advertised in newspapers, whenever circumstances required a family to move or to give up its farm. The barn shown here was a typical bank barn style, allowing direct entry to its upper level. The remnant foundation of this structure can still be spotted near Clove Road by the watchful eye.

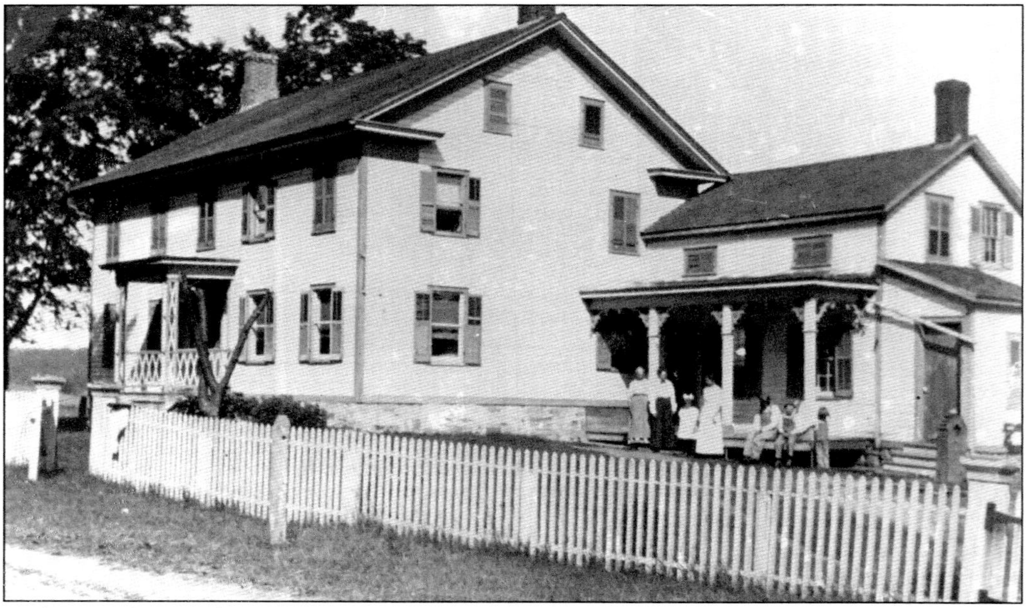

Right next door to the Grangers was this frame house on a large tract of farmland. The property originally had belonged to the vast Nearpass holdings. Across the road, on the east side of Clove Road, remains a small limekiln. It was the Schneider homestead when the photograph was taken in 1912. The house was last lived in by members of the Theodoseau family and was demolished after falling into disrepair.

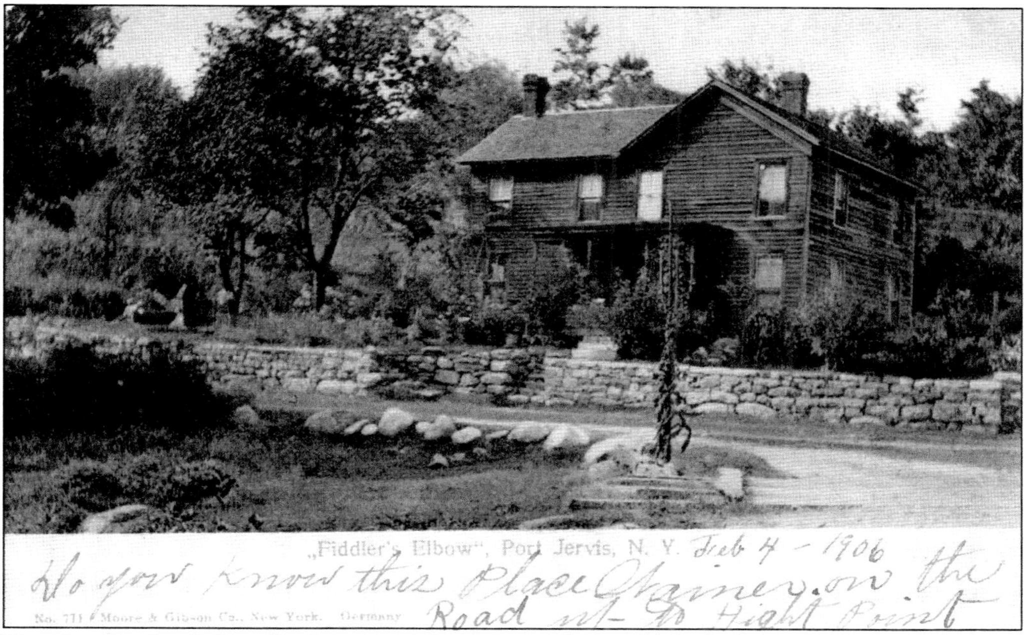

Travelers on the Colesville-Carpenters Point Turnpike would find a looped portion of the road called Fiddler's Elbow, which led by this home once owned by Julia Jones. The turnpike was chartered in 1851 and with it the incorporation of the Rutherford Turnpike Company. John Rutherford was its principal and controlling stockholder. It served as a mail and freight route between Port Jervis and Colesville, then an important locale for the sale of lumber.

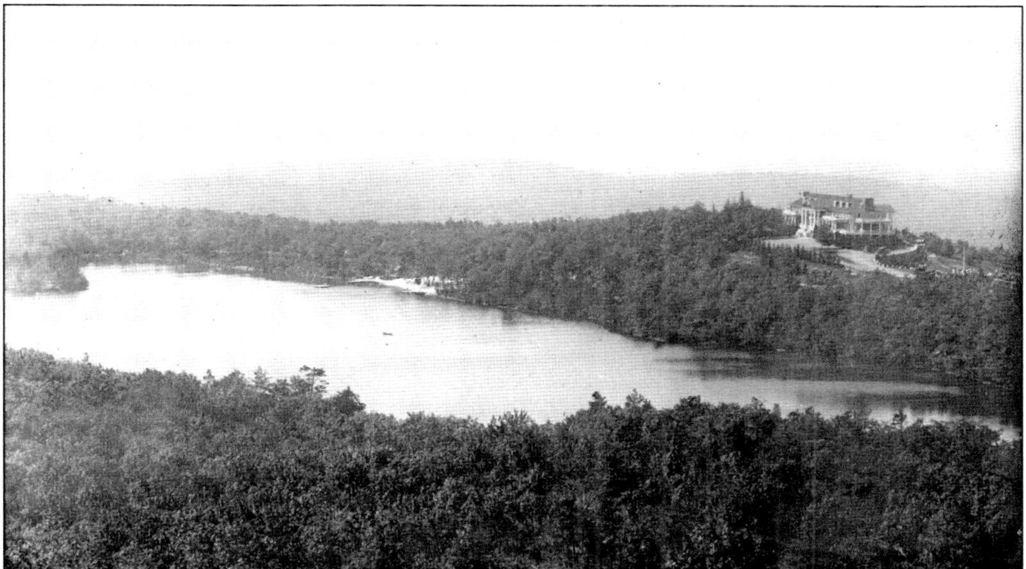

High Point Inn opened in 1890 and looked out on Lake Marcia. The 20-acre glacial lake was named by geologist Dr. William Kitchell for his childhood sweetheart and fiancée, Marcia Smith. It remains a favored spot for swimming in the summer, as well as ice-fishing and ice-skating in winter, and is the highest lake in New Jersey. (Courtesy of Brian J. Lewis collection.)

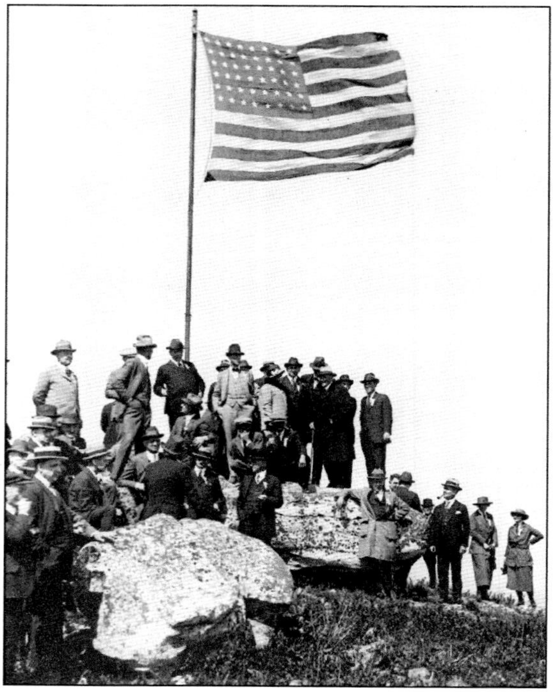

This photograph commemorates a dedication, showing a number of the park commissioners and Col. Anthony Kuser leaning on a cane. Off to the side are adult Girl Scouts wearing the uniforms of the era. A history detective would note that the American flag being flown shows 48 stars and represents a period from 1912 to 1959. (Courtesy of High Point State Park.)

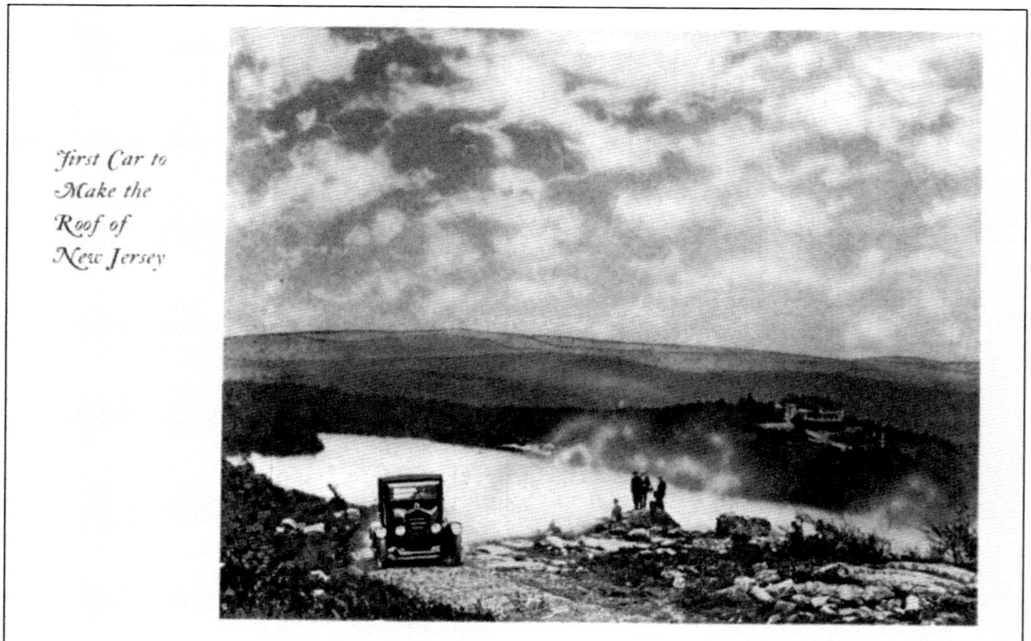

Once automobiles were more widely produced, the area saw an influx of tourists. While today's cars with better-powered engines still find the steep climb up High Point Mountain challenging, particularly in inclement weather, imagine the sense of accomplishment this driver felt on being the first. The creation of the Dryden and Kuser estates into a preserve prompted the improvement of adjoining roads. (Courtesy of High Point State Park.)

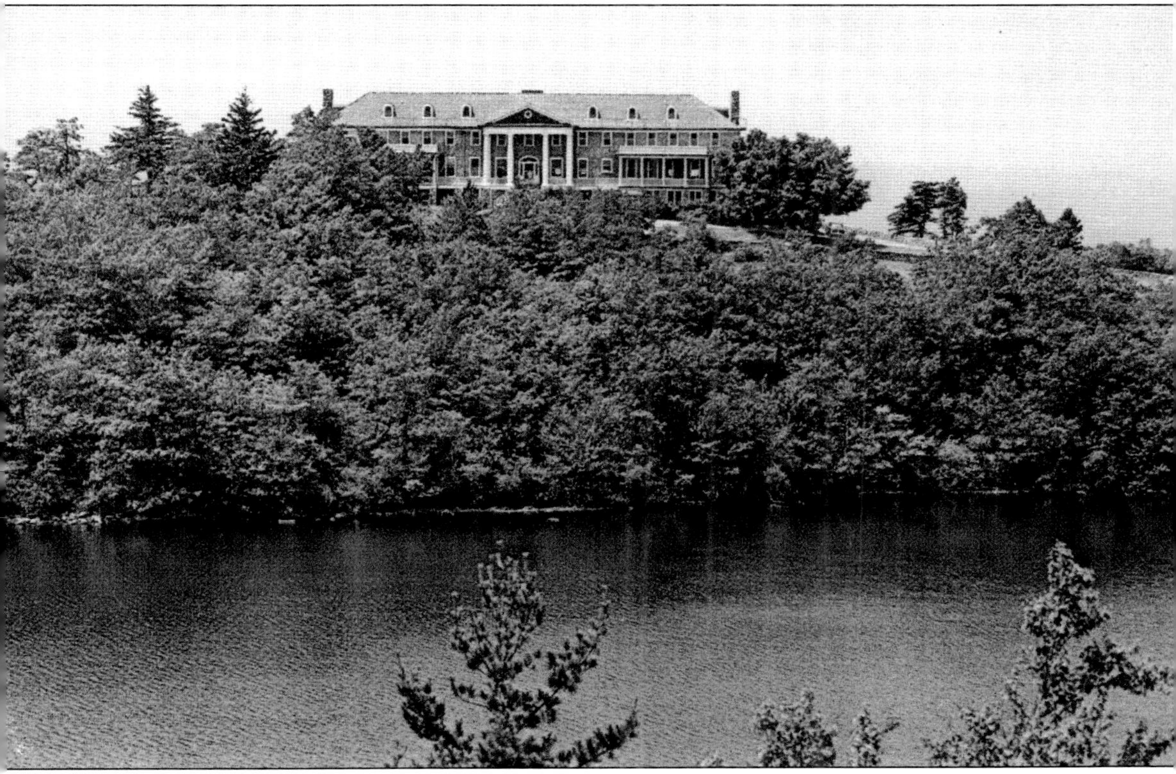

Kuser Mansion, within High Point Park, was given to the people of the state of New Jersey by Col. Anthony Kuser in 1923. It was an expansion of High Point Inn built in 1888, which became Kuser Lodge in 1911. The Kusers remodeled the inn from its former Adirondack style to reflect more of a Colonial Revival, similar to their Bernardsville estate. As part of the park it saw use as a visitors' center, museum, and inn. After falling into disrepair, it closed to the public in 1977. Despite outcries for its preservation, the once-stately building was in disrepair and was demolished in 1995. An interpretative panel currently indicates its former location.

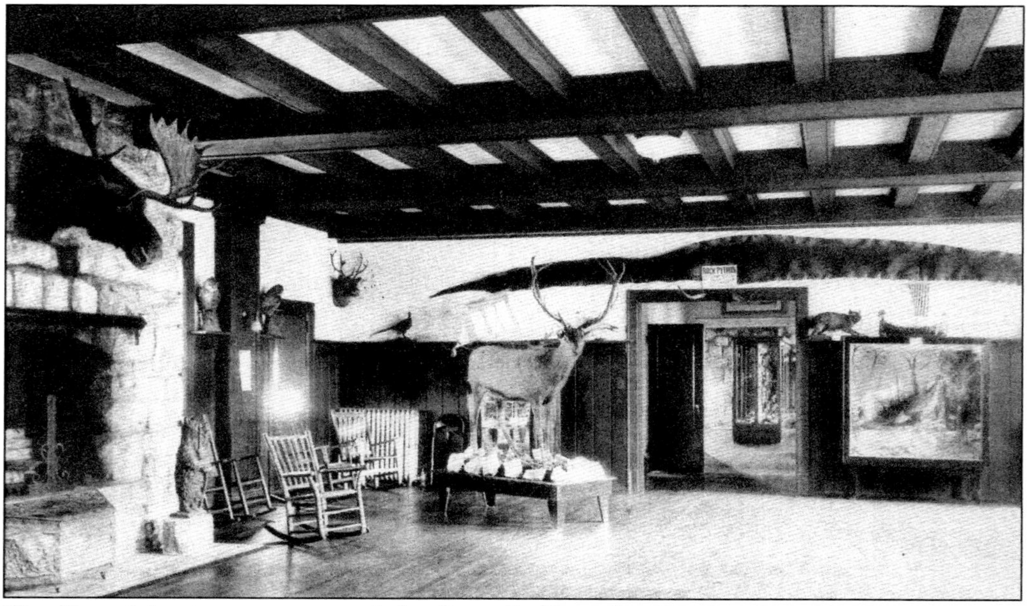

The Kuser Mansion was renamed the State Building shortly after Susie Dryden Kuser and her husband presented their tract to the State of New Jersey in 1923. Part of its first floor was transformed into a museum to show off a wide array of exhibits, artifacts, and collections for the public's enjoyment. The building saw limited use after 1969 and closed a few years later. (Courtesy of High Point State Park.)

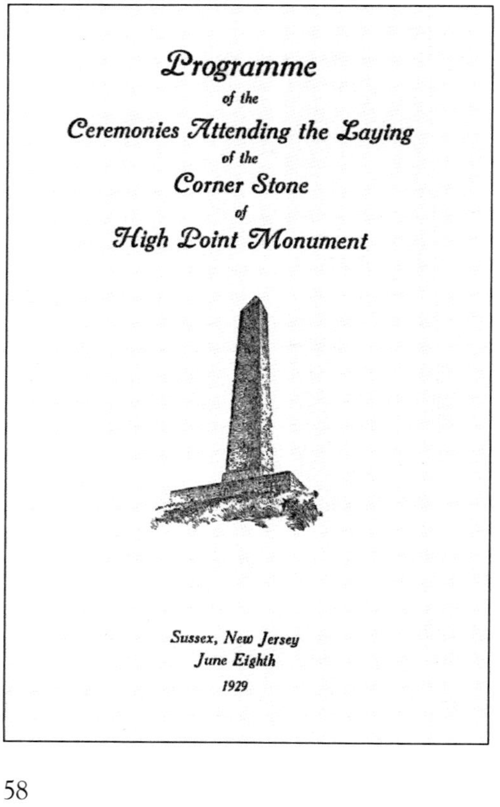

Programme
of the
Ceremonies Attending the Laying
of the
Corner Stone
of
High Point Monument

Sussex, New Jersey
June Eighth
1929

The dedication of the cornerstone for High Point Monument was held in 1929, although the actual construction of the base had started the prior August. Afterward, the shaft would be built of granite with a quartzite filling, which was used from the park property. At the time, a state police headquarters and an emergency hospital were located in the Girl Scouts building. (Courtesy of Minisink Valley Historical Society.)

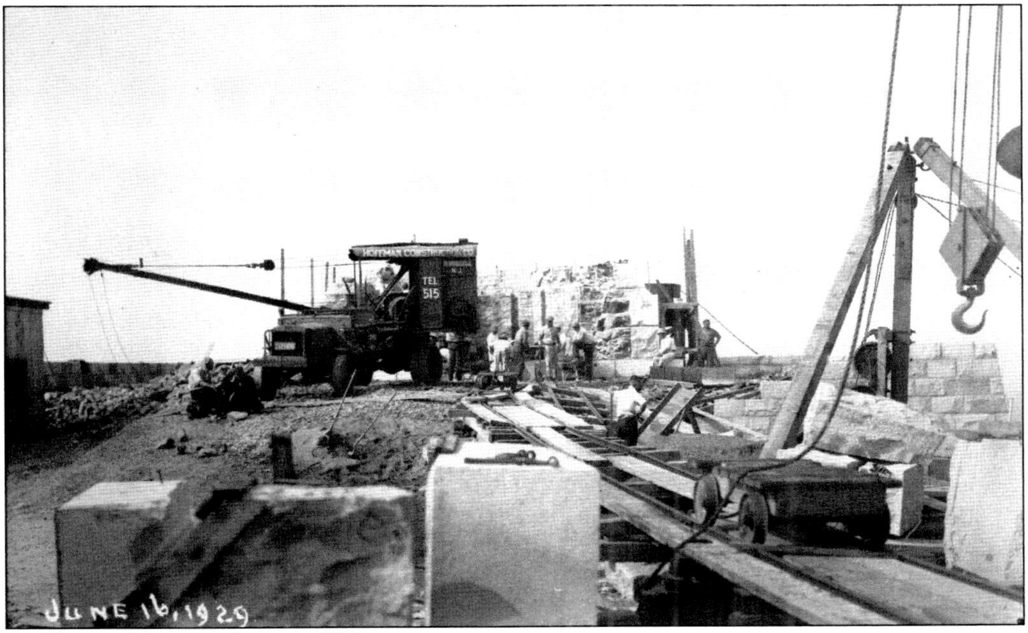

The Hoffman Construction Company of Bernardsville was hired to build the Soldiers and Sailors Monument, utilizing granite brought in through Tri-States and sand from Huguenot, New York. Many local residents were employed in assembling the obelisk, and the work was able to progress at a rate of three feet of height gained per day. This records the status on June 16, 1929. (Courtesy of High Point State Park.)

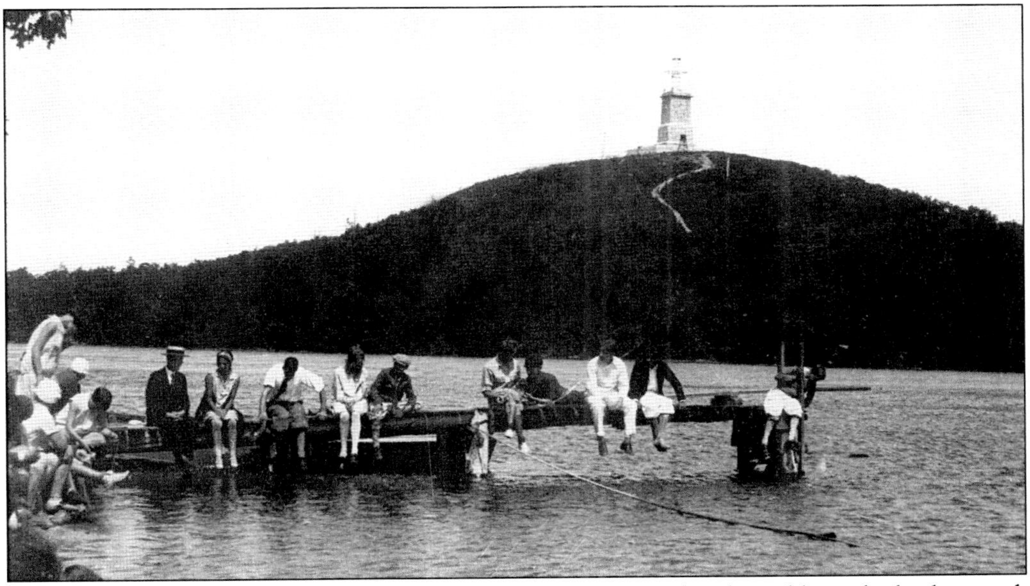

With the completed base and lower portion of the monument already visible in the background, the summer of 1929 visitors relax on a dock by the lake. Note the younger men wearing knickers, the women stylishly sporting typical short bob haircuts and flapper-style cloche hats, and the properly suited young gentleman wearing a straw boater. (Courtesy of High Point State Park.)

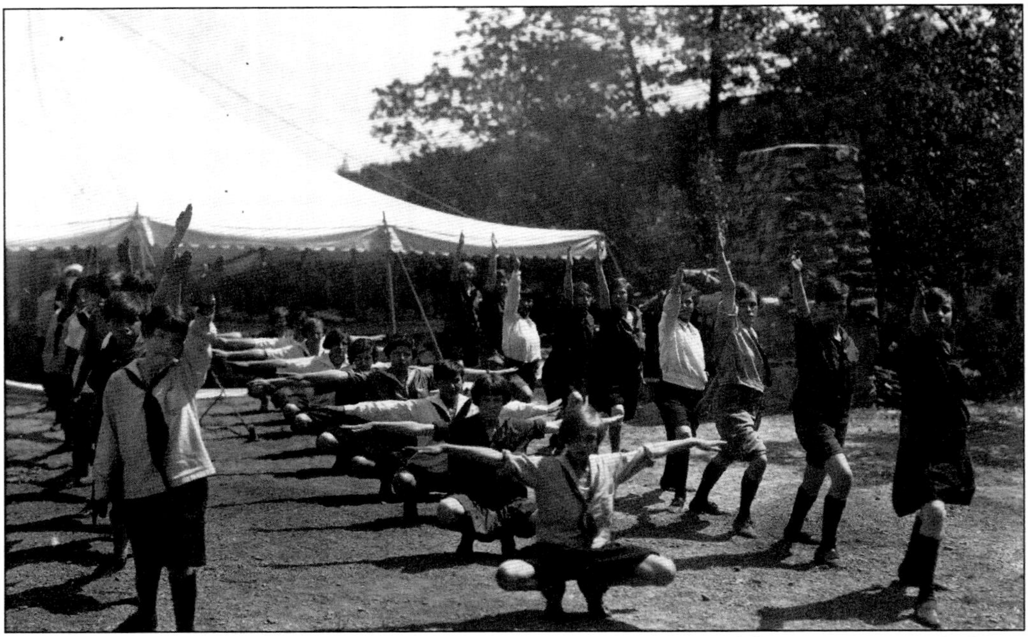

After the Dryden-Kuser tract opened as a state park in 1923 and modifications were made for its broader use, groups sought use of the grounds. The Girl Scouts opened Camp Kalmia about the mid-1920s. Here a group of Scouts is doing its morning calisthenics out in the clear mountain air. (Courtesy of High Point State Park.)

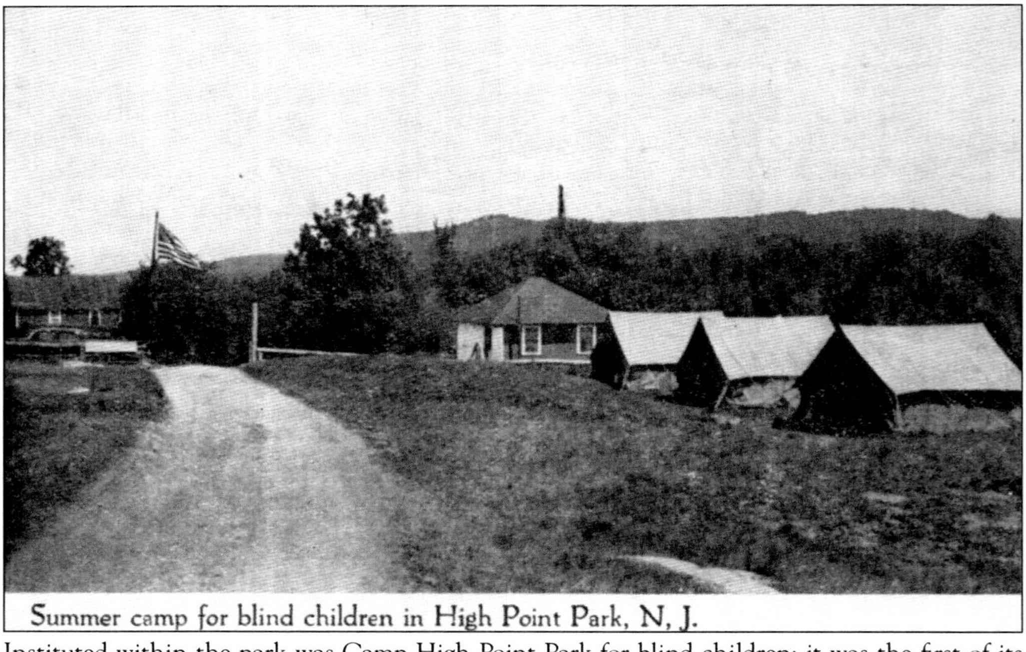

Instituted within the park was Camp High Point Park for blind children; it was the first of its kind in New Jersey. The first campers would attend in the summer of 1937. Individual groups of girls were followed by the boys' groups, and each stayed for a two-week period. These buildings were located near a group camping area currently used. (Courtesy of Beth Jones.)

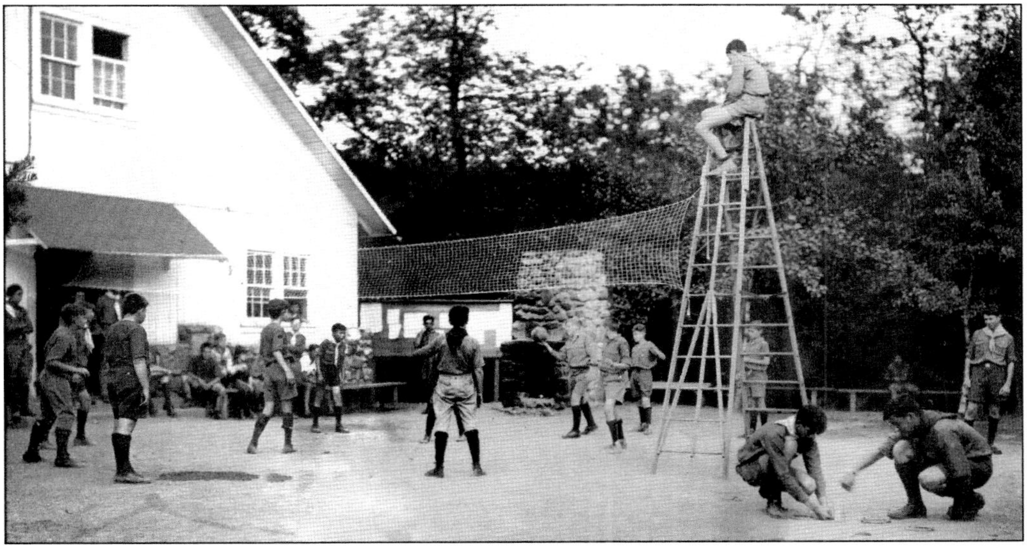

The Boy Scouts ran Kamp Henry Kohl from 1930 to 1951. The camp was named in honor of the president and founder of the National Grocery Company. Volleyball is played outside the camp mess hall while other Scouts tend to the horseshoe stakes nearby. A local Montague resident, Robert E. Quinn, recorded the memories of camping there in his book titled *On My Honor*. (Courtesy of High Point State Park.)

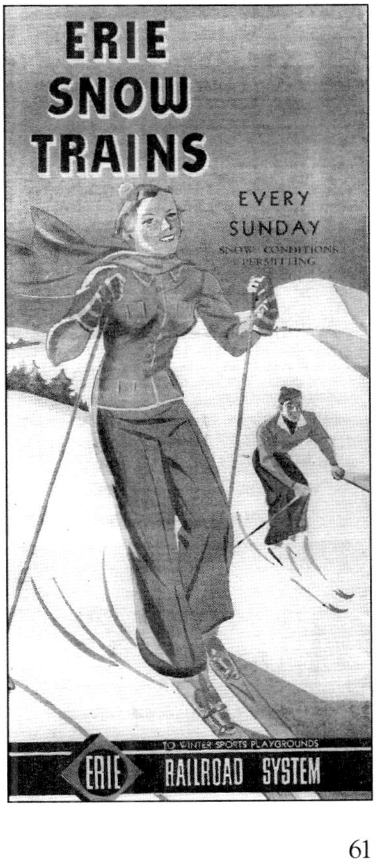

The Erie Railroad line sponsored snow trains from New York City and Jersey City to High Point. A 1923 train trip from New York City to Port Jervis took about 2 hours and 15 minutes, with the balance of the trip from the train depot to High Point "on the roof of New Jersey" by motor carrier. Round-trip fare on the "Snow King" cost $2.50. (Courtesy of Alicia C. Batko.)

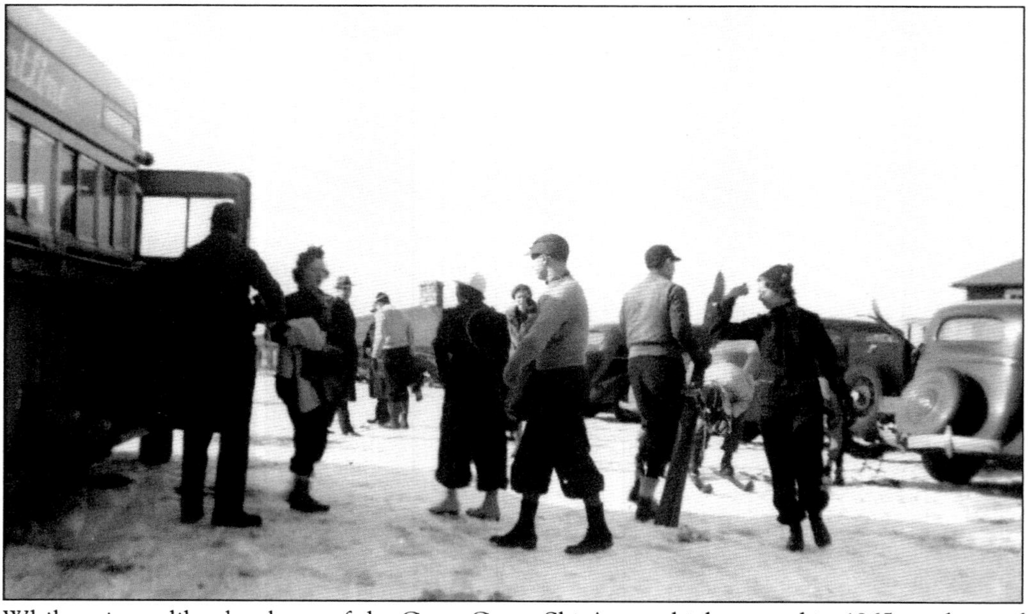

While quite unlike the slopes of the Great Gorge Ski Area, which opened in 1965, or those of Vernon Valley and Mountain Creek that followed, High Point attracted adventurers ready to hit the slopes by the late 1930s. Tour buses brought those ready to attempt ice-skating, tobogganing, or downhill skiing on the trails the Civilian Conservation Corps had created for such uses. (Courtesy of High Point State Park.)

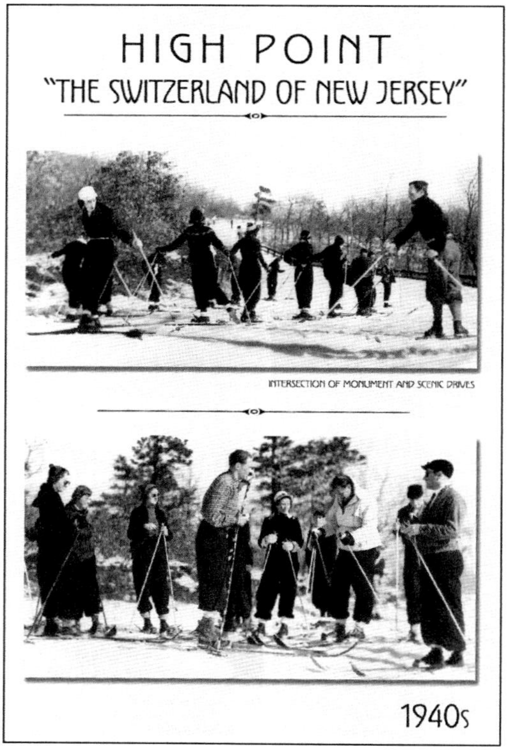

This display commemorates a time when High Point Park was promoted as "the Switzerland of New Jersey," a title first mentioned in local newspapers in 1937. The photographs were taken by the intersection of Monument and Scenic Drives, and the panel was created by interpretive specialist Kate Foord. Cross-country skiing still attracts participants to the park. (Courtesy of High Point State Park.)

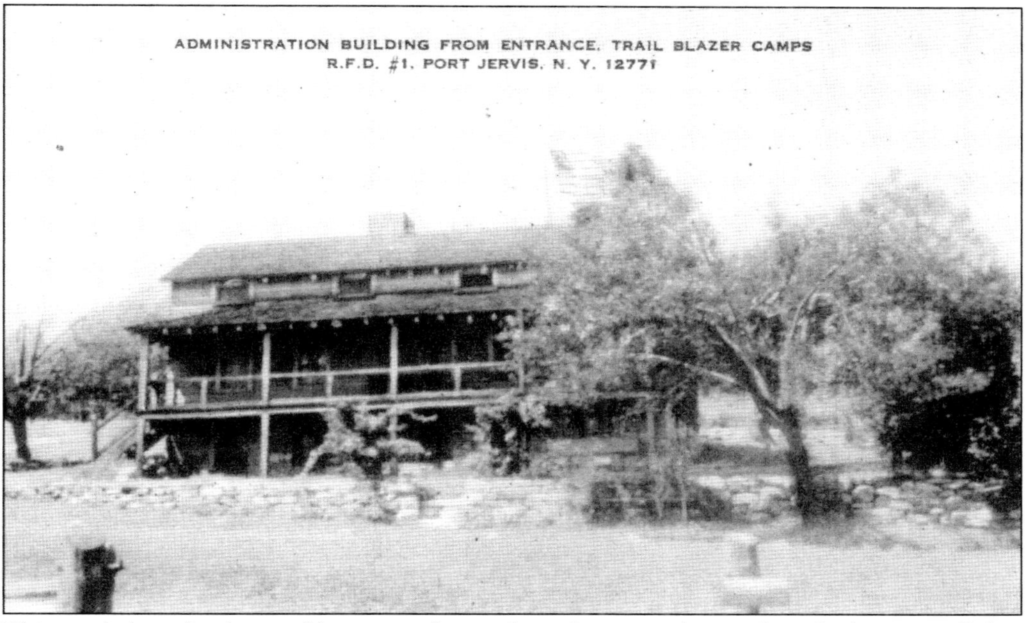

This was believed to be an old stagecoach inn along the original turnpike, which ran parallel to the existing route of Deckertown Turnpike at the eastern end in Montague. It veers a little bit to the north of the present route. When the road was realigned and the property turned over to use by campers, this became a counselors' cabin.

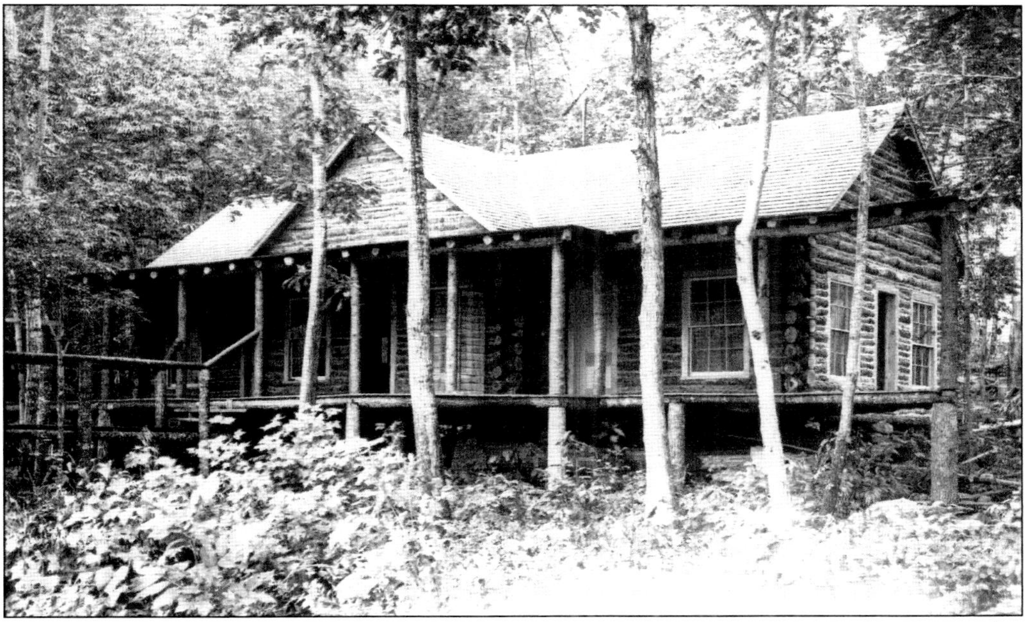

A rustic clubhouse was built nearby by prominent residents of New York and Orange, who incorporated the Mashipacong Club in 1901. Its location boasted being only a two-hour drive from the Erie Railroad in Port Jervis. The land around the lake was platted into lots, with 100 feet of frontage. Although acquired by Charles Robinson, after 20 years it was sold to Charles Orben.

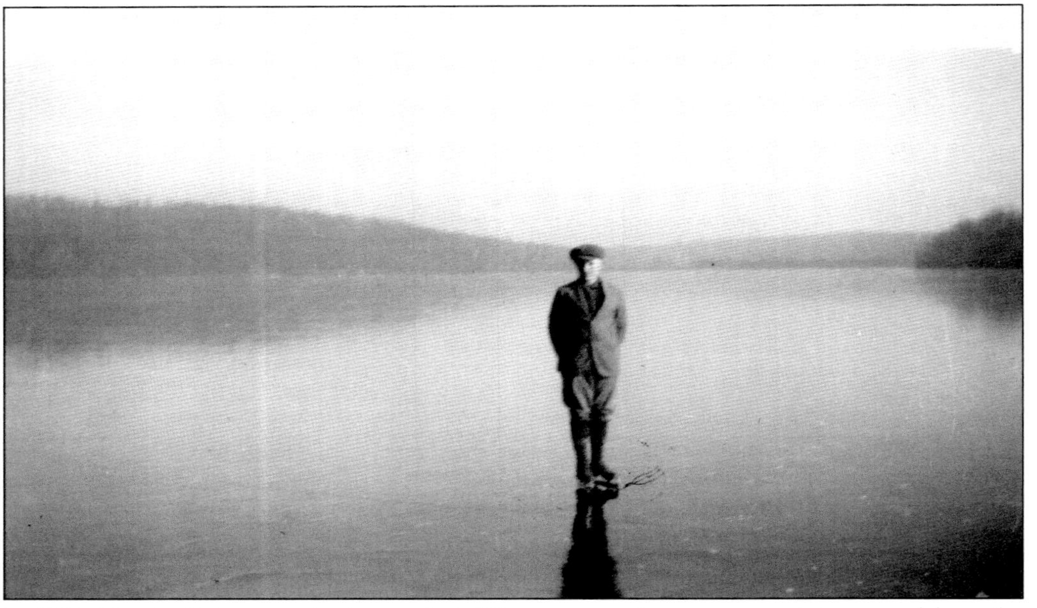

In 1929, Charles Orben acquired a nearly 1,000-acre tract that was a remaining parcel from the Sussex Allotments. Great lot No. 15 sat on the ridge heading toward Wantage. An impounded swamp had been transformed into a 46-acre lake in 1848 called Mashipacong Pond, to provide power to run two mills owned by John Rutherford. The parcel abutted High Point Park and Stokes State Forest.

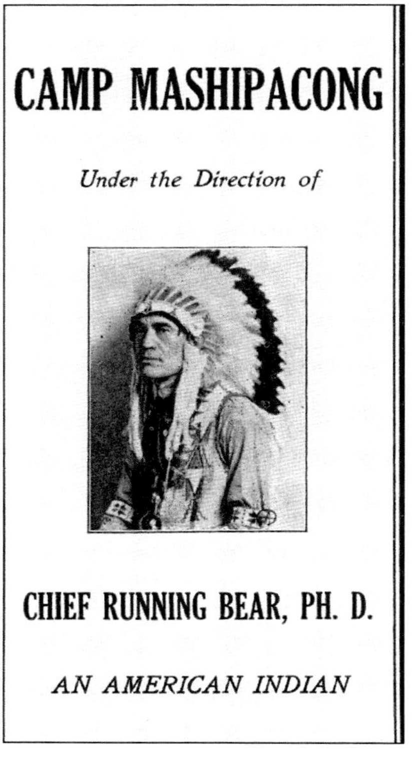

Trying to draw city people in to experience nature and learn Native American lore, Camp Mashipacong boasted of being an ideal camping location. It was run under the direction of Chief Running Bear, Ph.D., and claimed the camp catered "to a select clientele." The chief was described as being a Powhattan Indian and a Mason.

Orben and his son hoped to form an exclusive fishing and hunting preserve. The large parcel was advertised for sale by this mailing. It presented the asking price of $12,500 for the tract and related that it held three log cabins and the caretaker's house. Doris Duke bought the parcel in 1938 and leased it to Life Fresh Air Camps, which evolved into a National Camp training center for decentralized camping.

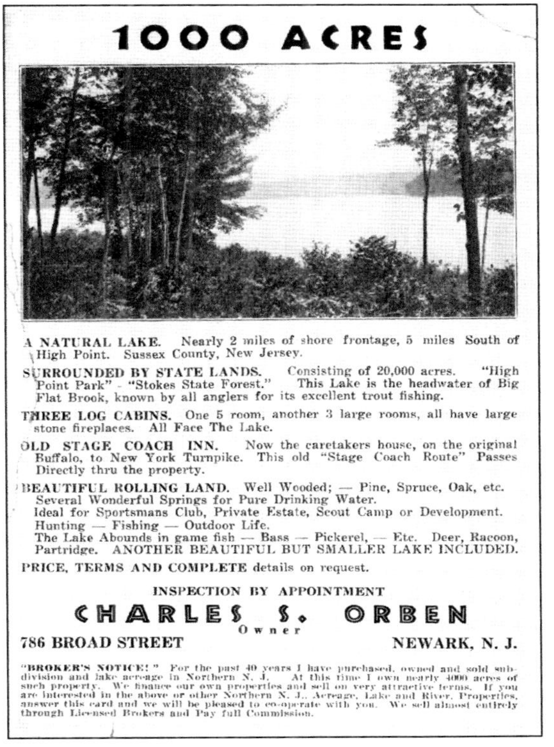

1000 ACRES

A NATURAL LAKE. Nearly 2 miles of shore frontage, 5 miles South of High Point. Sussex County, New Jersey.

SURROUNDED BY STATE LANDS. Consisting of 20,000 acres. "High Point Park" - "Stokes State Forest." This Lake is the headwater of Big Flat Brook, known by all anglers for its excellent trout fishing.

THREE LOG CABINS. One 5 room, another 3 large rooms, all have large stone fireplaces. All Face The Lake.

OLD STAGE COACH INN. Now the caretakers house, on the original Buffalo, to New York Turnpike. This old "Stage Coach Route" Passes Directly thru the property.

BEAUTIFUL ROLLING LAND. Well Wooded; — Pine, Spruce, Oak, etc.
Several Wonderful Springs for Pure Drinking Water.
Ideal for Sportsmans Club, Private Estate, Scout Camp or Development.
Hunting — Fishing — Outdoor Life.
The Lake Abounds in game fish — Bass — Pickerel, — Etc. Deer, Racoon, Partridge. ANOTHER BEAUTIFUL BUT SMALLER LAKE INCLUDED.

PRICE, TERMS AND COMPLETE details on request.

INSPECTION BY APPOINTMENT

CHARLES S. ORBEN
Owner

786 BROAD STREET NEWARK, N. J.

"BROKER'S NOTICE!" For the past 40 years I have purchased, owned and sold subdivision and lake acreage in Northern N. J. At this time I own nearly 4000 acres of such property. We finance our own properties and sell on very attractive terms. If you are interested in the above or other Northern N. J., Acreage, Lake and River, Properties, answer this card and we will be pleased to co-operate with you. We sell almost entirely through Licensed Brokers and Pay full Commission.

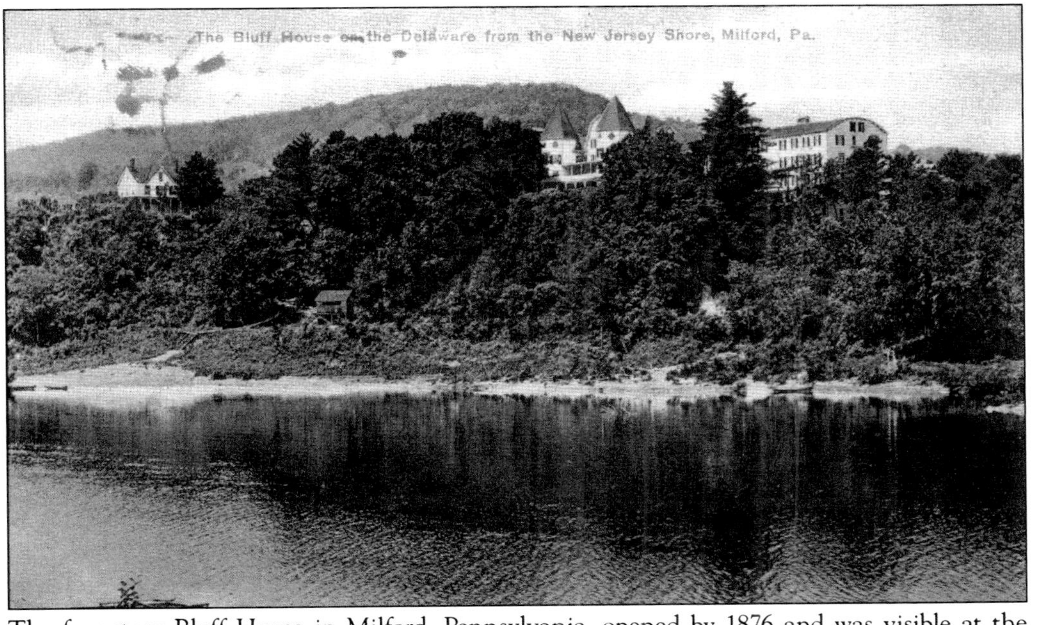

The four-story Bluff House in Milford, Pennsylvania, opened by 1876 and was visible at the river's bank. It would undergo expansions to accommodate up to 350 guests and boasted of superior accommodations and social advantages. Local Montague residents found employment there until it burned down in a 1947 snowstorm. Its inferno became so intense that brushfires ignited on the Jersey side of the river.

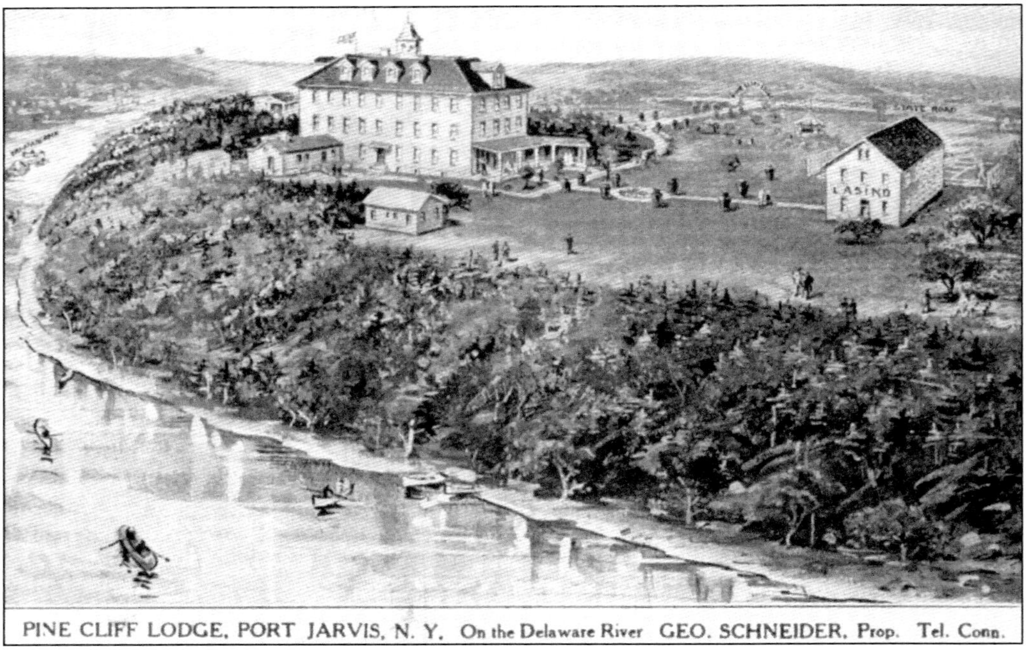

This Landis postcard presents Pine Grove, which was located on the west side of River Road, just prior to the New York state line. It also went by the name of Pine Cliff Farm in the 1920s, when George Schneider was proprietor and during which a fireproof garage and dancing pavilion were advertised. (Courtesy of Brian J. Lewis collection.)

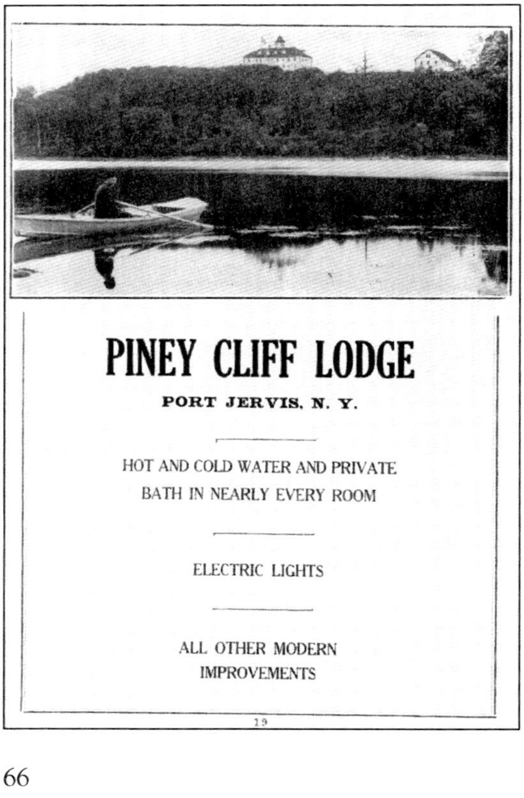

The resort sat 200 feet above the Delaware River and was a stone's throw from Tri-State Rock where thousands of summer people sought the privilege of standing in three states at one time. Its advertisements invited people to enjoy its entrancing views and to partake of its own farm products and artesian well water. (Courtesy of Minisink Valley Historical Society.)

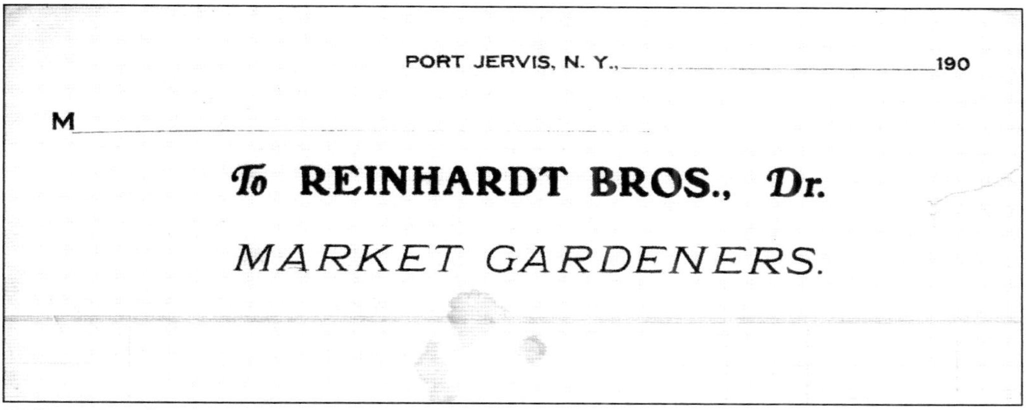

PORT JERVIS, N. Y., ____________ 190

M ____________

To REINHARDT BROS., Dr.

MARKET GARDENERS.

William Reinhardt came to the United States from Germany and served with the Union forces. He was a landscape gardener and florist by trade and moved to Sussex County where he followed farming. He married Katherine in 1887, and they raised a family of eight. His wife's cooking became well known, and people found excuses to come and enjoy her fine meals. In 1895, sons August, Frederick, George, William, and Charles rented the farm from their father and expanded their homestead to accommodate guests. It was in this manner that Rock View Farms began and their business evolved into the famed Rock View Hotel. (Courtesy of Betsy Reinhardt.)

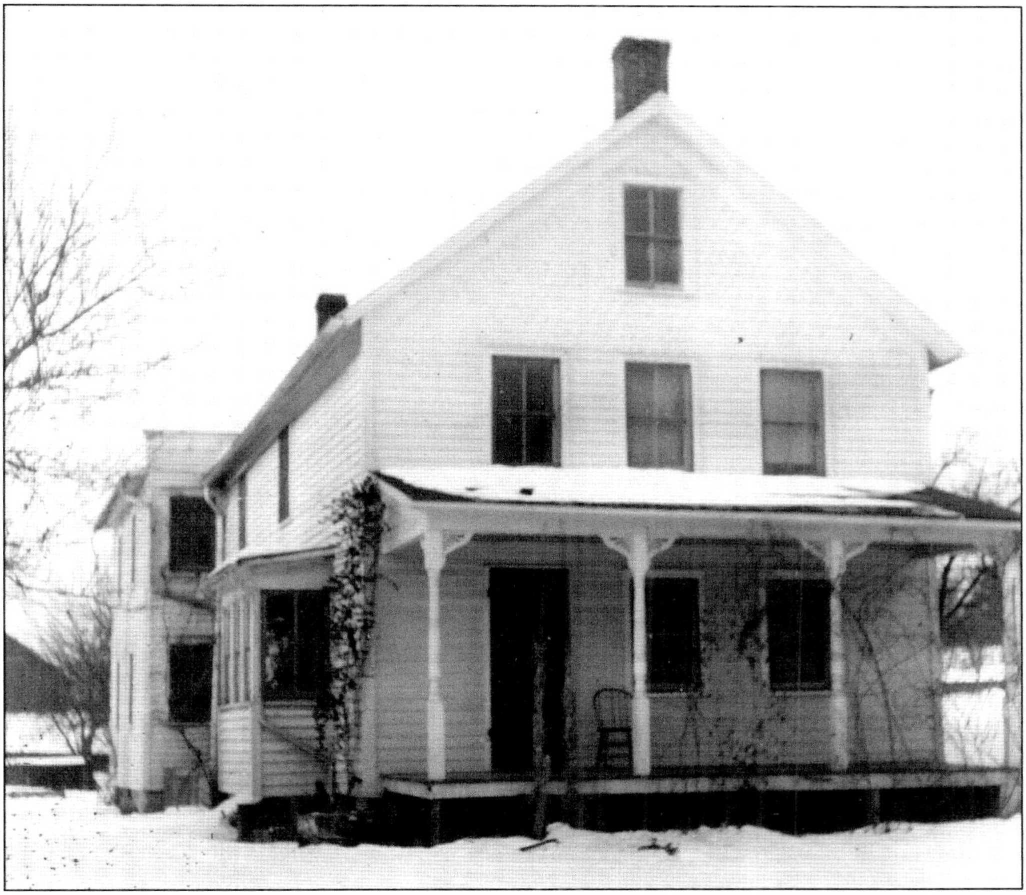

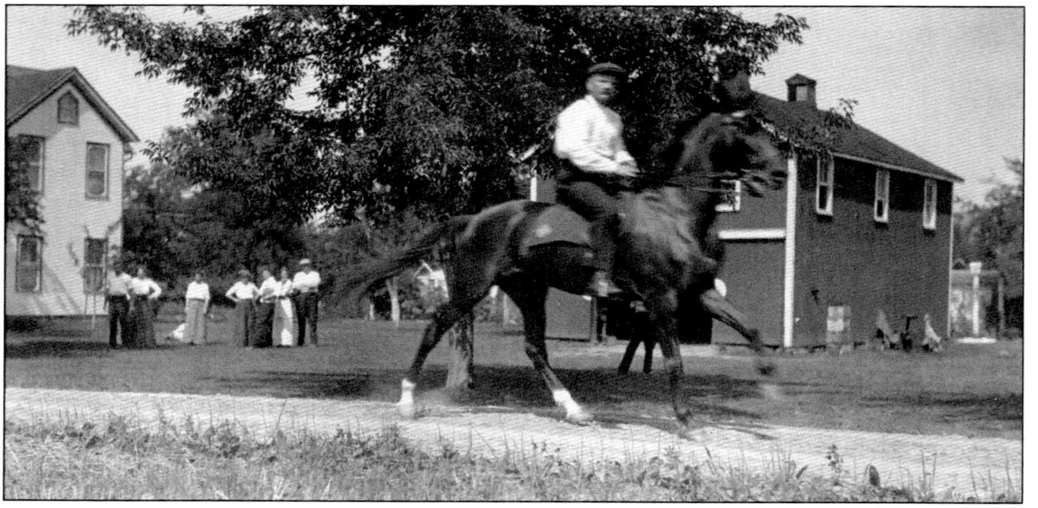

Summer boarding homes in Montague, such as Riverside Farm (page 97), existed since 1890. It became more prevalent for area farmhouses to also rent their extra rooms to accommodate those who sought to escape the crowded city environment. It was not unusual for guests to remain for several weeks and return yearly. Horse riding was popular, as was watching horses race on the mile tracks in the area.

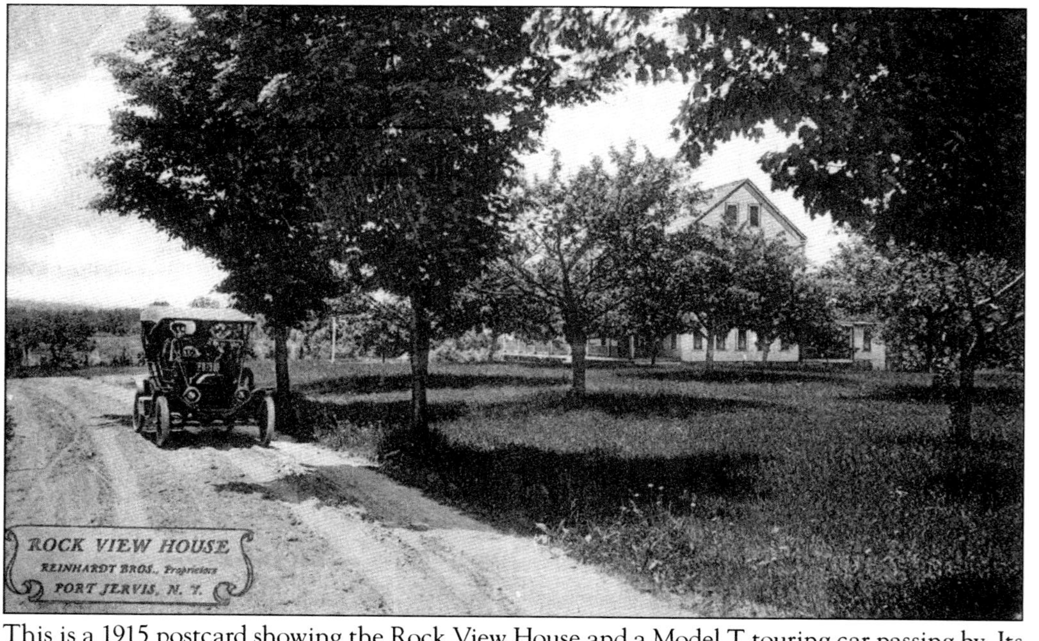

This is a 1915 postcard showing the Rock View House and a Model T touring car passing by. Its drivers are goggled to avoid the dust kicked up on predominantly dirt-packed roads. These slowly replaced the horse-and-buggy days and were made for travel on a gravel road or a grassy field, at speeds of 20 to 25 miles per hour. (Courtesy of Alicia C. Batko.)

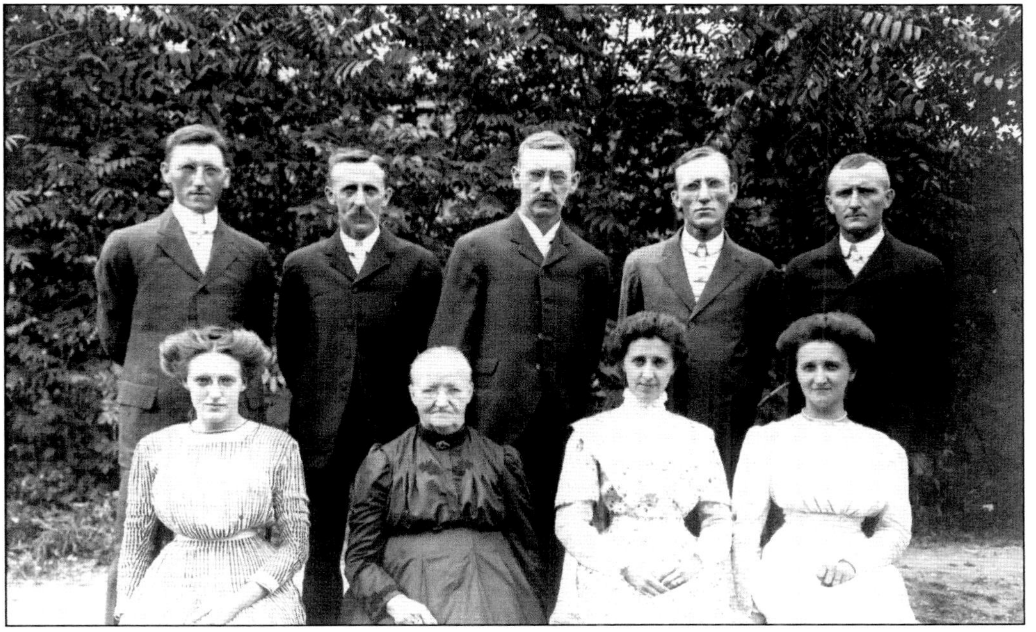

Katherine Reinhardt and her husband, William, had come to this country in the early 1800s. The Reinhardt family posed for this photograph, likely taken at the hotel's opening. Shown from left to right are (first row) Rose, Katherine, Mary, and Louise; (second row) sons Charles, Frederick, August, George, and William. (Courtesy of Betsy Reinhardt.)

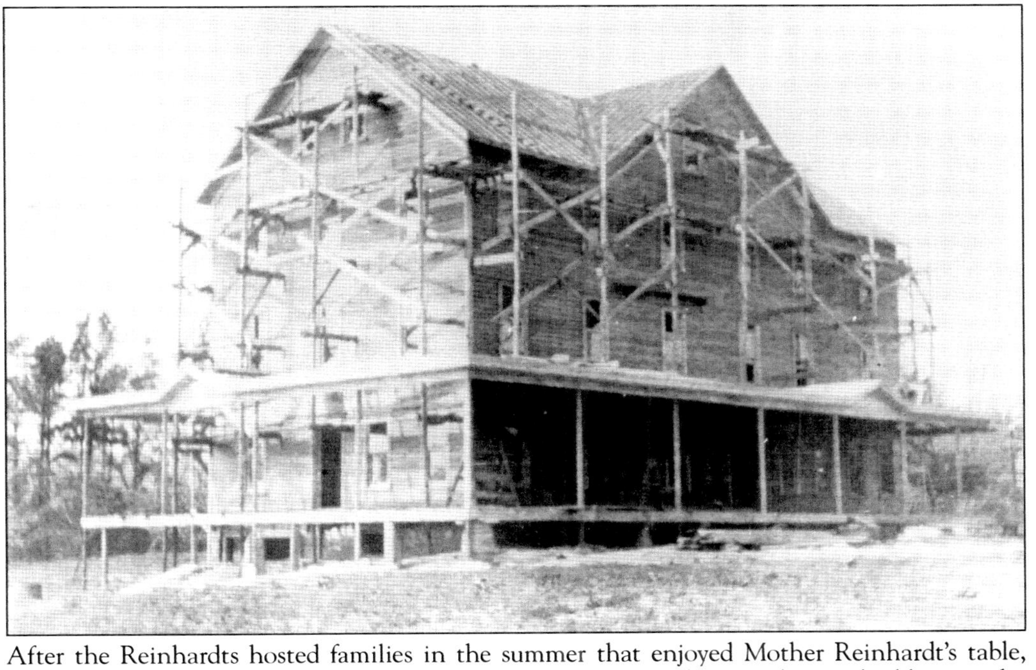

After the Reinhardts hosted families in the summer that enjoyed Mother Reinhardt's table, they decided to build a hotel. This photograph shows the first of the Rock View buildings under construction in 1911. This was a prominent site along the river, premiering with running water in each room, and was built to accommodate 175. (Courtesy of Betsy Reinhardt.)

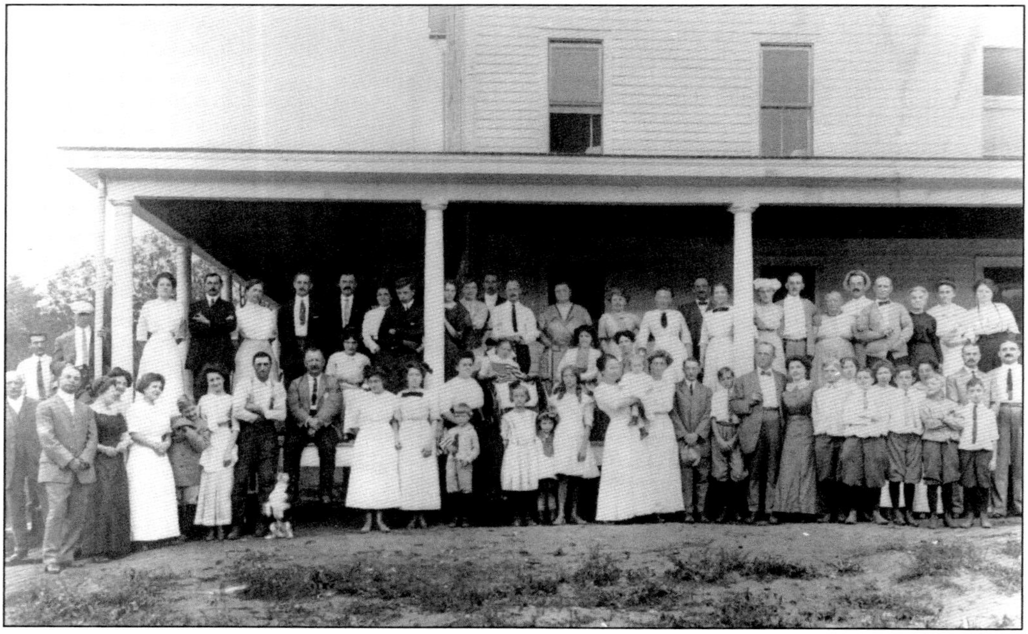

This photograph was taken at the grand opening on June 12, 1912. Members of the family, staff, guests, and neighbors all gathered to celebrate the opening. Mother Reinhardt can be seen standing on the porch, the sixth person from the right. The hotel would remain active well into the 1960s. (Courtesy of Betsy Reinhardt.)

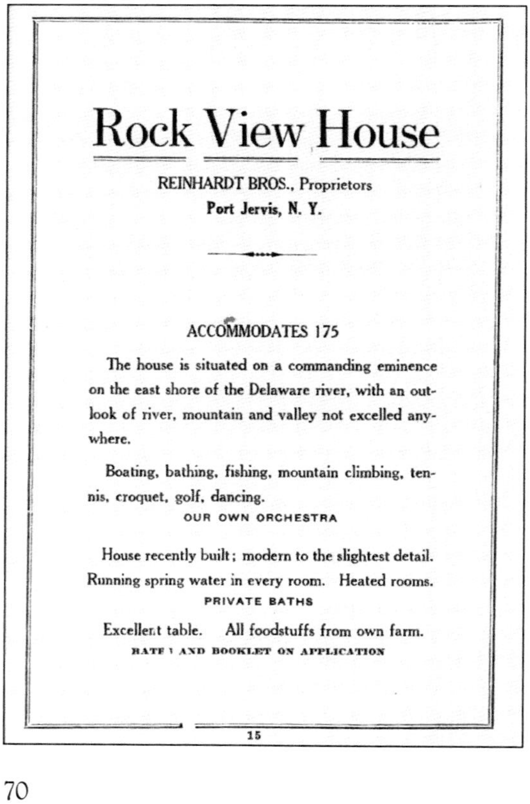

Rock View House

REINHARDT BROS., Proprietors
Port Jervis, N. Y.

ACCOMMODATES 175

The house is situated on a commanding eminence on the east shore of the Delaware river, with an outlook of river, mountain and valley not excelled anywhere.

Boating, bathing, fishing, mountain climbing, tennis, croquet, golf, dancing.

OUR OWN ORCHESTRA

House recently built; modern to the slightest detail.
Running spring water in every room. Heated rooms.

PRIVATE BATHS

Excellent table. All foodstuffs from own farm.

RATES AND BOOKLET ON APPLICATION

15

This announcement ran in advertising that featured the Delaware and Neversink Valley resorts in 1927. It describes the hotel shortly after it first opened and gives an idea of the fine service that clients obtained. Due to the postal service being from Port Jervis, New York, it reflects that address. (Courtesy of Minisink Valley Historical Society.)

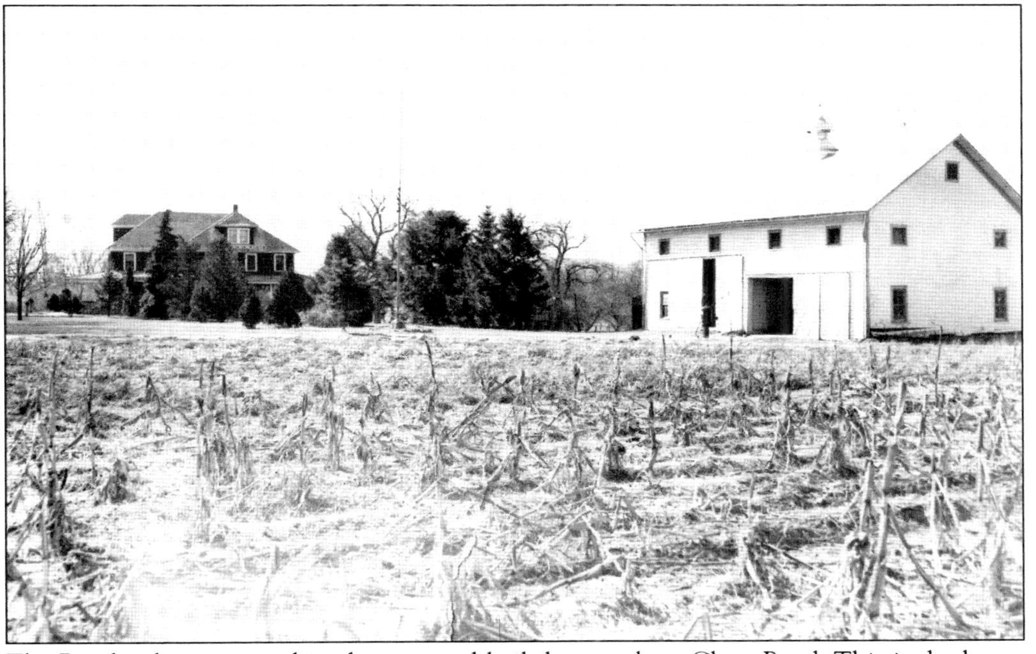

The Reinhardt sons stayed in the area and built homes along Clove Road. This is the house and barn of Frederick Reinhardt. It sat across the way from his brother William's property, on an upper terrace along the river. August moved to the Nearpass-Bigart farm on Clove Road that his son, Goyn, would later also live on. The Reinhardts, in addition to raising vegetables that were used at the hotel, also raised chickens along with many of the local farms. The scene below from the 1920s would have been a familiar sight at harvest time. (Above, courtesy of Betsy Reinhardt.)

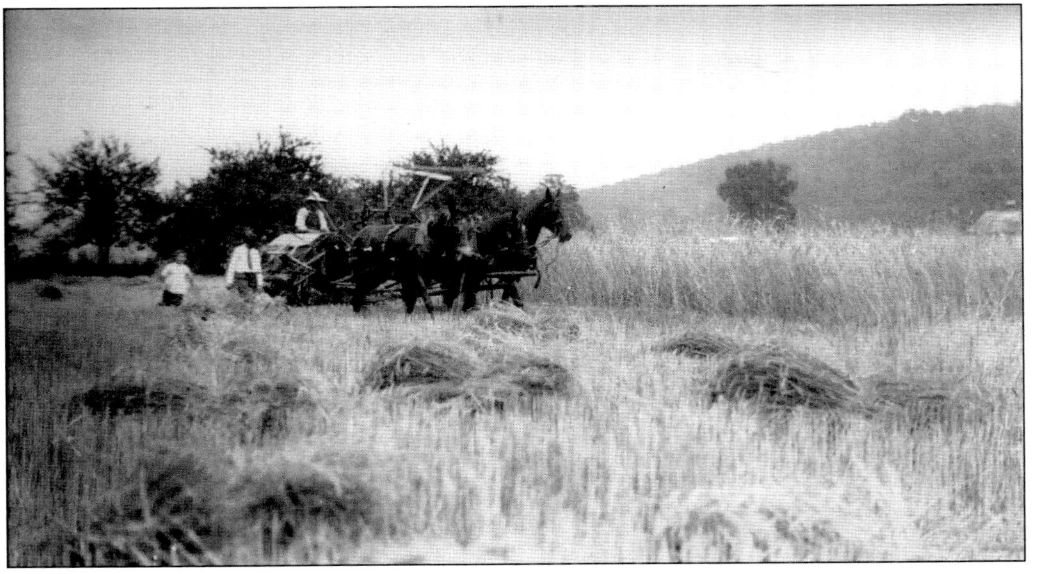

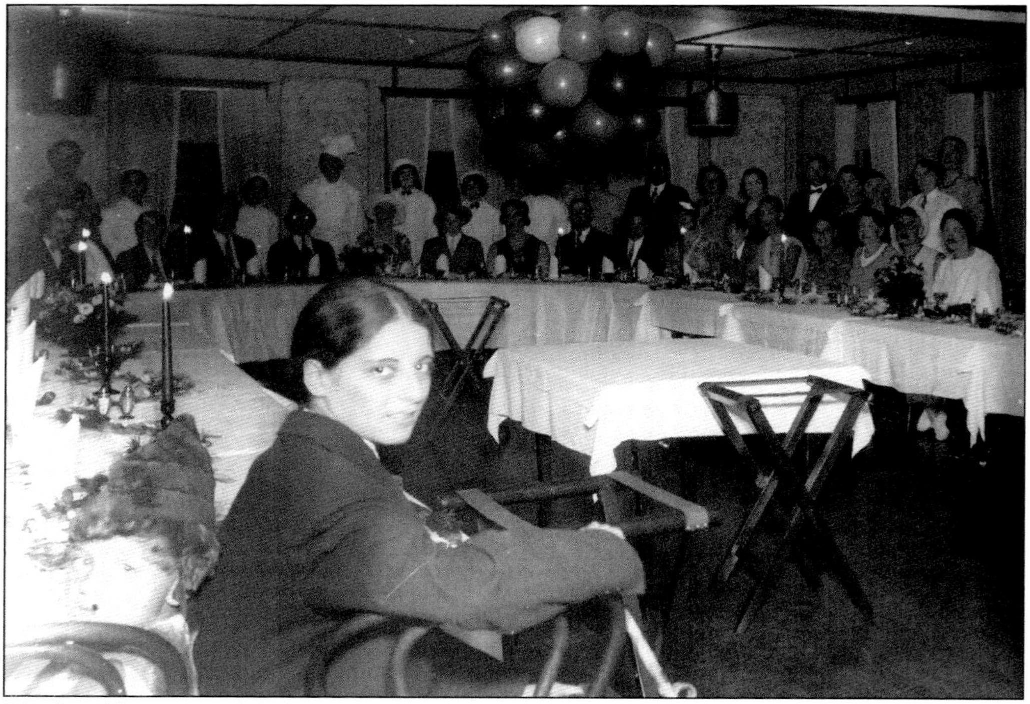

The hotel became widely known for its fine entertainment. Its casino was designed by William Van Alen, the famed architect who designed the Chrysler Building in New York City. The resort also had its own Rock View Playhouse and Grill. Here the guests and staff are shown at a costume party held in the main dining room. (Courtesy of Betsy Reinhardt.)

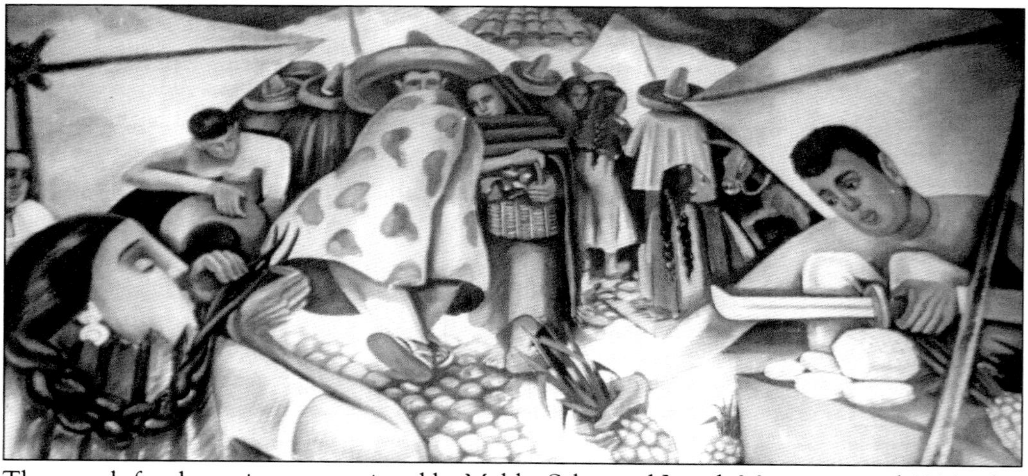

The murals for the casino were painted by Maltby Sykes and Joseph Marino around 1936. This shows but one of the panels that were commissioned by Louise Reinhardt when she ran the hotel. It hosted many large gatherings, and its guests frequently held reunions in New York City. (Courtesy of Betsy Reinhardt.)

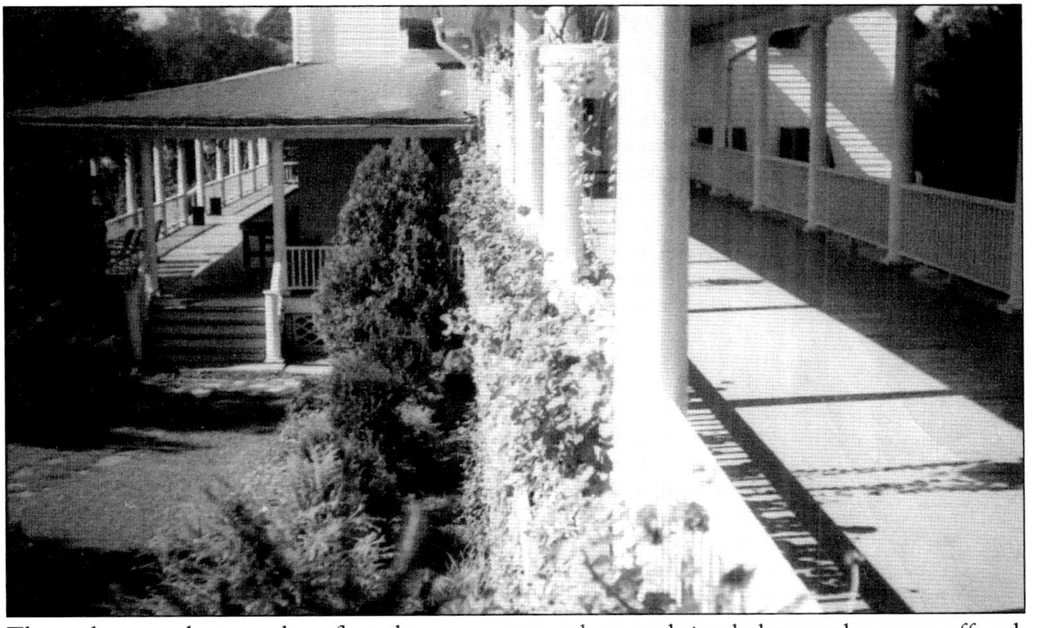

These close-up photographs reflect the serene atmosphere and simple luxury the resort offered. The second building was added in 1926 and connected by the covered promenade. The site was highlighted with its floral gardens. The Pioneer Bar and Grill was part of the main building, a casino began as the Circus Pavilion, and a playhouse was added by 1935. The hotel also offered golf, tennis, swimming, shuffleboard, and badminton for recreation. Louise Reinhardt, its last proprietor, frequently visited New York and traveled to Germany to gather ideas of how the hotel should be run. It was Montague's largest employer through the 1960s but changed ownership in 1963, and many structures were removed by the early 1970s. (Courtesy of Betsy Reinhardt.)

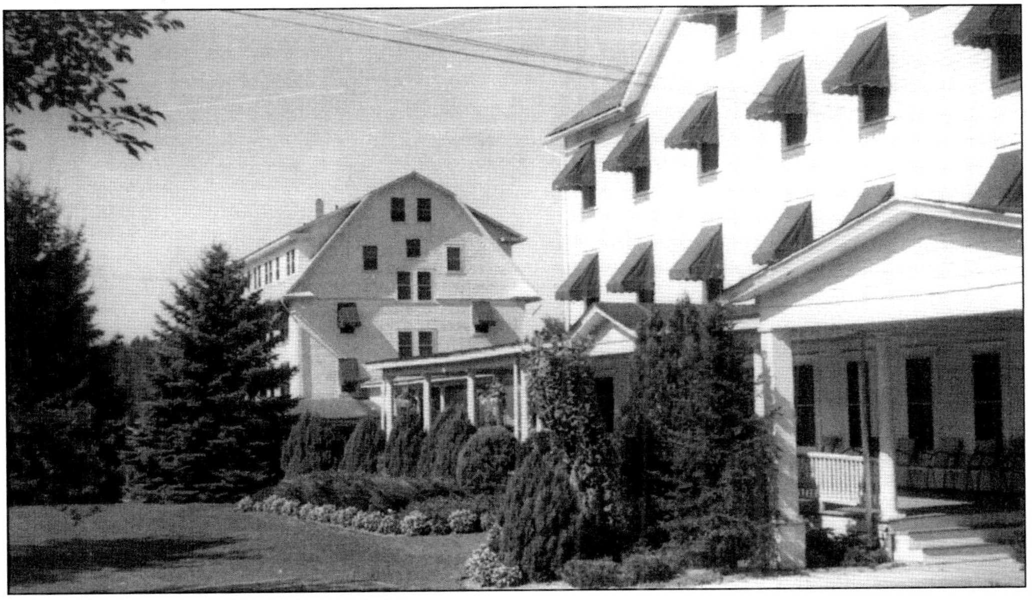

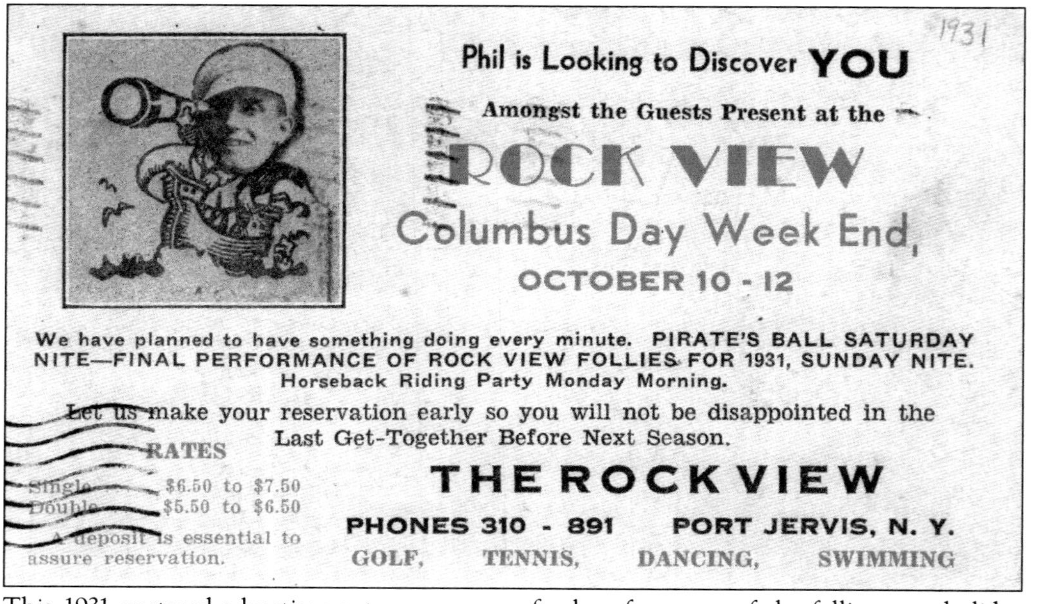

This 1931 postcard advertisement announces a final performance of the follies on a holiday weekend. Normally the season ran May to November. Peter De Rose, a composer who wrote several popular songs during the 1930s, performed here, along with well-known orchestras and bands. (Courtesy of Betsy Reinhardt.)

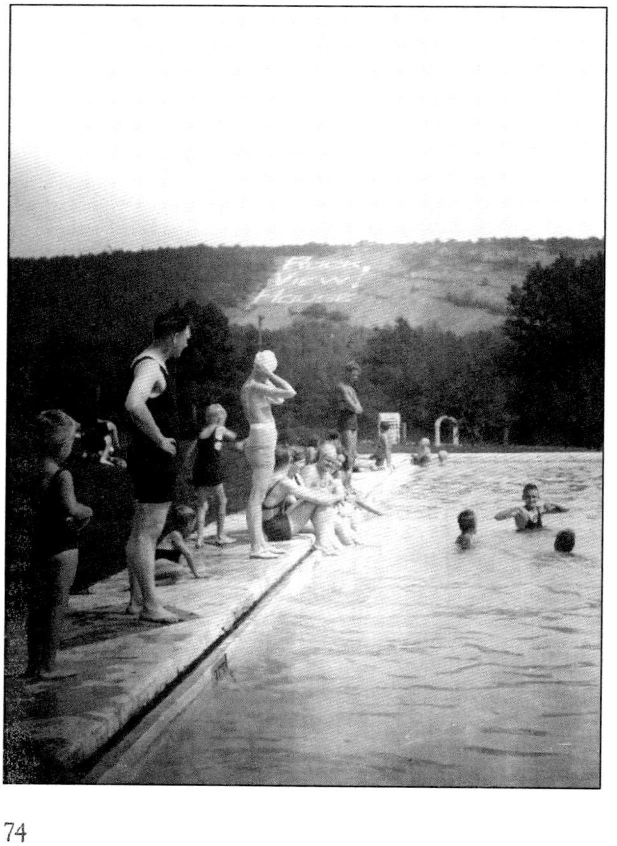

The swimming pool with its artesian water was welcomed refreshment on hot summer days. The resort's name was annually painted on the sheer rock face, which remains visible for miles around. This was visible from Point Peter in Port Jervis, New York, and is still recognizable from the Pennsylvania side in Westfall Township.

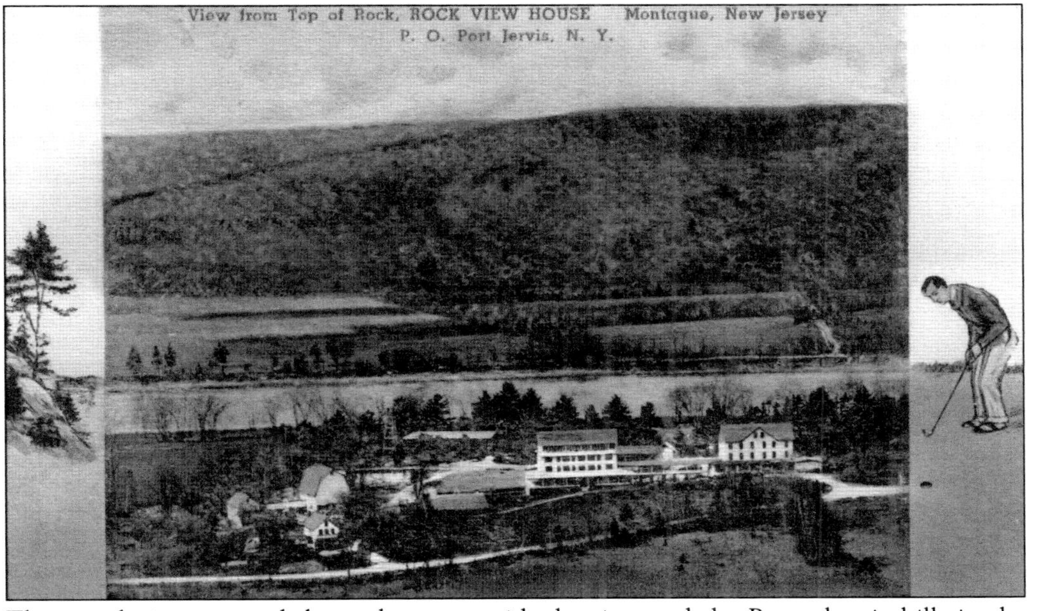

This aerial view postcard shows the resort with the river and the Pennsylvania hills in the background. It was quite a complex in its time. After being sold, the golf course was maintained and the lowest floor of one building retained for the Rock View Golf Course. (Courtesy of Alicia C. Batko.)

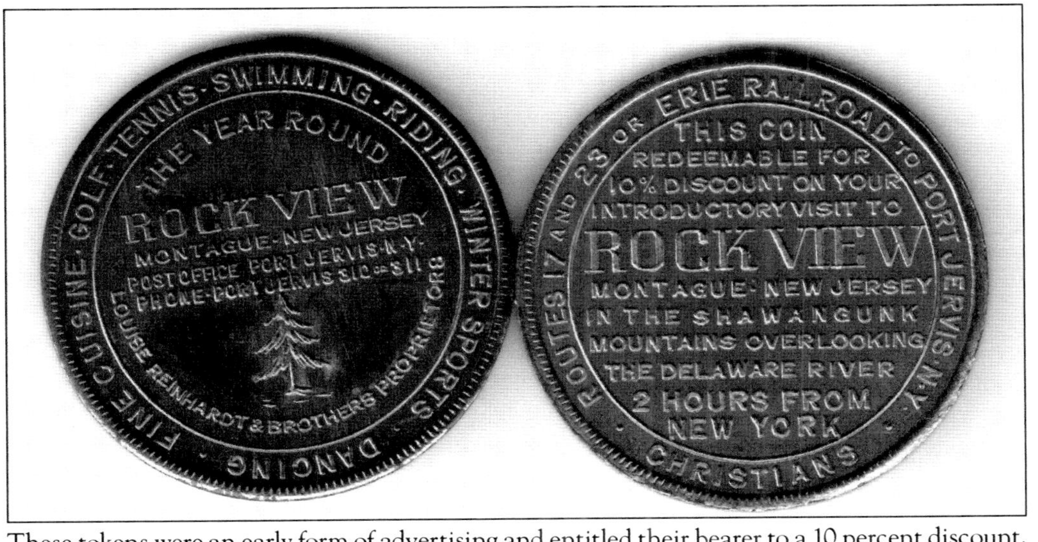

These tokens were an early form of advertising and entitled their bearer to a 10 percent discount. As winter sports are noted, this must have been from the later period when the resort was popular for beginning skiers. The Erie Railroad snow train afforded Newark and New York residents a quick getaway.

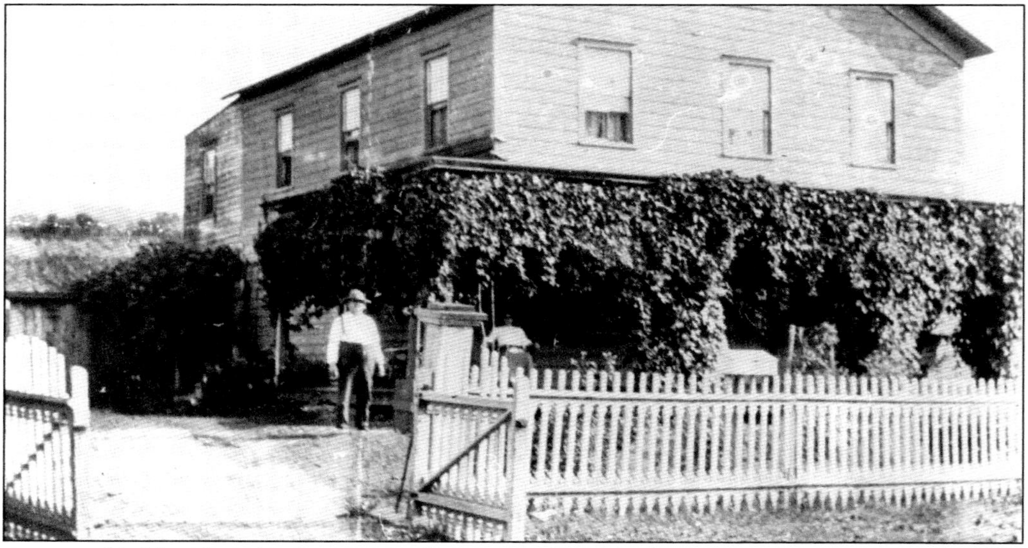

Artemus Vail lived at this home, which sat near the old Clove Road, prior to that section of road being vacated in 1934 following a realignment. Vail was connected with running a hotel at Tappentown, and it is presumed it was one that sat across the stream. The house would be owned by the Meloi family and eventually burned down some years later.

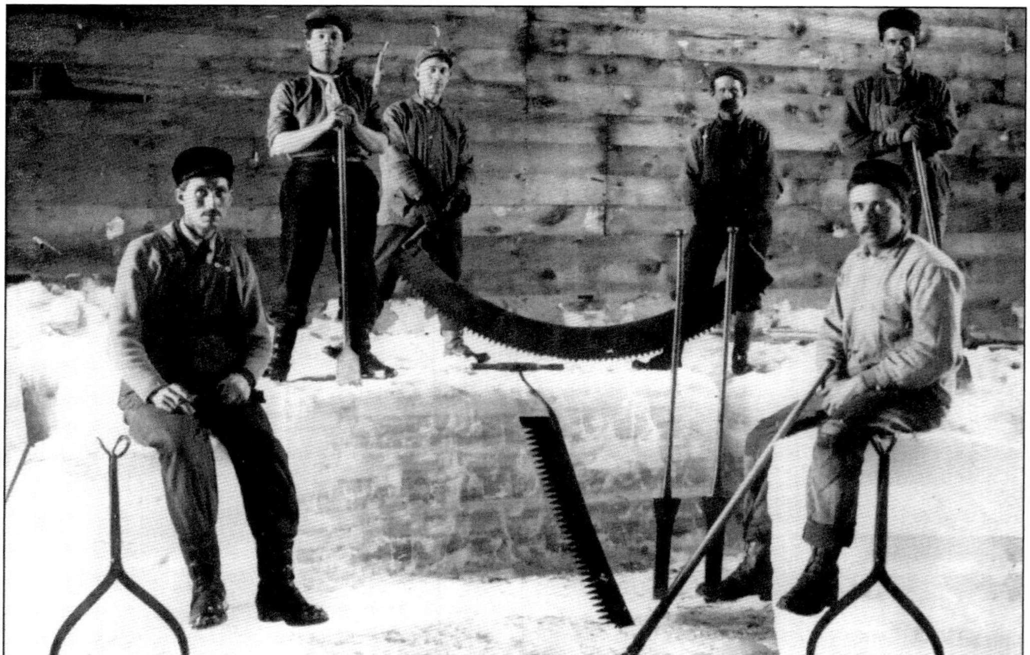

Local ponds, frozen lakes, and *binnekills* were harvested for ice, prior to streams being impounded to create ice ponds for that purpose. Vail's ice pond from which this ice was removed was located right on Mill Brook. The workmen would extract the large ice chunks and saw them into cakes for delivery to refrigeration units. The ice was kept insulated in sawdust, which helped it stay frozen through the summer. (Courtesy of Miriam Carpenter.)

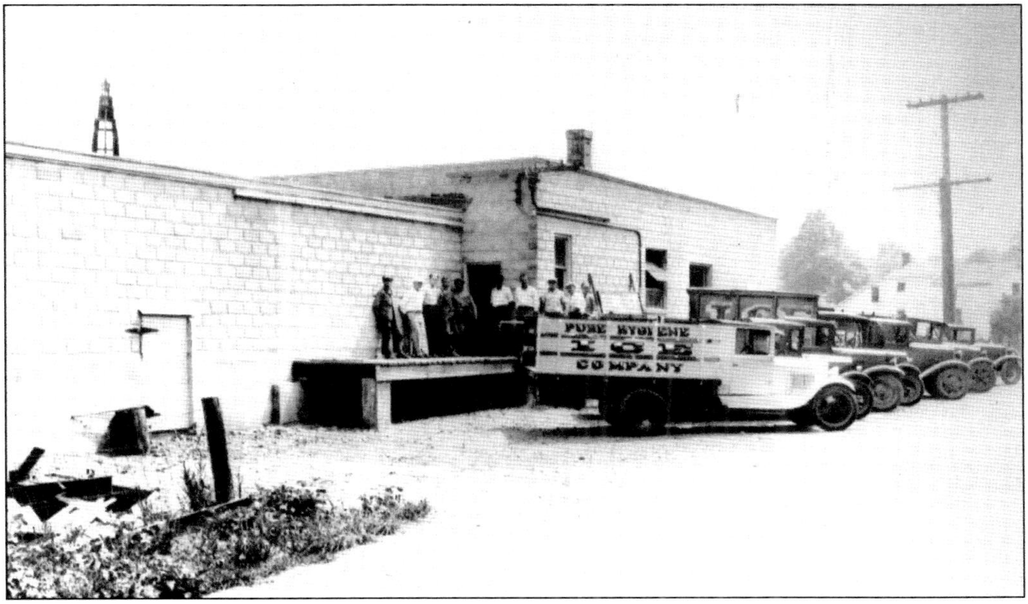

An earlier Vails' Ice House in Tappentown was replaced by this compressor-driven plant, the Pure Hygiene Ice Company. In addition to local deliveries, the company provided ice to the Erie Railroad. This helped keep perishable food from spoiling, until home use of the electric refrigerator began to gain popularity around the 1920s. To some it was known as Judd's Ice House. He also owned a gas station nearby.

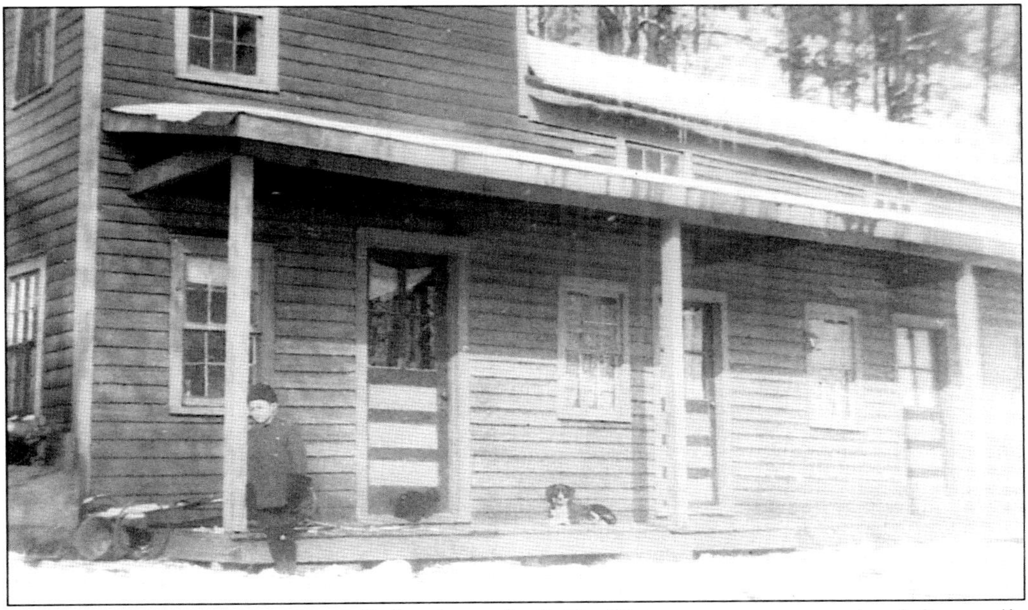

The area was renamed Duttonville by the early 1900s. This structure once existed diagonally across from Judd's Ice House. Both South of the Border on River Road and this site were run as taverns at one time and straddled the New York/New Jersey border. That feature allowed their customers to shift positions on the bar to accommodate the states' different drinking laws. (Courtesy of Tivon Meir.)

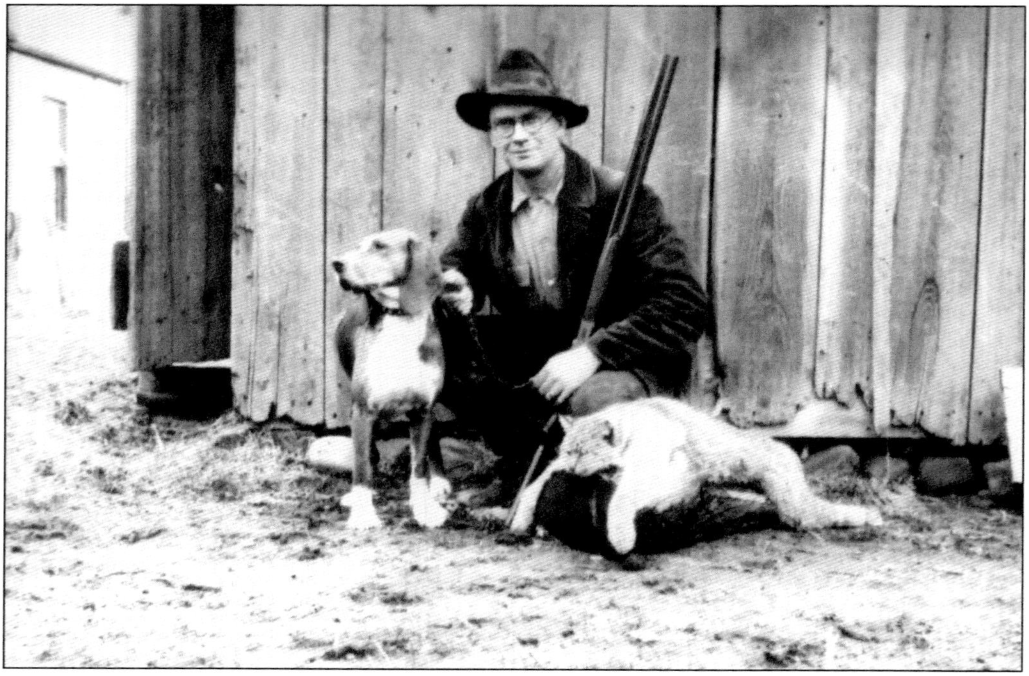

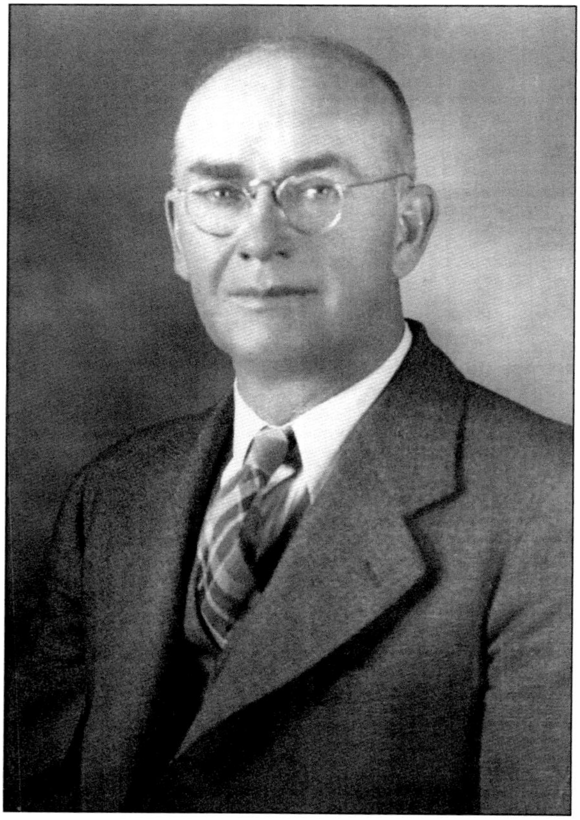

One of the more popular local pastimes was hunting. While deer and pheasants were not as prevalent in prior years, bobcats could still be seen. Joseph Judd proudly displays his trophy, along with his hunting hound and a double-barreled shotgun in hand. A contractor by trade, he was an avid sportsman and lived where the Tri-State Mall now exists. He was known in the building profession for having constructed many area churches, schools, and other buildings. Among them were St. Peter's Lutheran Church in Port Jervis and Grey Rock in High Point. A well-known businessman, Joseph Judd belonged to many sportsmen's, civic, and fraternal organizations and served on the township committee. (Courtesy of Miriam Carpenter.)

Four

Rural America at Its Best

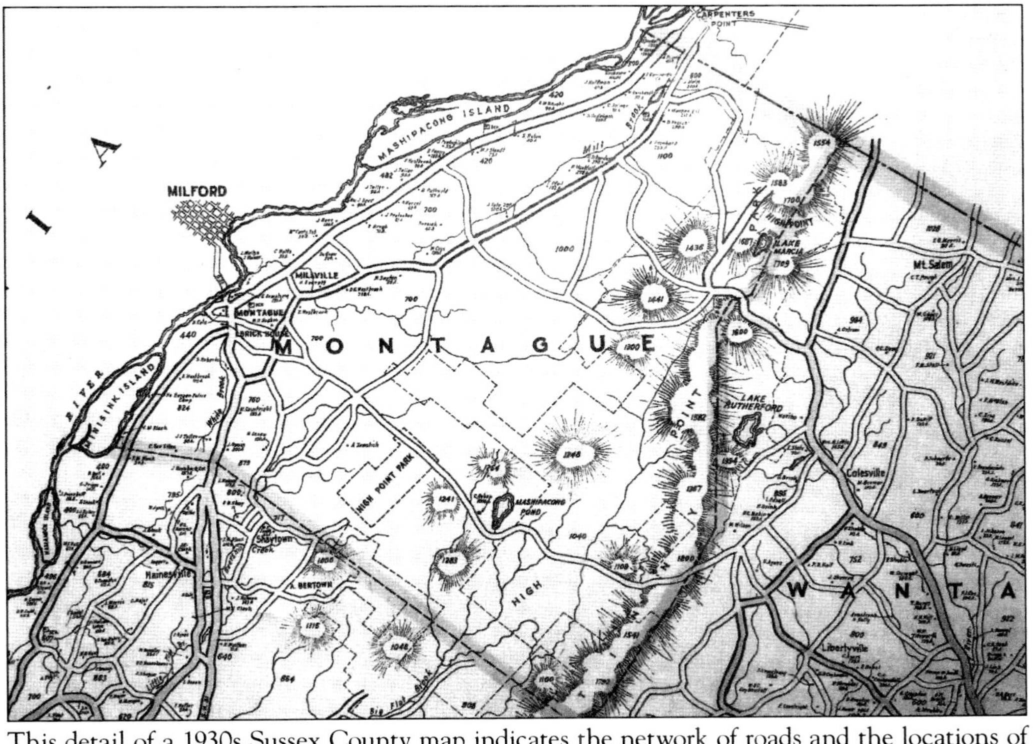

This detail of a 1930s Sussex County map indicates the network of roads and the locations of residences. Like the Hopkins map of 1866, it shows the majority of the township population living near the river. The outline of the High Point Park boundary reflects the park taking up most of the eastern bounds of the township.

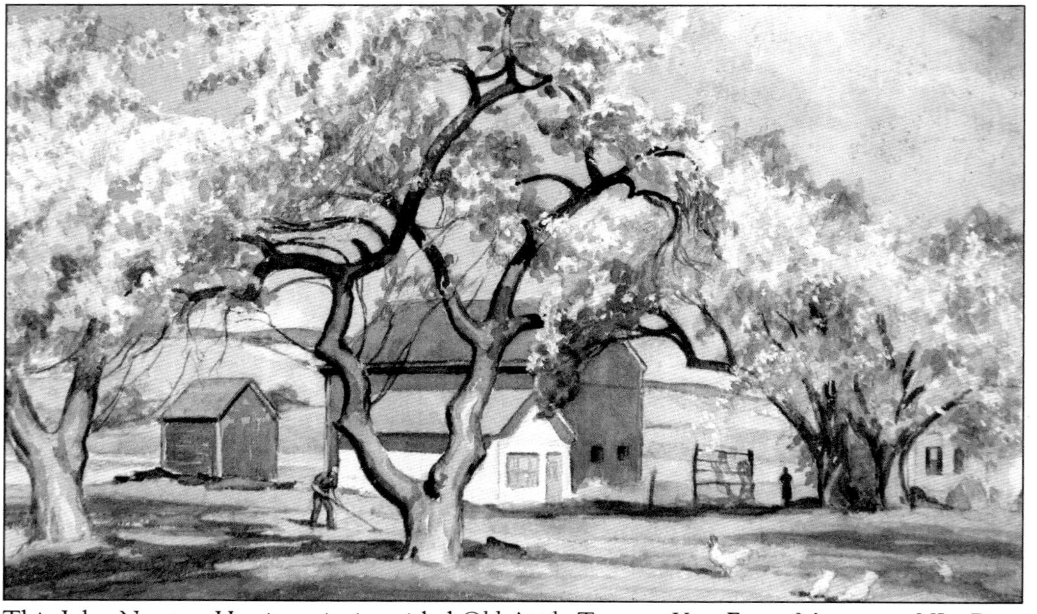

This John Newton Howitt painting titled *Old Apple Trees on Kerr Farm, Montague, NJ - River (Delaware) Rd.* captures a scene from River Road. Howitt was a nationally renowned artist who lived in Port Jervis and was best known for his pulp illustrations, as well as his landscapes and illustrations for magazines such as the *Outdoor Life*, the *Saturday Evening Post*, and *Country Gentleman*. (Courtesy of Greenwood Gallery.)

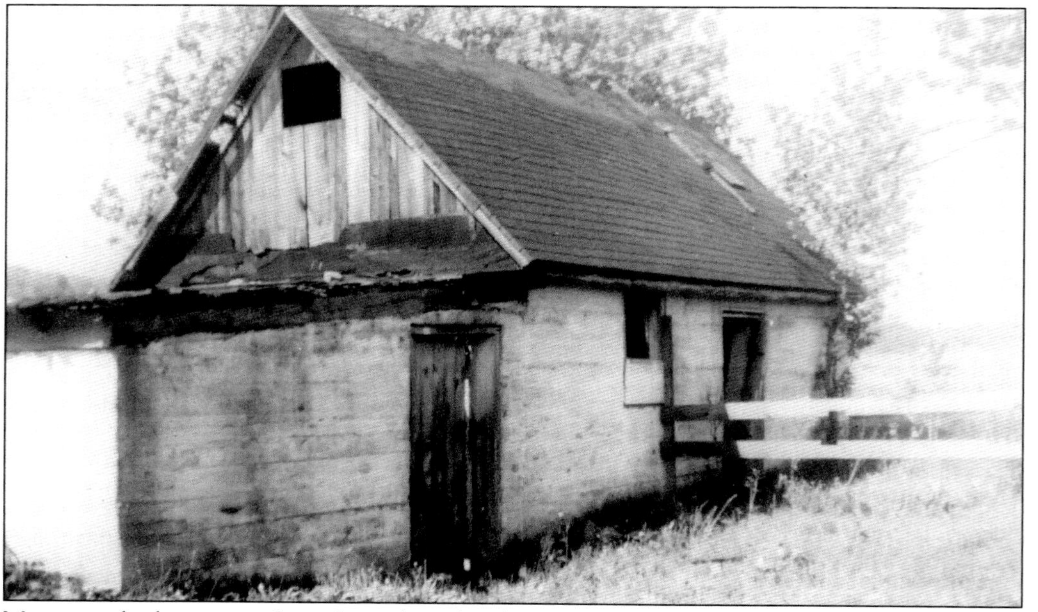

Montague had many apple and peach orchards. Those who had apple presses would welcome neighbors coming to assist in the harvest. Families with smaller yields could also bring their own bushel of apples to those who could mill them. Fresh cider was a fall favorite, as was the occasional hard cider produced. This cider press was on the VanderWerf farm on upper Clove Road. (Courtesy of JoAnn VanderWerf Whitesell.)

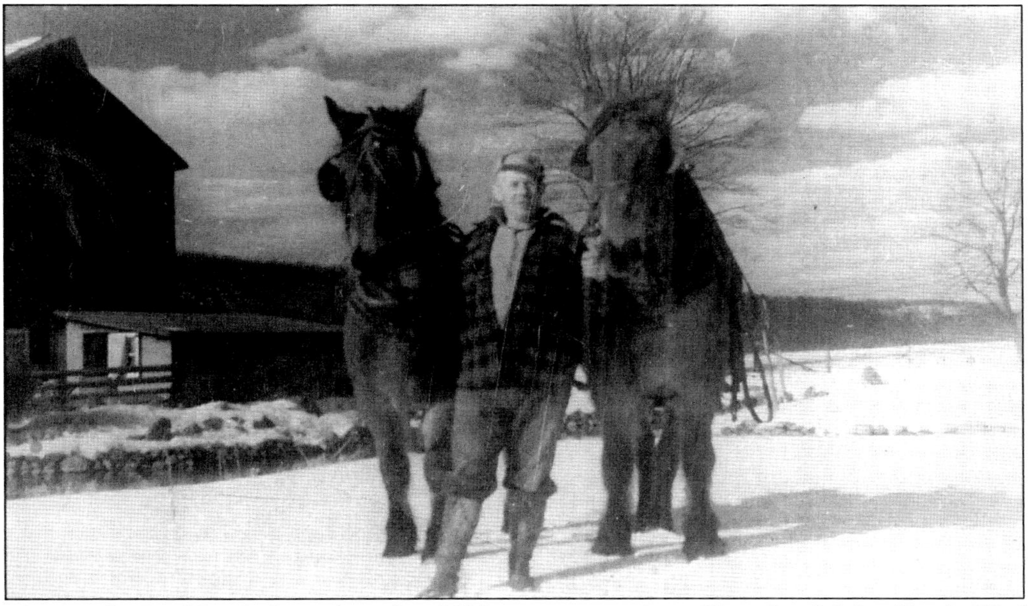

The VanderWerf family farmed on the old Nearpass tract along Clove Road. John VanderWerf holds his team. Horses were a key element for a farmer to have for the capability for plowing, tilling, harvesting, and hauling. Horses served the small farm until mechanized farm machinery became affordable and was later preferred, since one did not have to feed a tractor when it sat idle. (Courtesy of JoAnn VanderWerf Whitesell.)

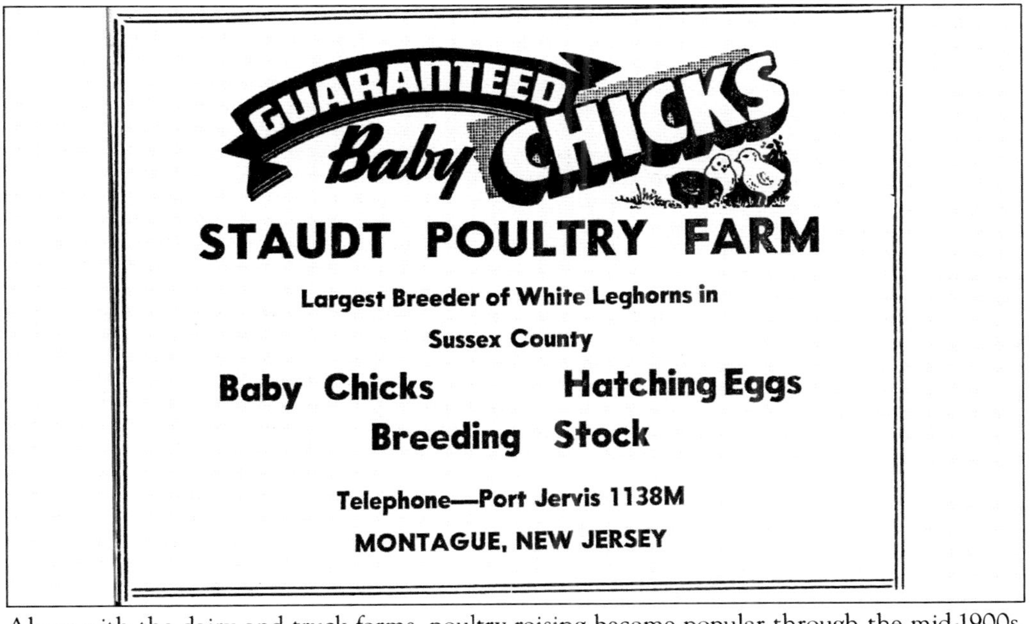

Along with the dairy and truck farms, poultry raising became popular through the mid-1900s. The Staudt, Pratschler, and Reinhardt farms were often in competition to be recognized as the best in egg and/or chicken production. All farms would vie for standing at the county fair held each summer, to earn ribbons and best-in-show status. (Courtesy of New Jersey State Fair, Sussex County Farm and Horse Show.)

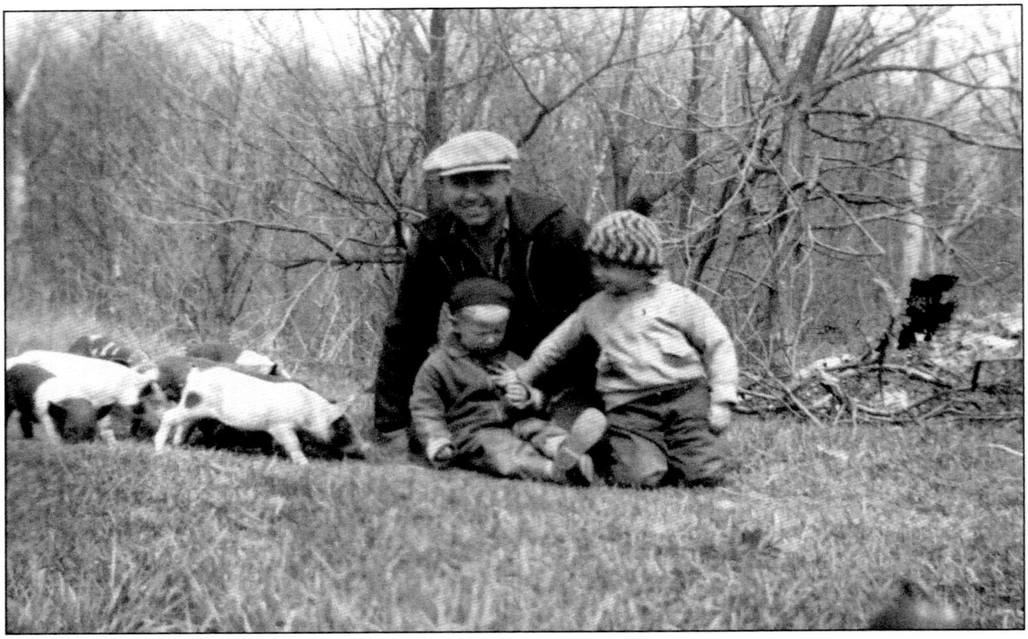

One of the enjoyments of life in a farming community is seeing calves, chicks, ponies, ducklings, and piglets such as these. Joan Forster Erb's uncle Tom and his children are seen amid this litter. Difficulties sometimes arose when slaughtering time came in order to put meat on the table. Often that was done under the guise of having "sold" the animal, if a fond attachment formed. (Courtesy of Joan Forster Erb.)

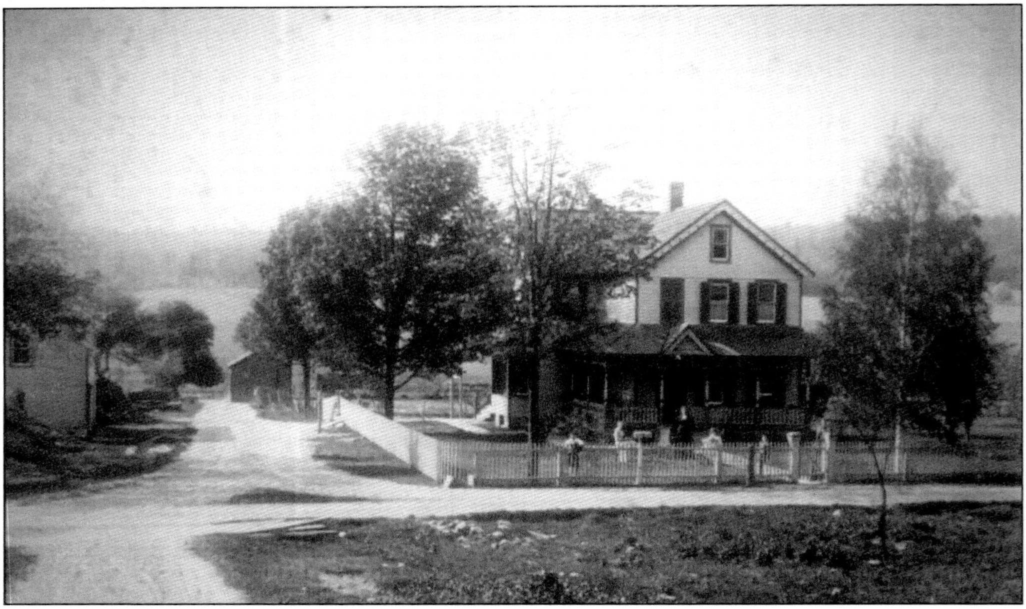

This farm belonged to Capt. James Cole of the Civil War era and was last held by his descendant James Cole, who was elected mayor of Port Jervis after he moved from Montague. There does not appear to be any road cut through at this period to head over the ridge, nor is the later horse barn erected.

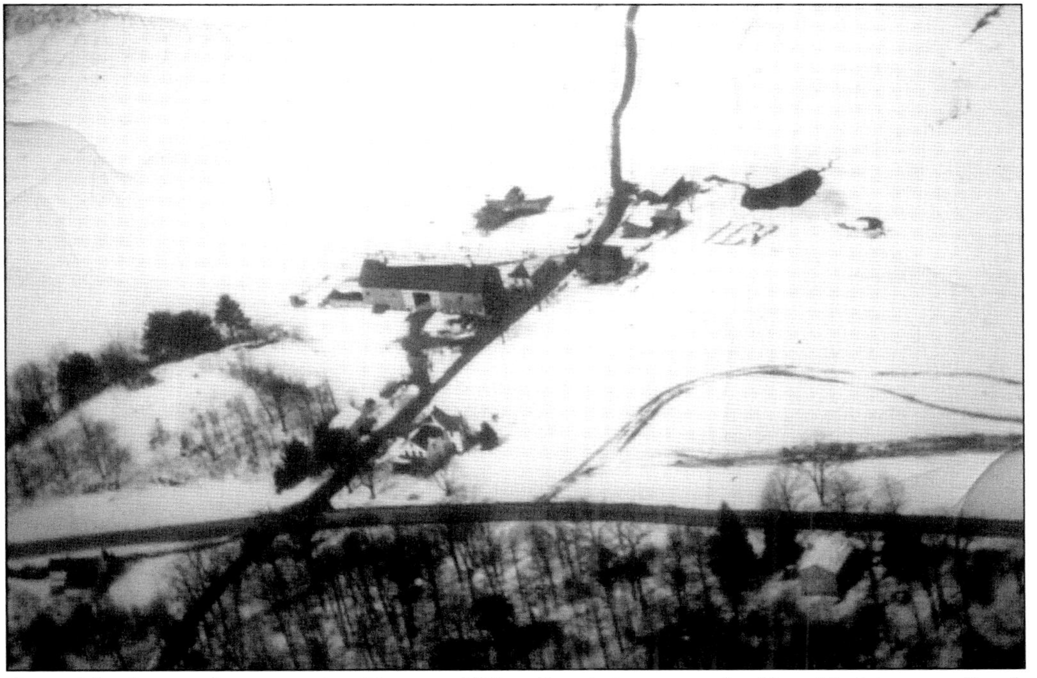

One of the few roads connecting Clove and River Roads is present-day New Mashipacong Road. This aerial view shows its predecessor cutting through the Cole farm. Prior to its realignment, the road ran to the left of the existing house. The large barn still stands, and modern horse barns have since been added to Big Z Stables. The structure visible in the lower right-hand quadrant is likely the Church School.

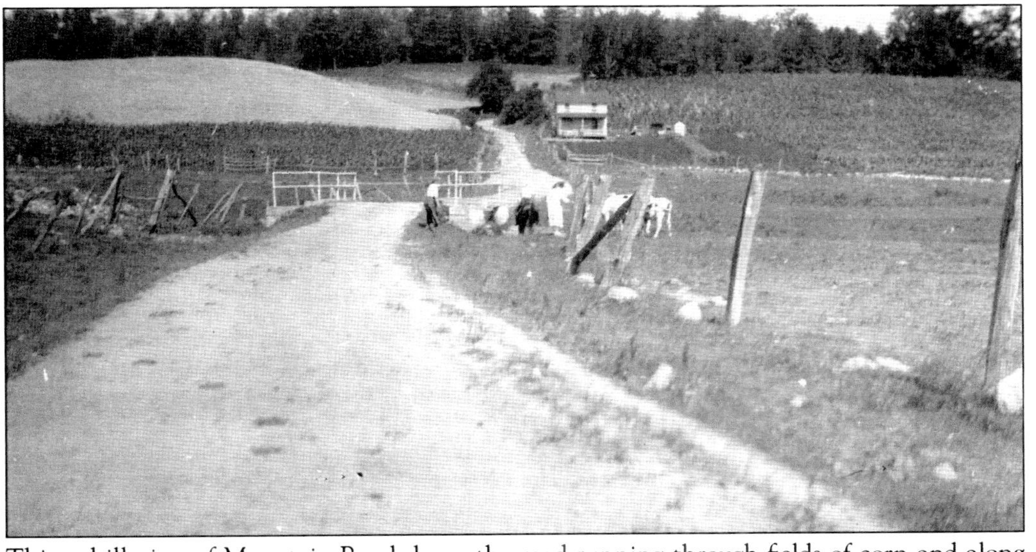

This uphill view of Mountain Road shows the road running through fields of corn and along barbed-wire enclosures where cows were once pastured. Homes were spaced a good distance apart and such pastoral scenes abounded. Most roads were not paved, and men were given responsibility for maintaining the roads within a district.

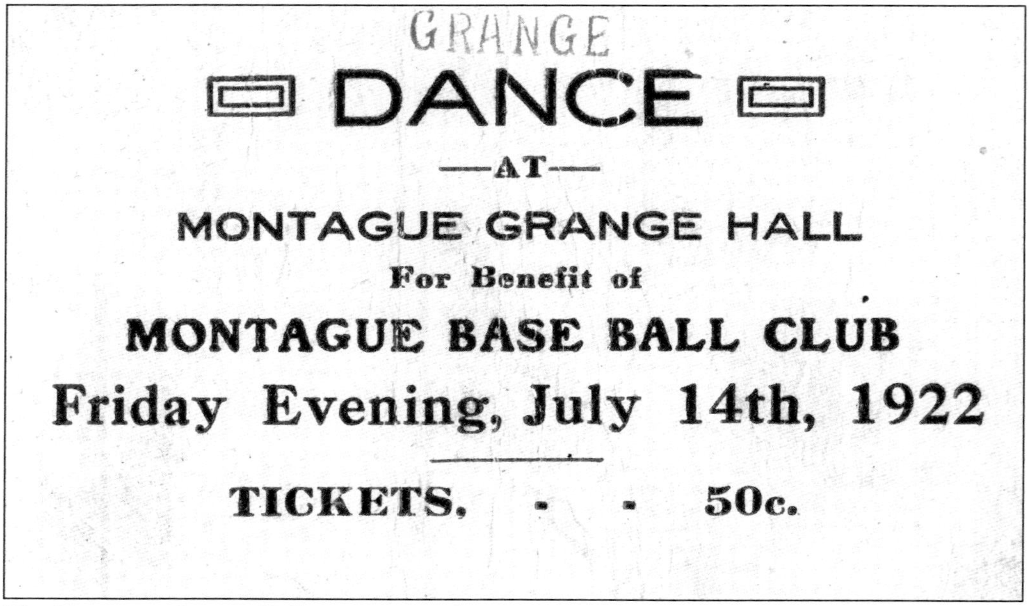

GRANGE

DANCE

—AT—

MONTAGUE GRANGE HALL

For Benefit of

MONTAGUE BASE BALL CLUB

Friday Evening, July 14th, 1922

TICKETS, - - 50c.

The Montague Grange Hall was a center for many township activities. Among those held were dances, such as one to benefit the Montague Base Ball Club in 1922. It was the center for many social activities, having a kitchen and a meeting room with a stage. It also featured a spacious room on the second floor. (Courtesy of Montague Township.)

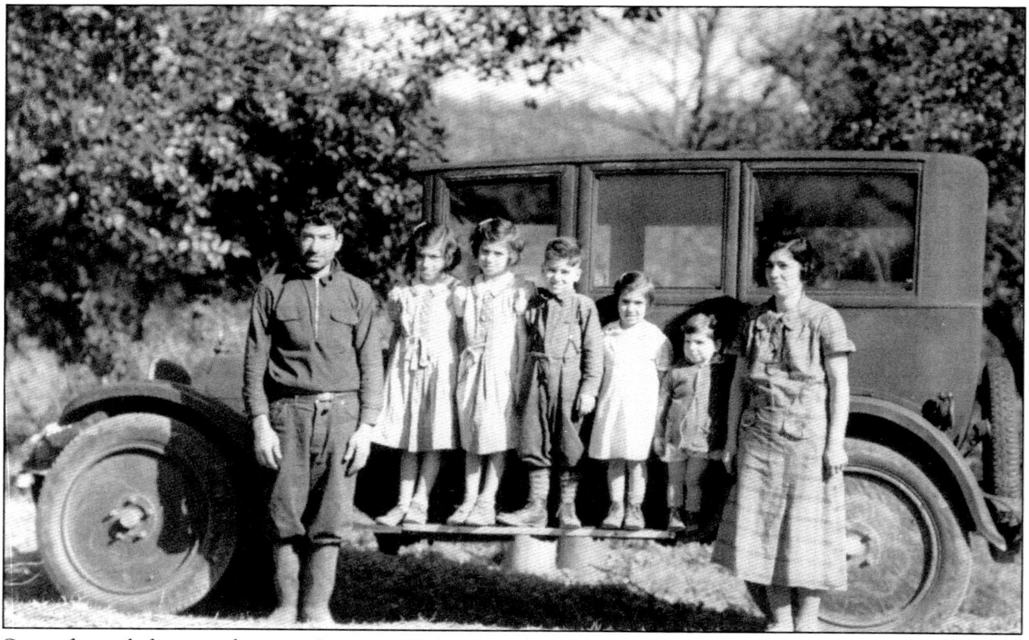

Seen from left to right are George, Helen, Evelyn, Joseph, Joyce, Edward, and Mary Zitone. George and Mary Zitone immigrated to this country, settling in Montague by the 1930s. They survived the lean times of the Depression. The family's name became well known after the sons opened the Zitone Construction Company, on return from military service during the Korean War. (Courtesy of Helen Zitone Gassman.)

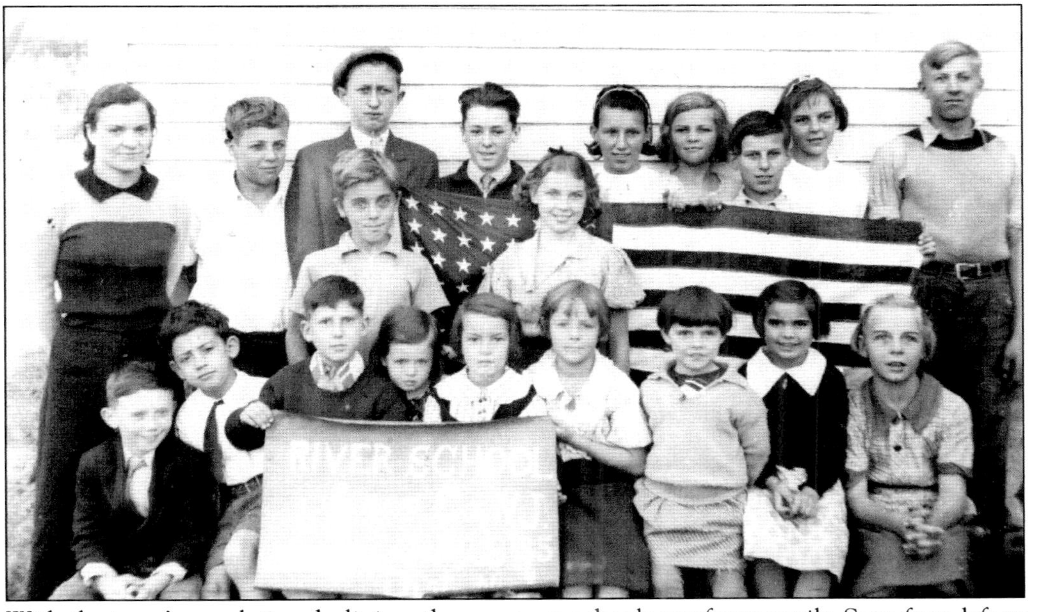

With the town's population declining, the one-room schools saw fewer pupils. Seen from left to right are (first row) Walter Duffy, Robert Early, Steven Jerger, Beverly Duffy, Shirley Burg, Jane Irwin, Clara ?, Mable ?, and Earleen Emrich; (second row) Charles Page and Loraine Burg; (third row) teacher Olive Middleton, unidentified, Ken Bradshaw, Russell Owens, Marie Ayers, Doris Irwin, Bucky Ayers, Gladys Emrich, and Stanley Buczek. (Courtesy of Karen Ardler Cherapy.)

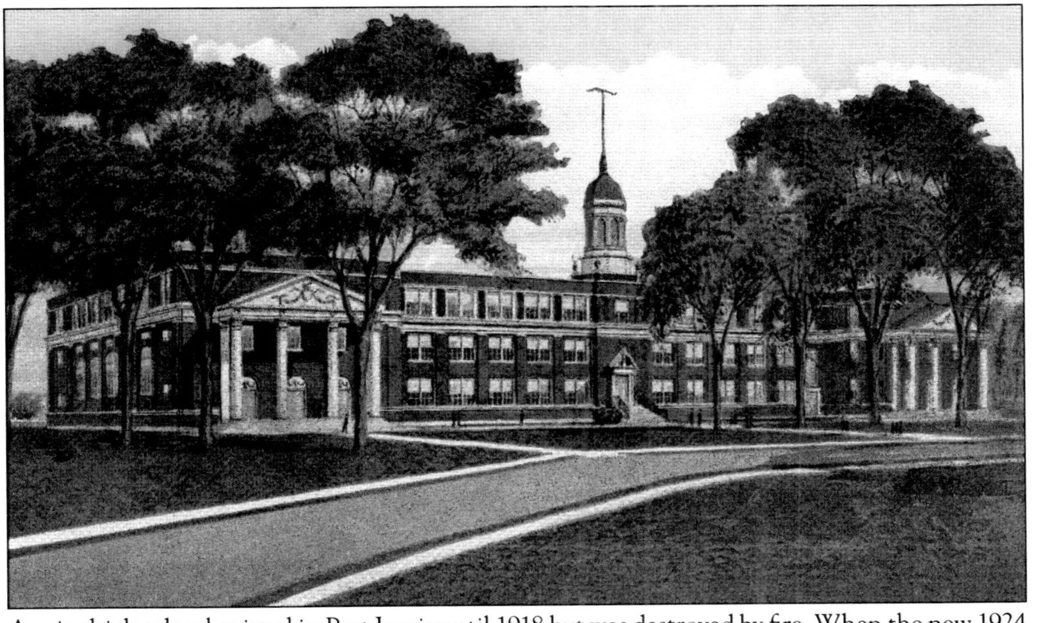

A prior high school existed in Port Jervis until 1918 but was destroyed by fire. When the new 1924 building opened, Montague considered sending its high school students to attend the secondary school. A small group of students had previously traveled to Branchville and proceeded from there by train to attend Newton High School. They spent their week boarding away from home. (Courtesy of Alicia C. Batko.)

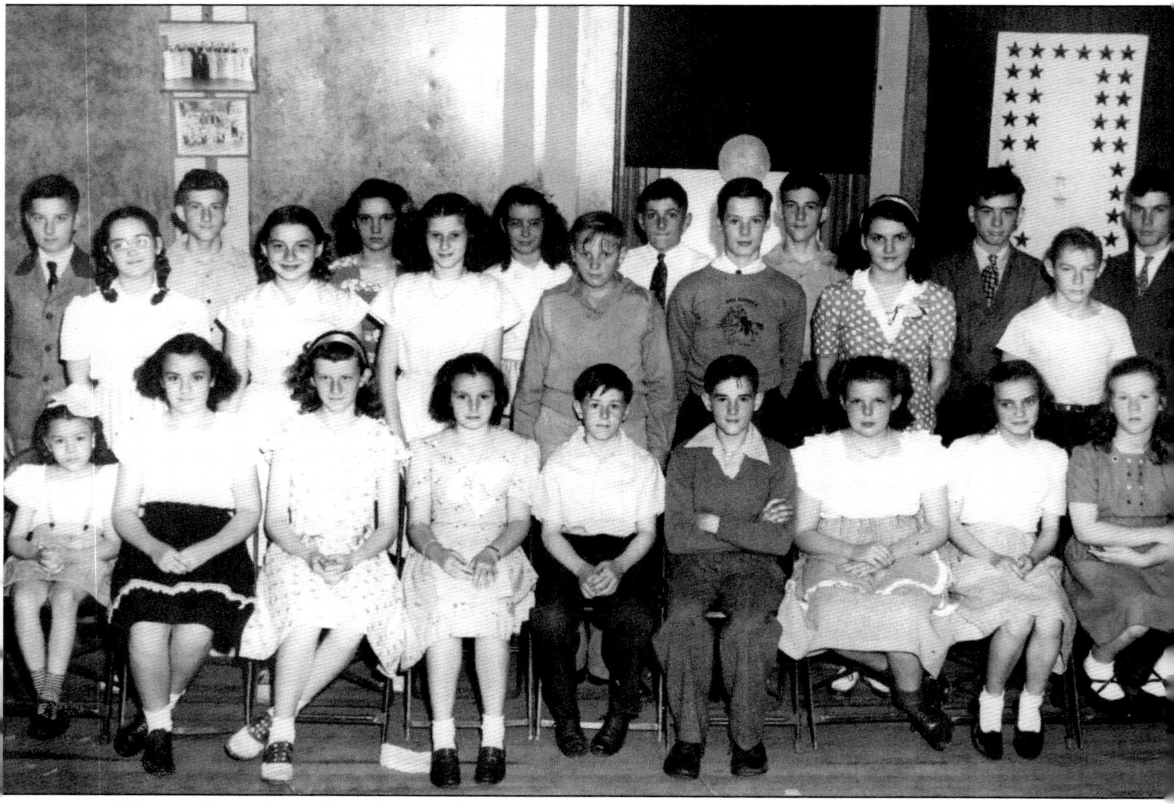

The students from the Clove and River Schools gathered together for a function at the Montague Grange Hall. Seen to the right, on the wall, is the banner with stars for each person who had enlisted in World War II from Montague and the known Gold Star casualties: Earl Irwin and Irvine DeRemer Jr. A classmate recalled the students as, from left to right, (first row) June Happ, Joyce Happ, Regina Miller, Sylvia Sumner, Eric Grau, Alan Tooley, Doris Schoeffel, Frances Jones, and Jean VanderWerf; (second row) June Aeberli, Barbara Pratschler, Mary Patricia Staudt, Harold Hawkins, Paul ?, Ella Smith, and Herbert Finch; (third row) Donald Poetsch, James Tooley, Johanna Reganess, Rosemary Aeberli, Thomas Teller, John Tooley, Durwood Biccum, and Harry Biccum. (Courtesy of Regina Miller Quinn.)

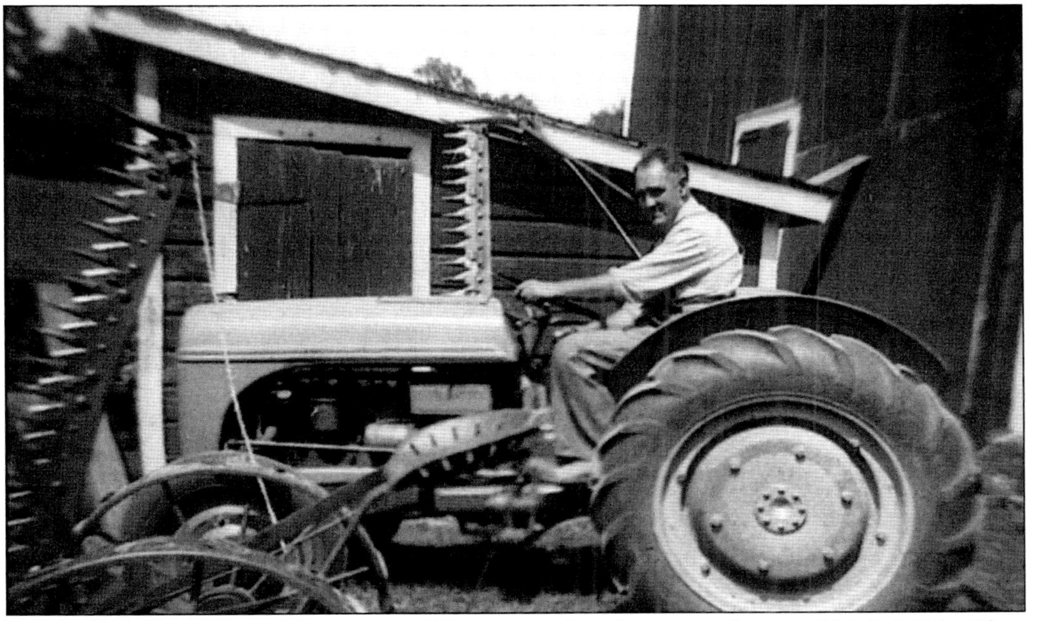

Stanley Roberts came as a cow tester to Montague, where he met and married Mabel Cole. They and their two sons, Robert and Hobart, remained an active farm family. They were known for their activities through the Montague Grange and the 4-H circuit and for their prize-winning cows exhibited at the Sussex County Farm and Horse Show. The farms they ran encompassed the former Nelden and Hornbeck tracts along U.S. Route 206 and River Road. The apple grove, near which they ran a summer camp, has had its trees dated. They are considered to be nearly 300 years old. An orchard restoration project is now in progress there. (Photographs by Robert W. Rowe, courtesy of MARCH.)

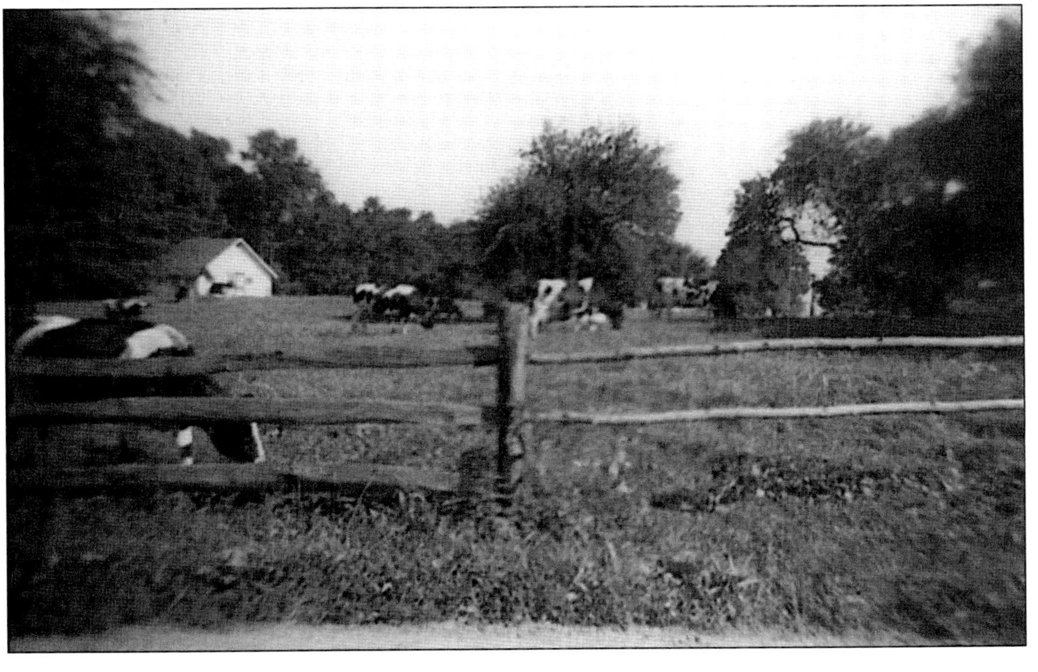

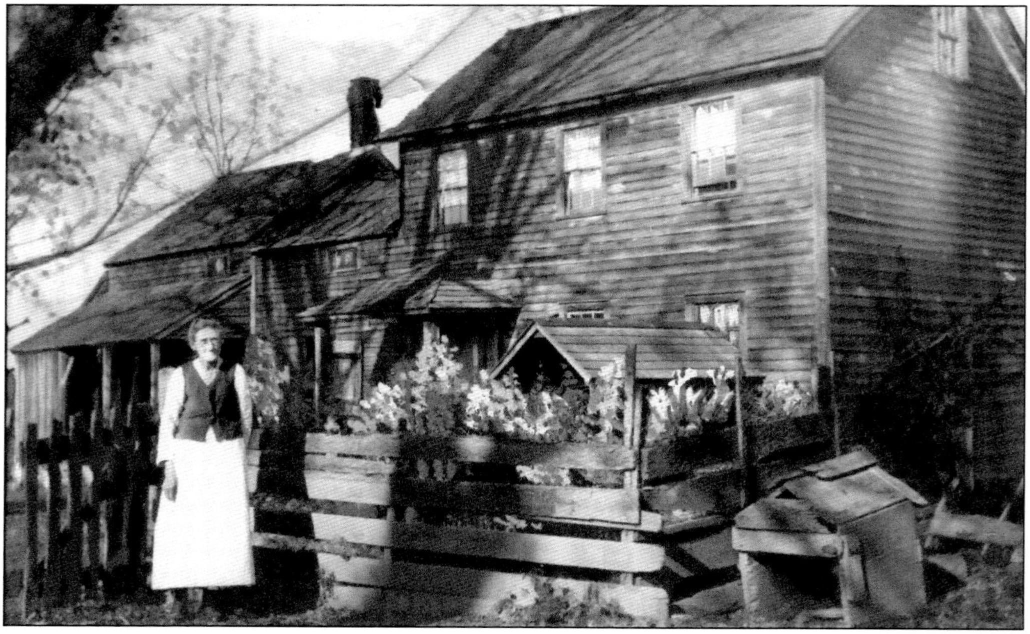

Parthenia Wainwright lived in this home, which sat a half mile east of Clove Road and was accessed by a short lane. The home had been erected by her father, Wallen. The small central portion was original, with an extension later added to the left. When times became more prosperous, the two-story structure on the right was constructed.

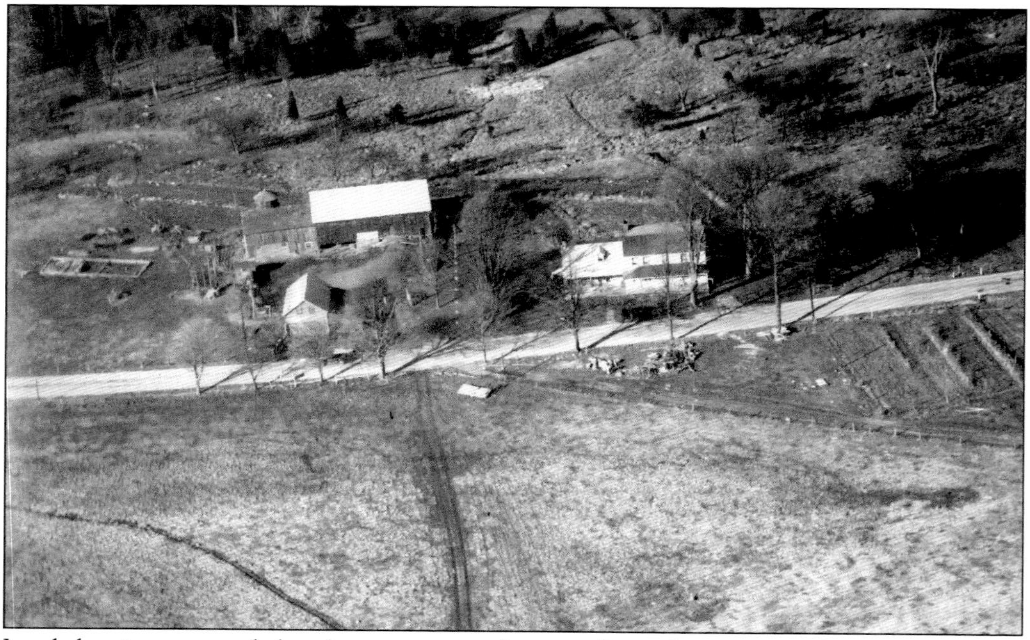

Land that is now wooded and overgrown no longer reflects the openness during its period of prior agricultural use, as this aerial reflects. With the removal or loss of outbuildings and barns, one cannot quickly identify old farms. This one was run by George Armstrong at the time the aerial was taken. (Photograph by Schulman's Air Photo Service, courtesy of MARCH.)

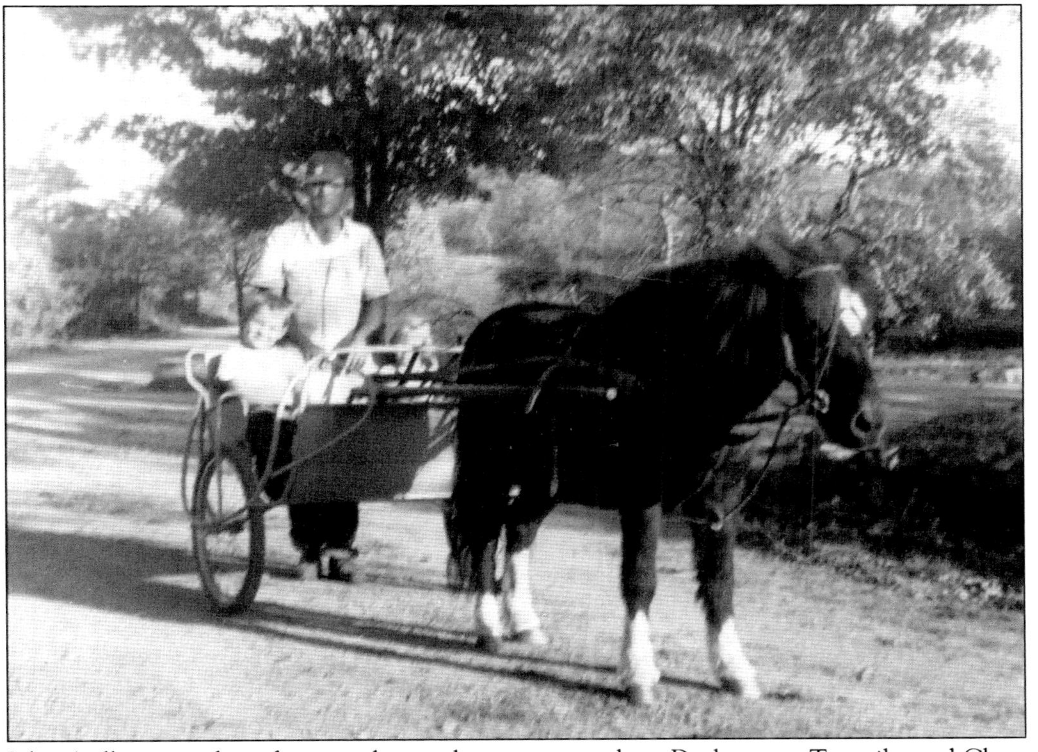

John Ardler ran a dairy farm on the northwest corner where Deckertown Turnpike and Clove Road currently intersect. He is shown standing behind the cart where his children, Karl and Karen, are seated. The gentle pony shown pulling the cart was named Diamond. The farm also had a team of workhorses. (Courtesy of Karen Ardler Cherapy.)

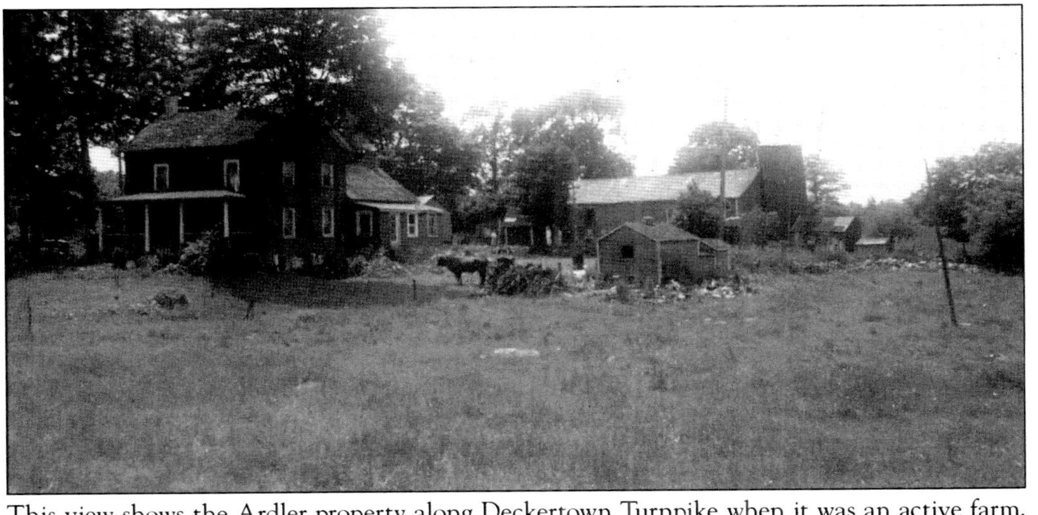

This view shows the Ardler property along Deckertown Turnpike when it was an active farm. Ardler was a founding member of the local volunteer fire department in 1950 and served his community in many capacities. Long gone are the silo and a greater portion of the barn. The porch facing Clove Road no longer exists, although the home remains. (Courtesy of Karen Ardler Cherapy.)

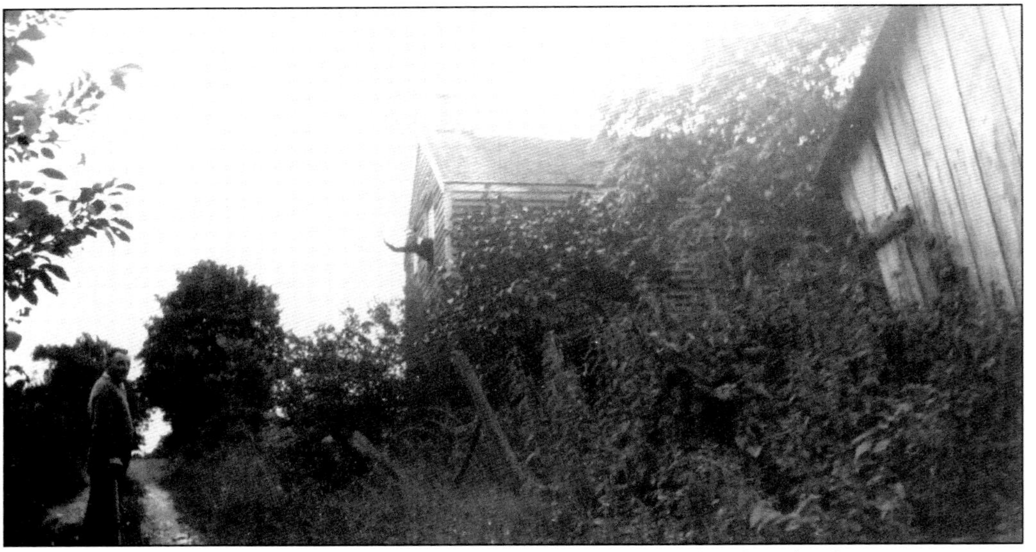

In the 1940s, this section of Deckertown Turnpike was a rutted path. This home remains on Deckertown Turnpike, although its clapboard was later hidden under shingles. Remodeling occurred and extensions were added after James Carpenter acquired it in 1949. He was employed on the Ardler farm just across the road and hauled milk to the Branchville Creamery. The old Hotalen shop is shown below it. (Courtesy of James and Miriam Carpenter.)

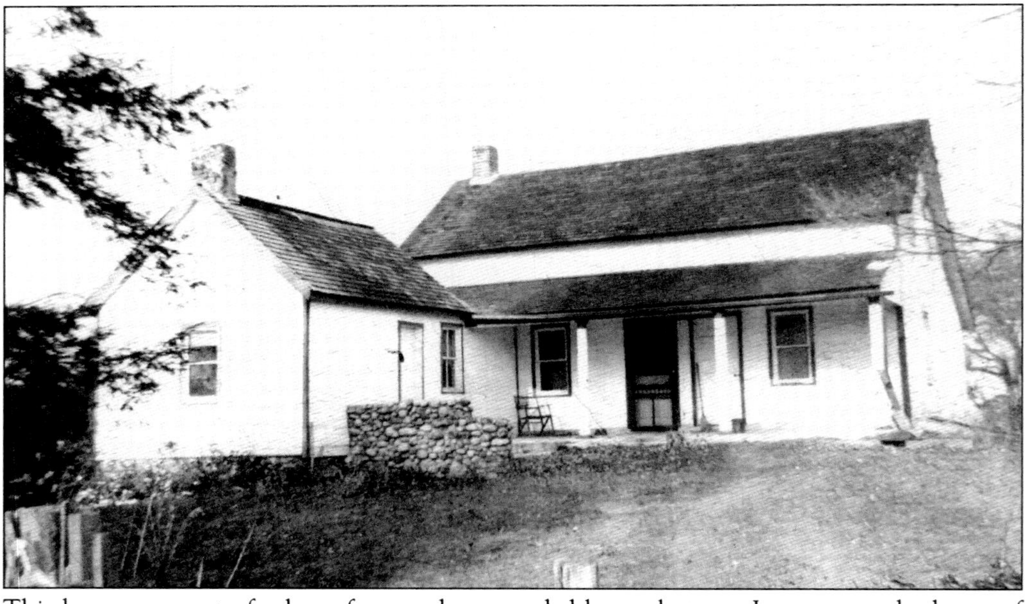

This home was part of a large farm and surrounded by apple trees. It was once the home of Arnold Cole, whose ancestors had acquired it many generations prior. The property extended across the street and once had sheds and a barn. Originally the land had belonged to the Thomas family. The home has been remodeled and the farm subdivided.

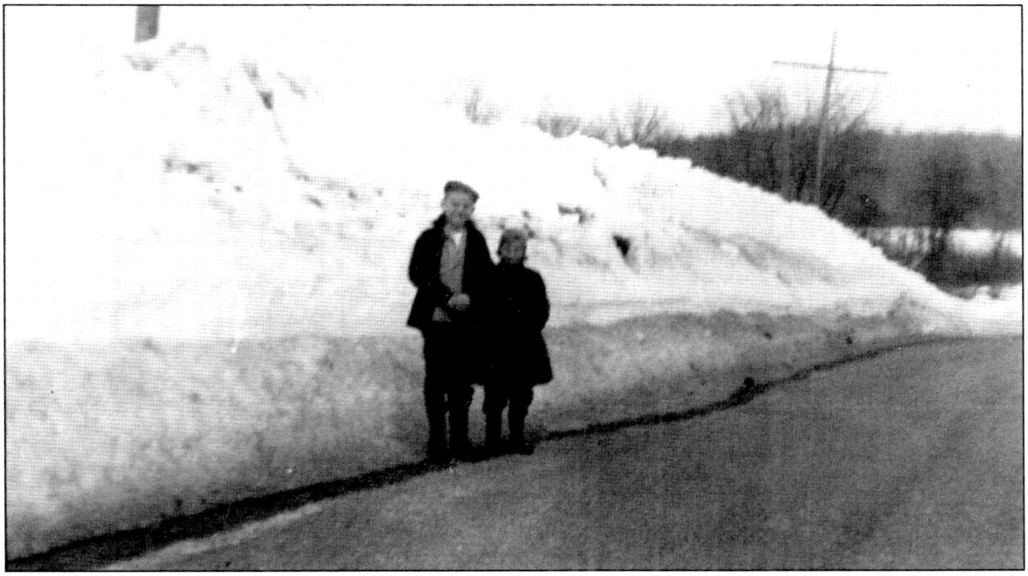

Montague has not seen as much snowfall as this in many winters. Longtime residents recall even being unable to get out of their homes. Such winters enticed tourists to come try varied winter sports. Attempts to expand on such opportunities, when Mother Nature delivered less-wintry precipitation, proved unsuccessful for rope tow skiing attempts near the Rendezvous Restaurant on U.S. Route 206 and at Holiday Lake. (Courtesy of Karen Ardler Cherapy.)

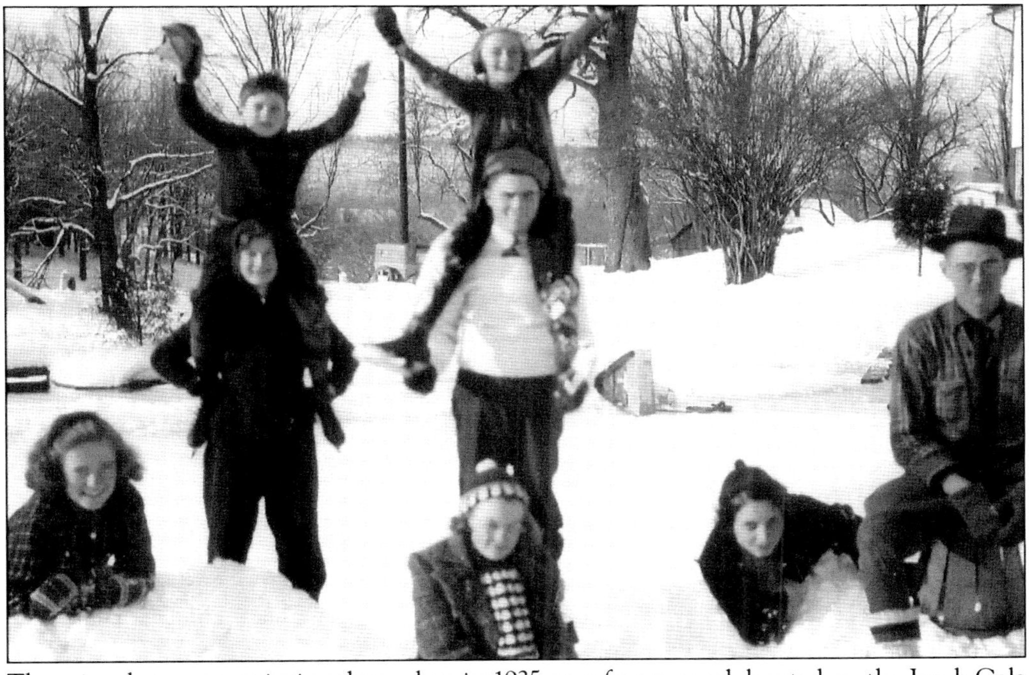

These ice-skaters are enjoying themselves in 1935 on a frozen pond, located on the Jacob Cole property off State Route 31 and Deckertown Turnpike. Shown from left to right are (first row) Jeanne Cole, Carolyn Cole, Isabel Hartrim, and George Armstrong; (second row) Helen Herman and Levi Cole; (third row) Ronald Hartrim and Mary Cole. (Courtesy of Marjorie Cole Shay.)

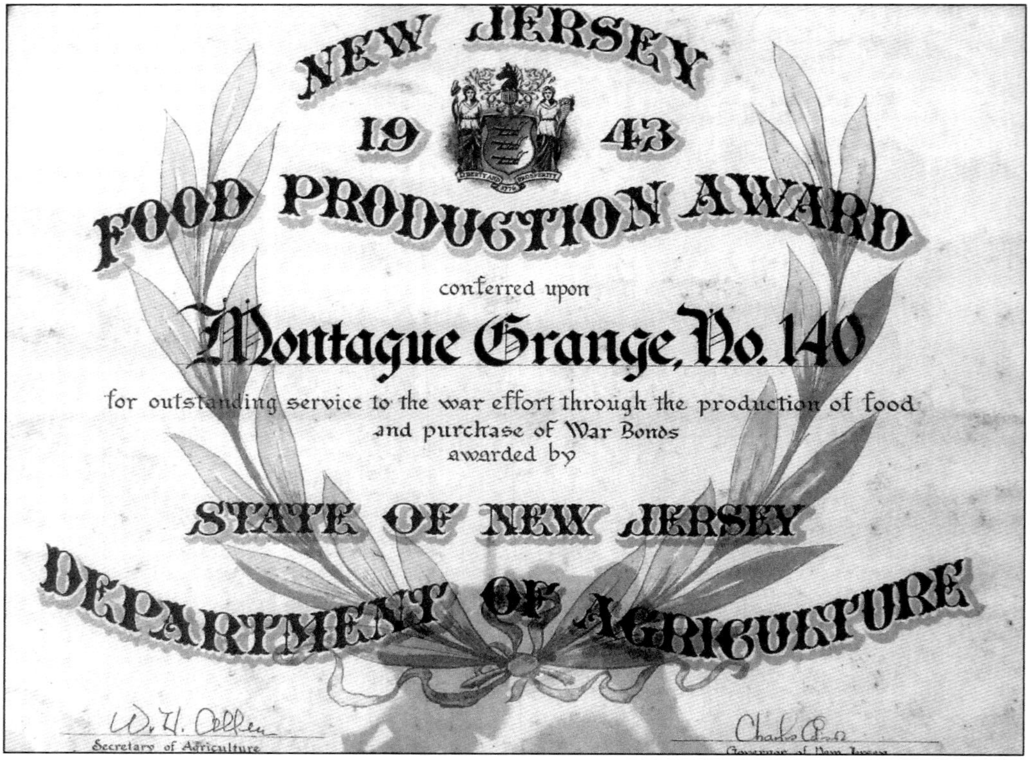

To help the local farm families and as part of the war effort, local canning centers opened. One was instituted at the Grange building, where the final preparation and preservation of food by this mechanized process was made available. For its service to the war effort, through the production of food and purchase of war bonds, the local Grange received this award in 1943. Such efforts had been initiated through the Sussex County Vocational School of Agriculture, which had opened as a school with no buildings in 1937. During the war, courses in food production and conservation were held at the Montague Grange Hall, where a community canning center opened. The Grange helped publicize the need to purchase defense bonds by this float. (Courtesy of Montague Grange.)

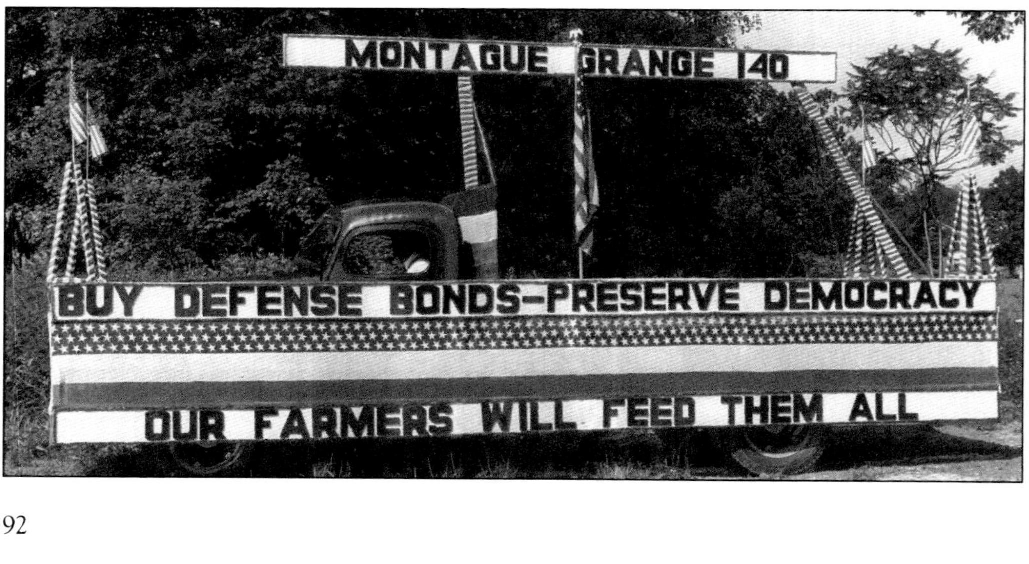

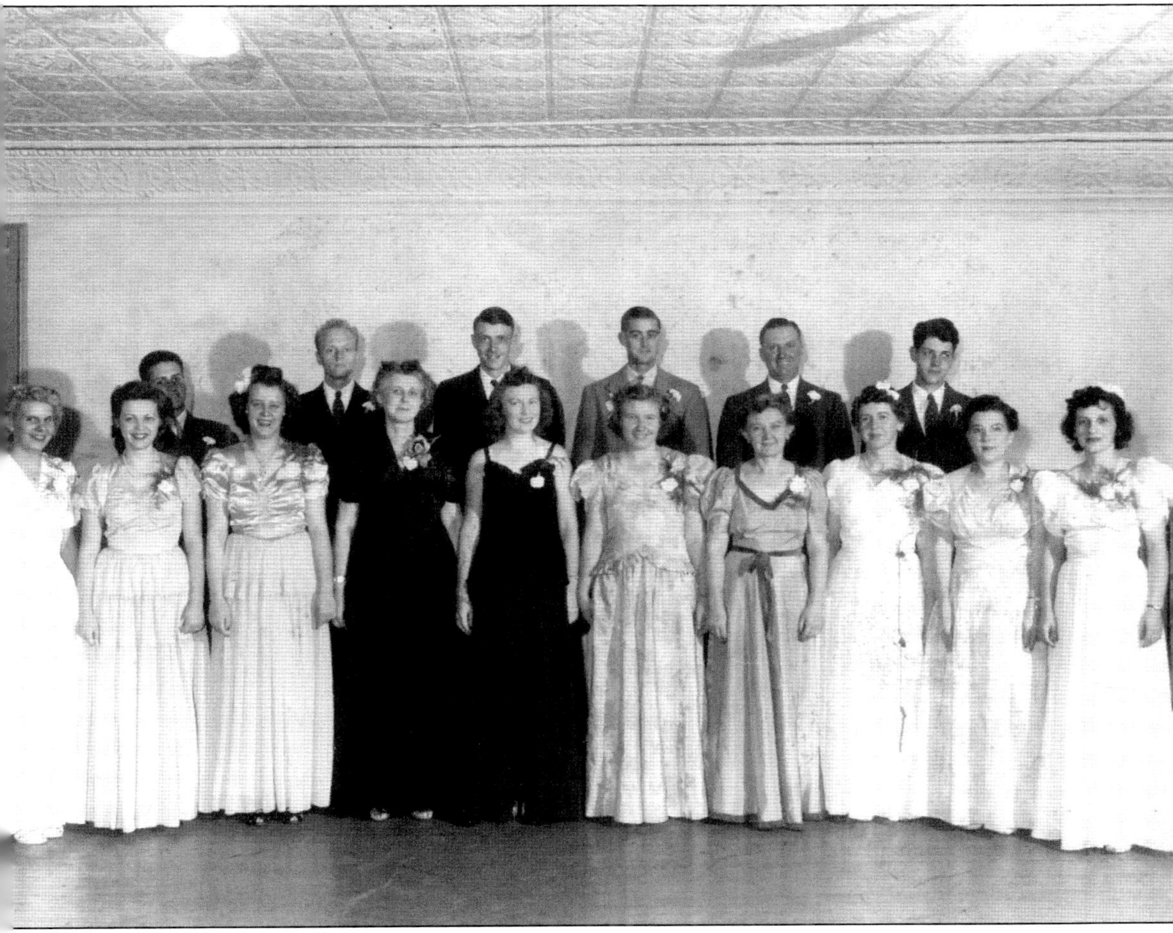

The 1944 degree team from Montague Grange No. 140 consisted of officers who had just conferred membership on Enterprise Grange's candidates. From left to right are (first row) Hazel Westbrook Irwin, Doris Irwin, Jane Irwin, Edna Westbrook, Marjorie Cole Shay, Elvira Pfiel, Anna Staudt, Ann Schneider, Gertrude O'Neil, and Isabel Hartrim; (second row) Robert Roberts, Robert Blasberg, master Robert Westbrook, George Armstrong, Carl Schneider, and Hobart Roberts. The degree team was formed of officers who served to initiate candidates into the organization. At this event, it welcomed new members of Enterprise Grange.

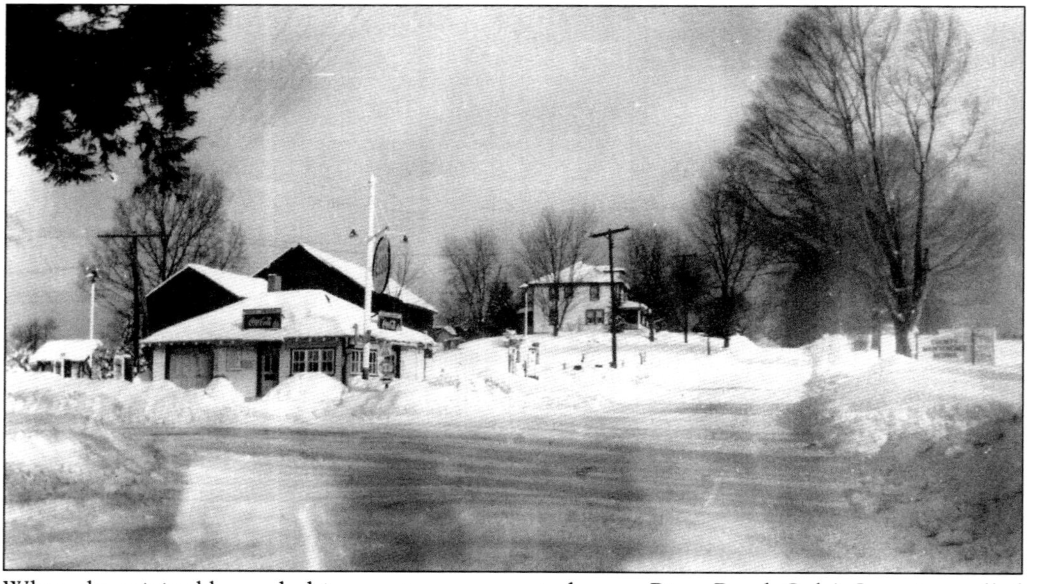

When the original burned, this new store was erected across River Road. Cole's Store is recalled for the sodas and ice cream it sold. It was an Esso station and the last stop for Jersey motorists headed to the old Milford Bridge. A Cole house is visible on the hill, prior to being moved across the street when the Tocks Island plan acquired this section. (Courtesy of Robert Myers.)

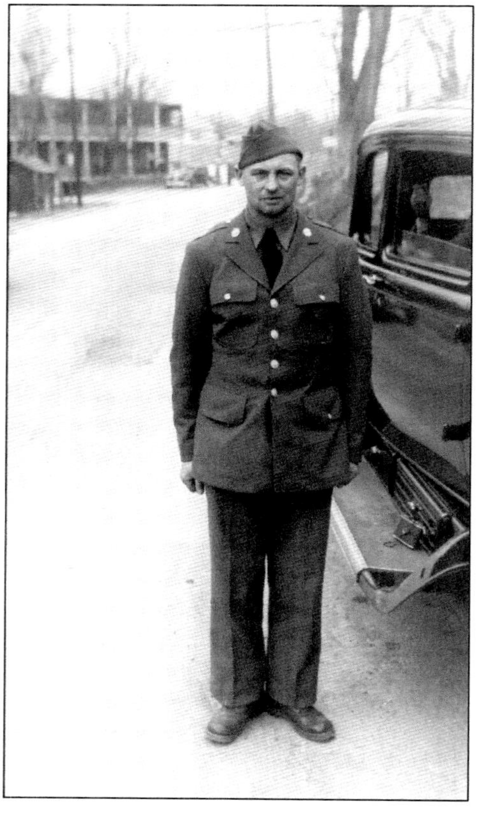

When World War II erupted, local young men and women enlisted to serve their country. Donald Shimer Cole's ancestors had defended the emerging frontier. He was awarded the Purple Heart for having been wounded and held as a POW in the European theater of operations. He served with the 3rd Army, 4th Armored Division, and returned to Brick House village with the rank of staff sergeant. (Courtesy of Marjorie Cole Shay.)

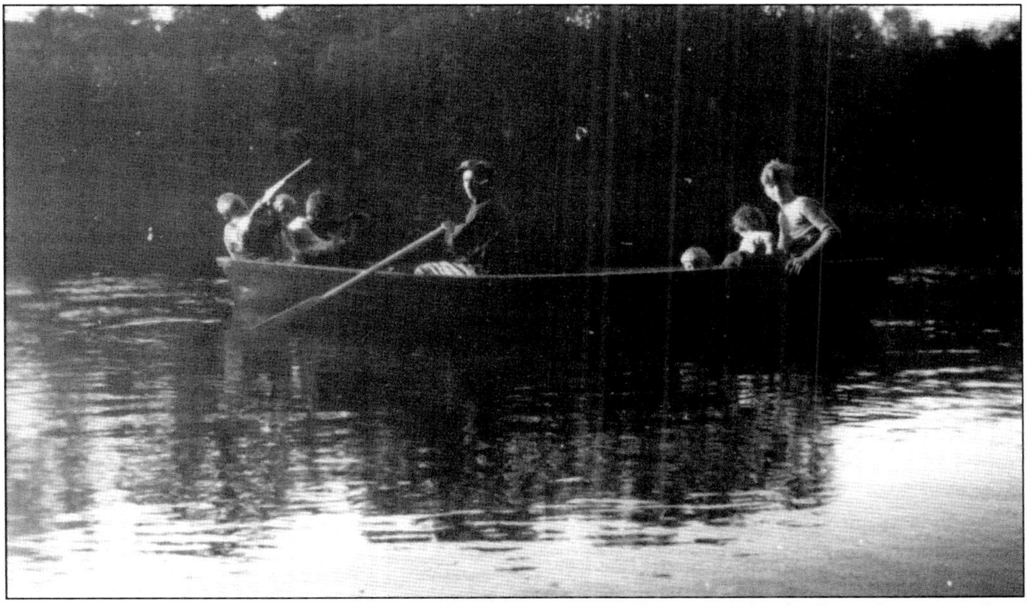

Not unlike the early settlers, these children are imagining being on the lookout for marauding bands or trying to shoot a duck for dinner. The river was a place where the native people, settlers, farmers, travelers, and tourists each gravitated toward. For some it provided water and fish for food, for others a means for transportation or irrigation, and for all a place of enjoyment. (Courtesy of Joan Forster Erb.)

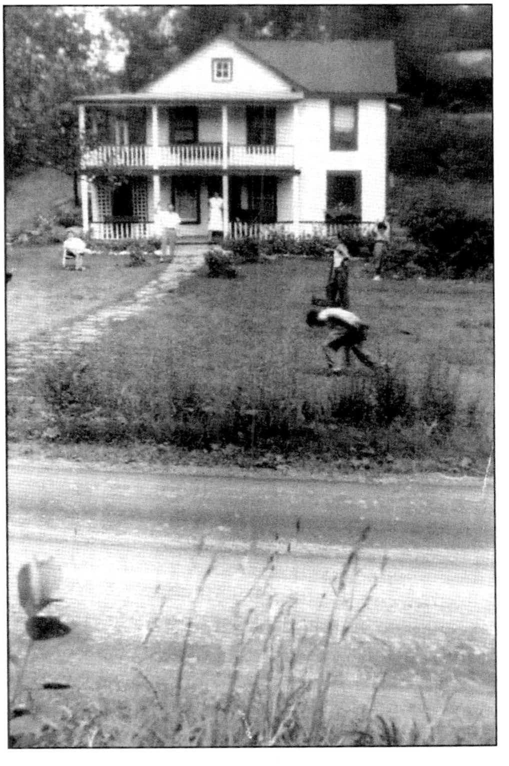

This shows a familiar scene on Sundays around town. Families would spend those days, prior to stores remaining open all week long, to enjoy each other's company and to play badminton or a game of catch. This is a memory recalled by the grandchildren of Joseph and Rose Trovato, who often came to visit. (Courtesy of Joseph and Rose Trovato family.)

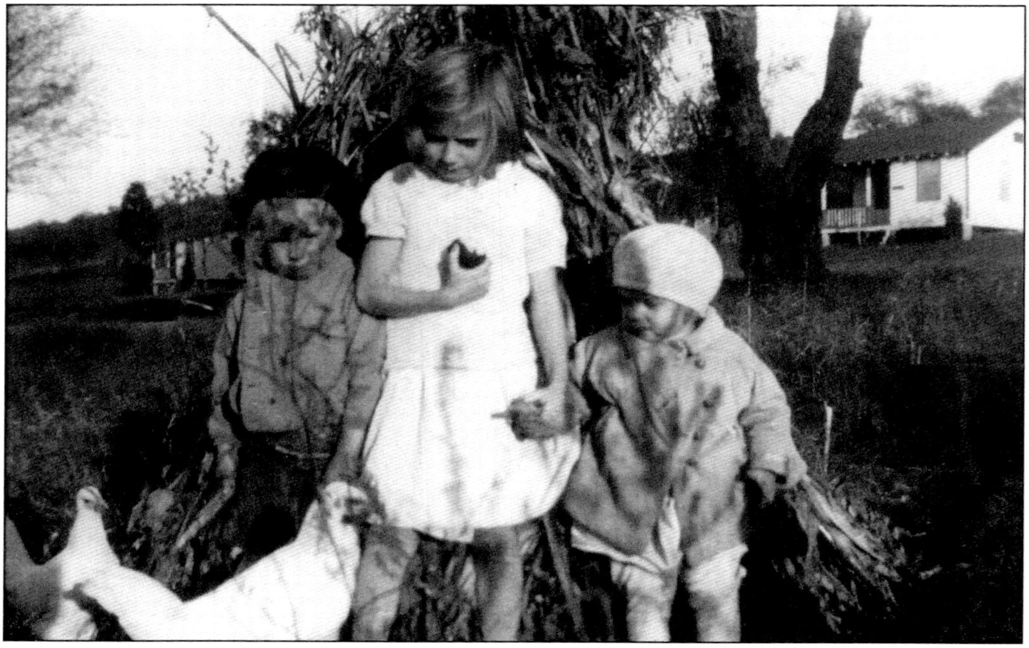

Along the Delaware Mine Road located below the Milford Bridge was the North Bergen police camp. It was used as a place where the families could spend some quiet time. From left to right are Richard, Marie, and Joan Forster watching the chickens that were often allowed to roam free-range on the small farms. (Courtesy of Joan Forster Erb.)

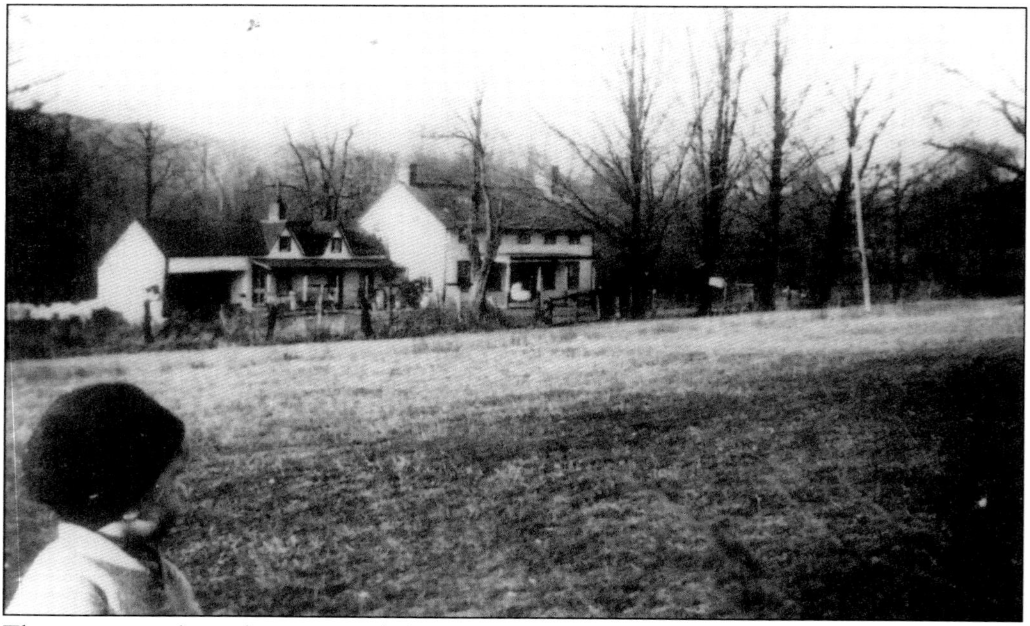

The camp sat along the river, and this was its main building. There were also a number of small cabins, as noted in the above image. It was a place of recreation and vacation for the North Bergen Benevolent Association Camp for Patrolmen but was also recalled as McCarty's. (Courtesy of Joan Forster Erb.)

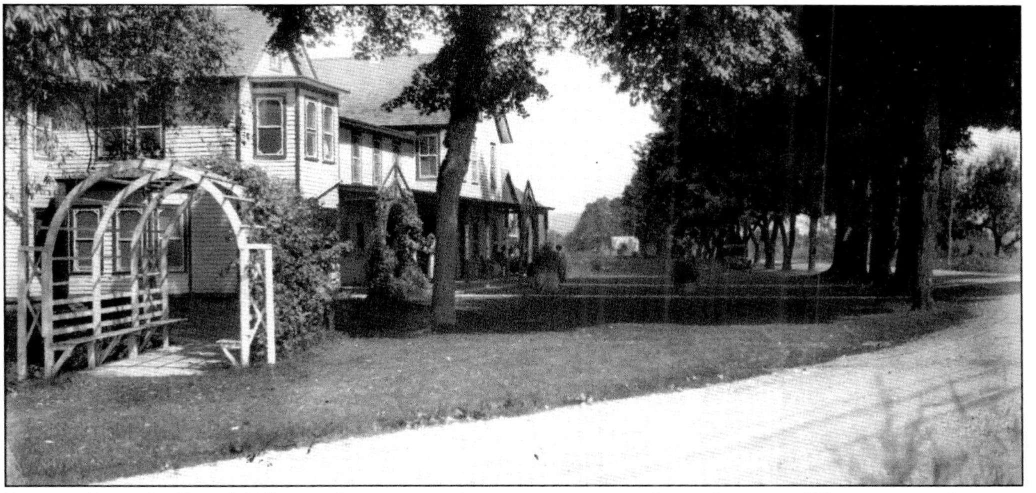

Dating from the late 1800s, such structures began to appear along the river. This one was known as Riverside Farm (page 68) and run by the Kerrs. It is hard to imagine where it once sat, as all evidence of its location is lost. An old newspaper account mentions the remains of a Native American burial being uncovered, when the Kerrs were digging foundations near here.

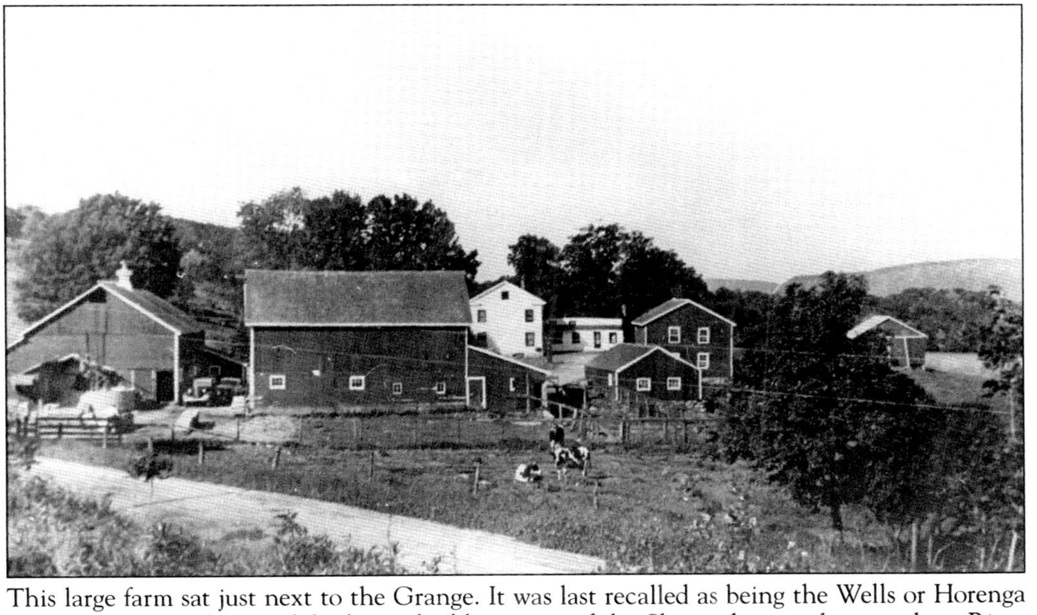

This large farm sat just next to the Grange. It was last recalled as being the Wells or Horenga place. The original part of the house had been one of the Shimer houses that sat along River Road. On this parcel is a small Westbrook family burial plot where Soveryne and Blandina Westbrook and others are buried (page 41).

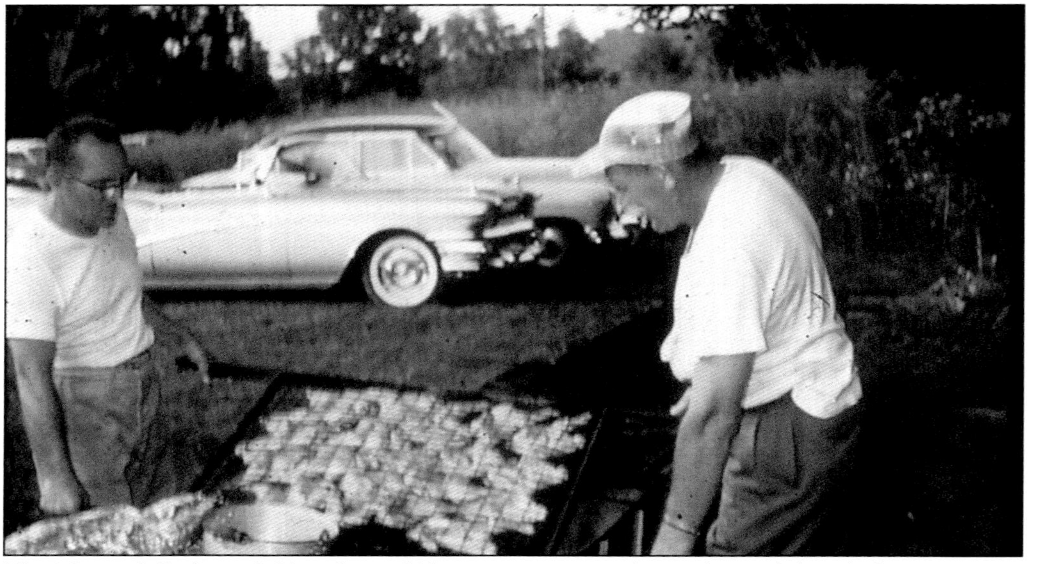

The Minisink Reformed Church would host many events that welcomed the whole community to participate. It frequently sponsored chicken barbecues or harvest home dinners. Such events enjoyed the bounty that local farms produced and promoted fellowship. These annual specials have been added to with a yearly vacation bible camp, a rummage sale, and an auction.

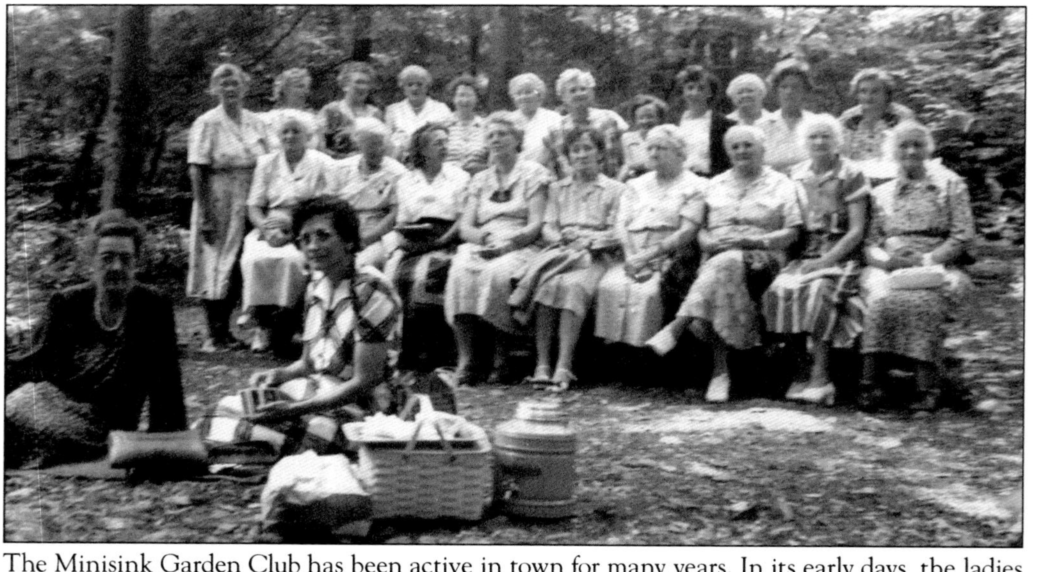

The Minisink Garden Club has been active in town for many years. In its early days, the ladies often toured neighboring clubs or traveled to see botanical gardens and other locations where they could admire flowers and learn about horticulture. But, aside from the club activities, such social events were also enjoyed. (Courtesy of James Heim.)

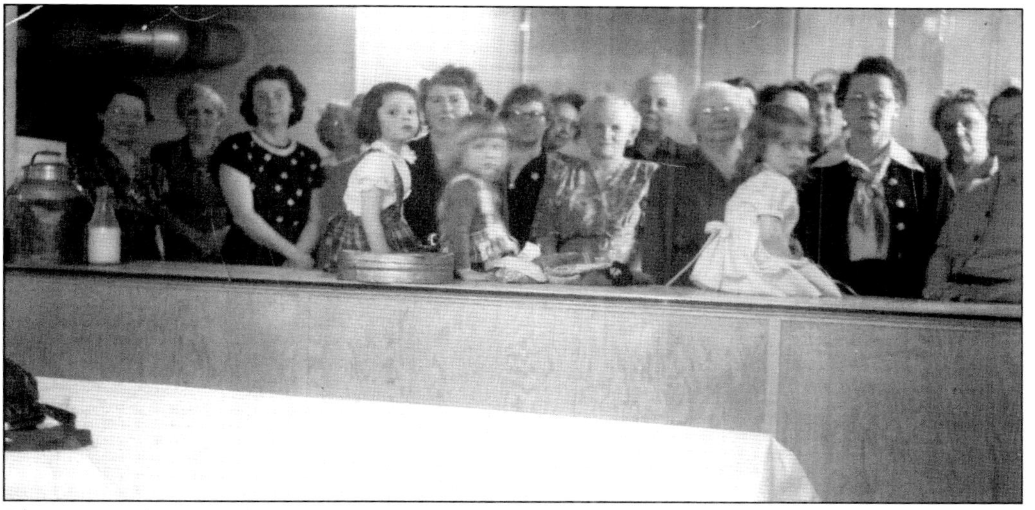

This group of women from the Minisink Reformed Church and the girls sitting on the counter pose for a photograph. Donie Cortright is seen second from left, and the lady wearing a polka dot top is identified as Marion Hough. On the left side, on the counter, are a milk jug and a glass milk bottle. (Courtesy of Minisink Reformed Church.)

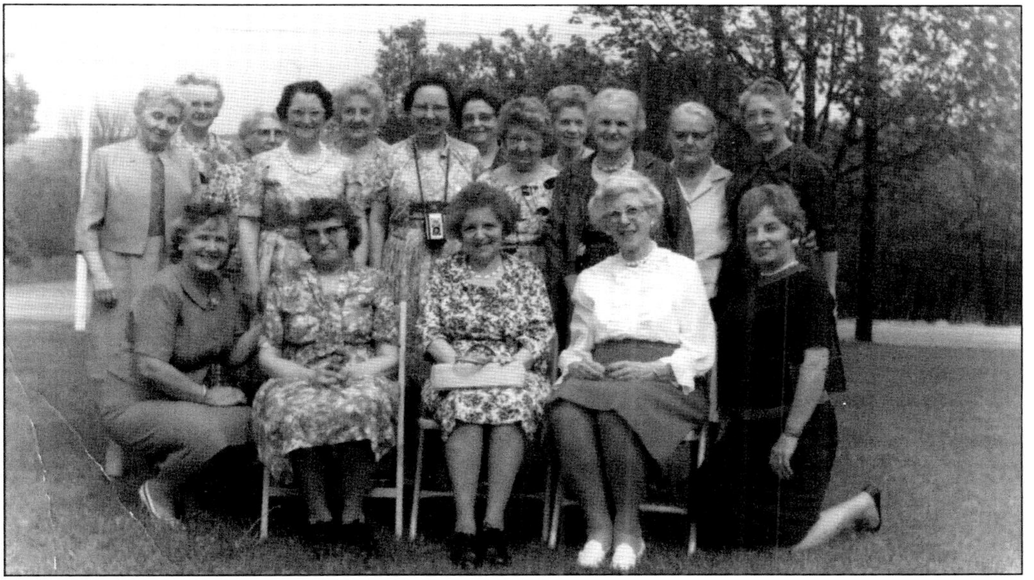

In the 1950s, the Minisink Reformed Church Ladies Guild posed, and from left to right are (first row) Helen Santina, Bertha DeRemer, Marie Rogers, Edna Westbrook, and Isabel Hartrim; (second row) Gladys Kerr's mother, Marion Aeberli, Roberta Schneider, Susan Garris, Mary Pollara, and Myrtle Benz; (third row) Marqueen Jasuilewicz, S. Weiner, unidentified, Esther Emrich, unidentified, and Clara Dickson. (Courtesy of Minisink Reformed Church.)

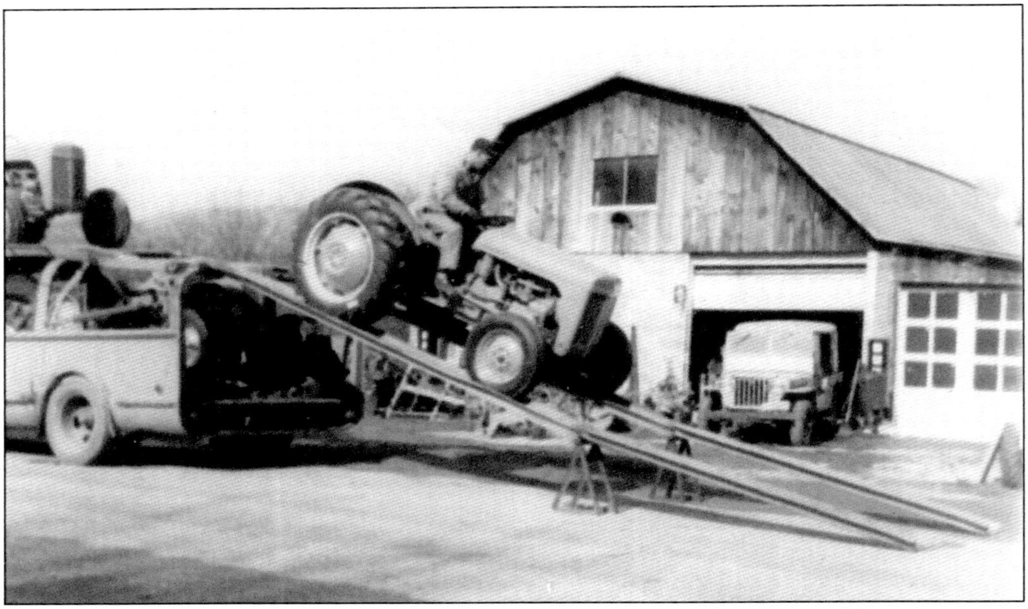

The William Reinhardt and Son business sold old army surplus in the 1940s and farm equipment by 1950. Its most popular item, the Ferguson tractor, was sought by Dutch farmers actively farming in the Sussex County area. This building caught fire in 1962. In 1965, it became the Reinhardt Equipment Company after being rebuilt and has been an antique store since 1993. (Courtesy of Betsy Reinhardt.)

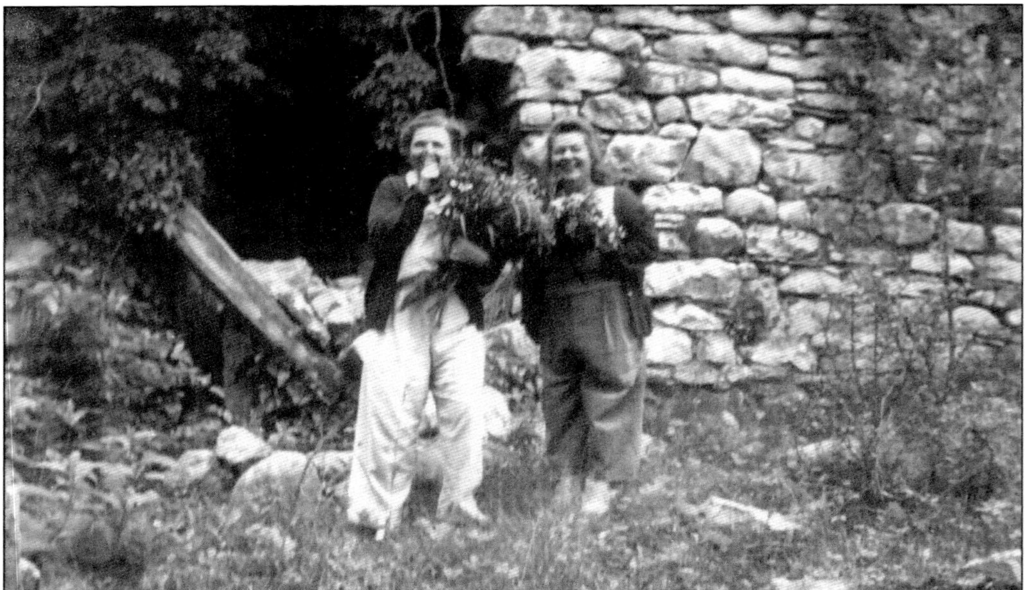

Long after the kilns were no longer in use, they stood as sentinels to the heritage of the Clove Valley. This one sides into the bluff and was a charcoal-burning kiln, unlike the others, which were basically all wood-burning in nature. Martha VanderWerf (left) and a friend are seen enjoying the countryside. (Courtesy of JoAnn VanderWerf Whitesell.)

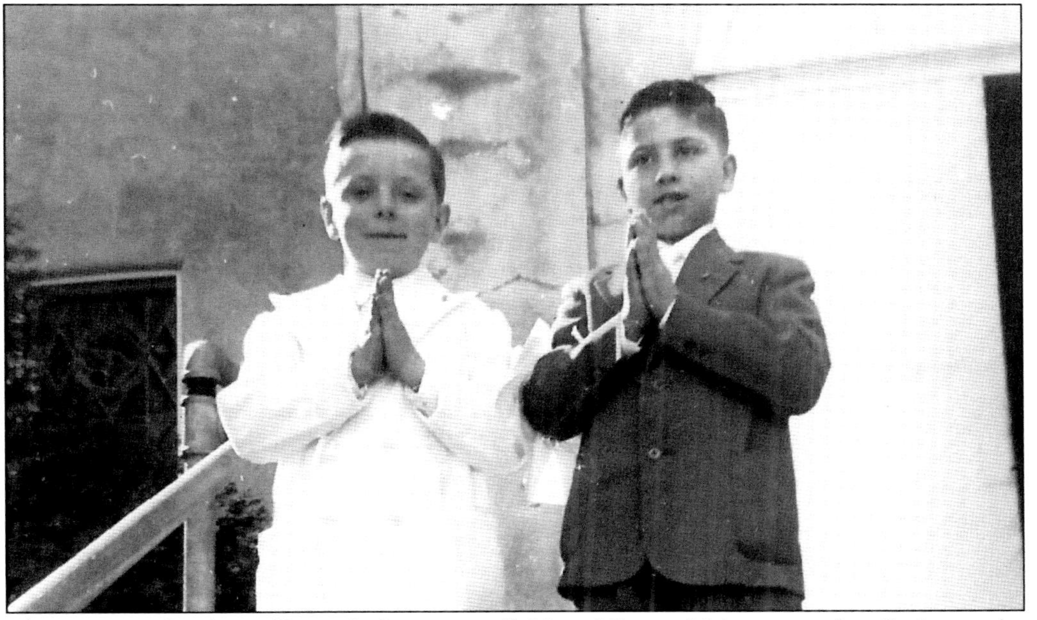

These young altar boys, Kenneth Sieperman (left) and Rocco Meloi, assisted at St. James the Greater Roman Catholic Church. The Reinhardt family had given the land so the church could be erected, and the first celebration of the Eucharist was held here on Christmas Day in 1945. A parish rectory was added later and finished by Peter Zazzi, while Rev. Sylvius Mancini was pastor. (Courtesy of Doris Sieperman.)

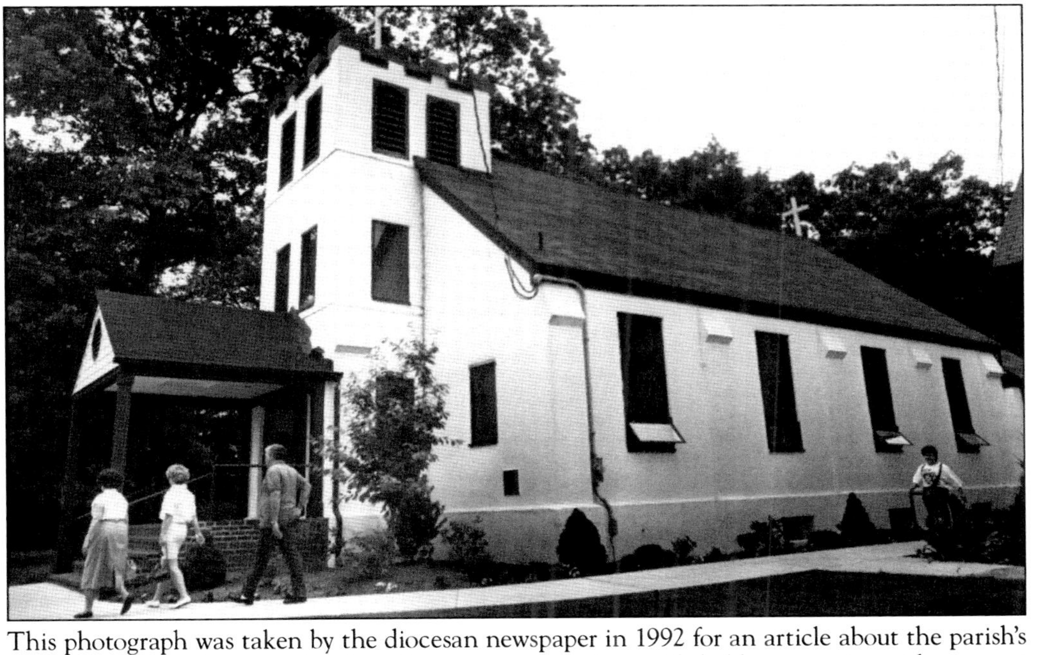

This photograph was taken by the diocesan newspaper in 1992 for an article about the parish's 50th anniversary. Prior to the church's construction, the parish held services in a side room at the home of Anna Staudt on River Road. Sunday masses had also been occasionally held at the Rock View Hotel. (Photograph by Tom Lynch, courtesy of the Beacon.)

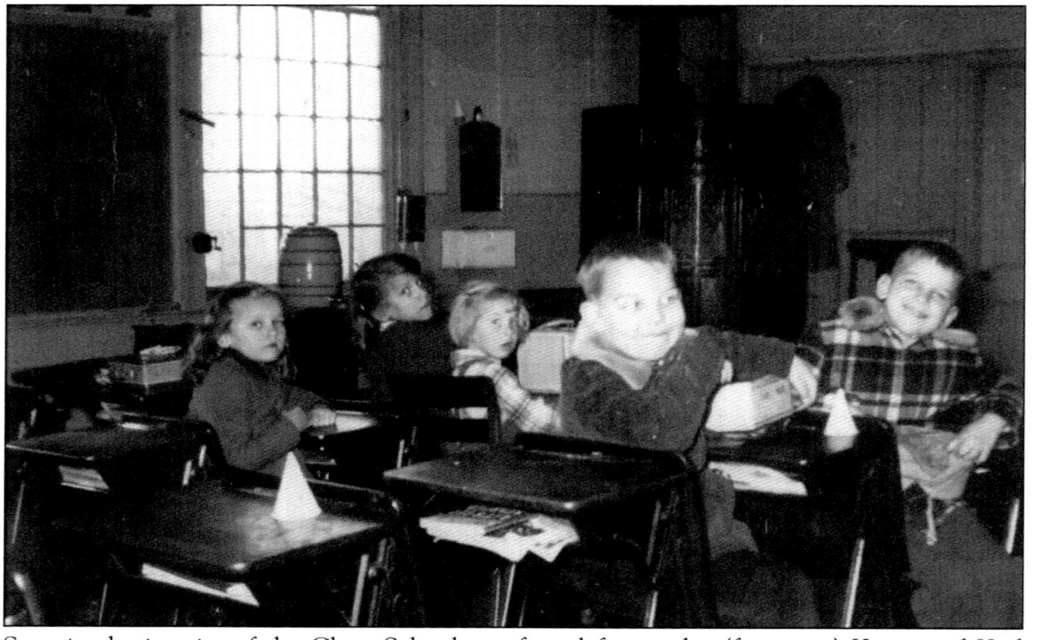

Seen in the interior of the Clove School are, from left to right, (front row) Karen and Karl Ardler and Wade Coss. The one-room classrooms had early woodstoves and corner furnaces that needed tending. Most pupils walked to the nearest schoolhouse as busing was only used for the children attending at greater distance or going to secondary school.

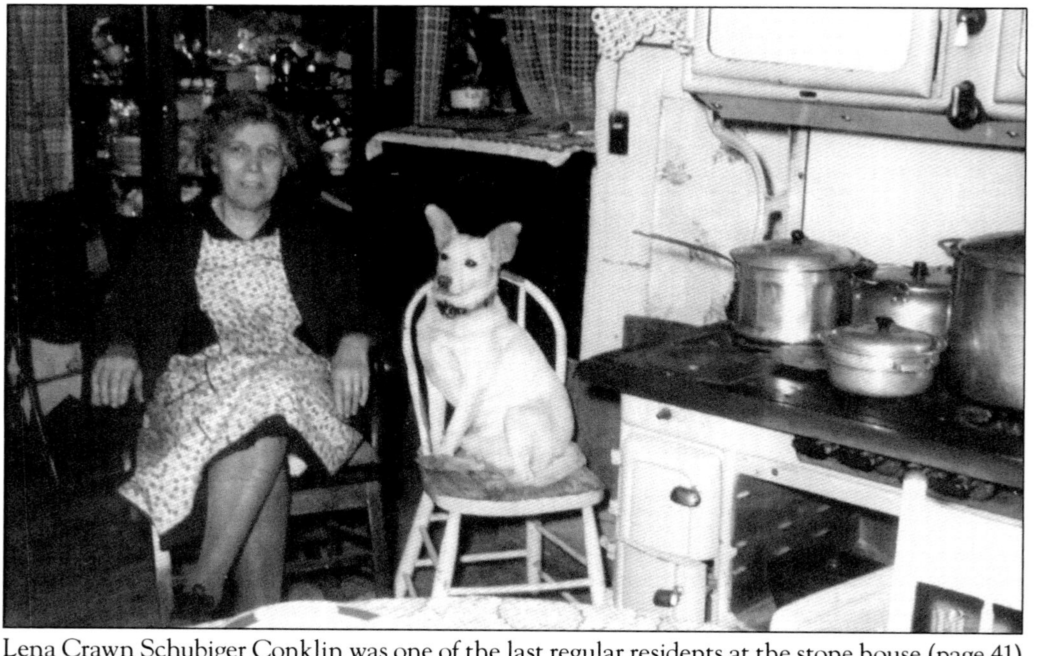

Lena Crawn Schubiger Conklin was one of the last regular residents at the stone house (page 41) on U.S. Route 206. It served as a tenant house to the farm across the way for many years. She was well known for her baking ability, and her pies were favorites at community functions. During hunting seasons, she allowed hunters to room on the upper floor.

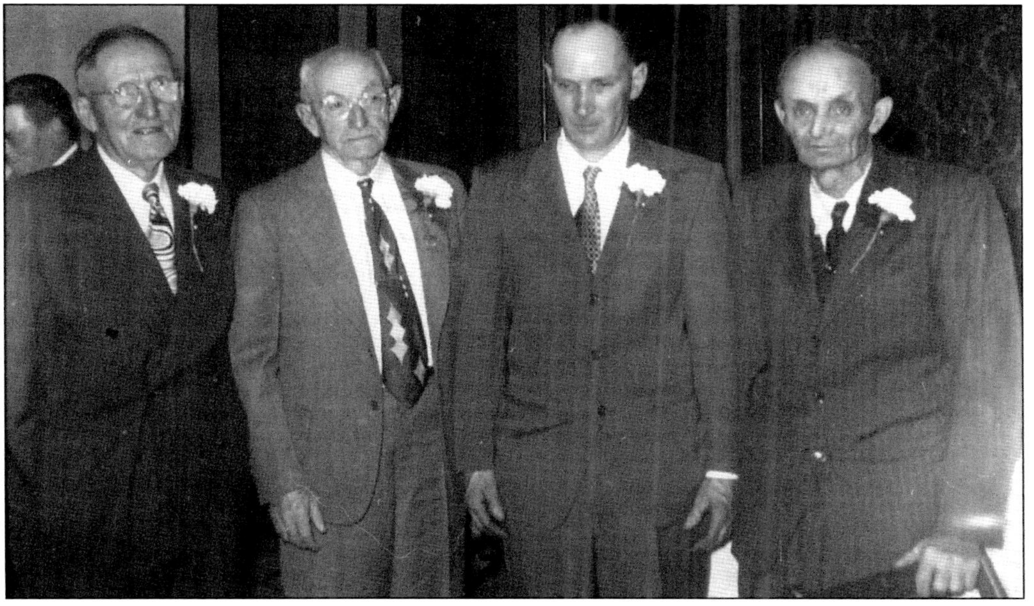

On February 2, 1954, Montague Grange No. 140 celebrated its 50th anniversary. The charter members, each wearing a carnation to indicate their longtime status with the group, are, from left to right, George Reinhardt, John Middleton, Arnold Cole, and Harry Cortright. (Courtesy of Montague Grange.)

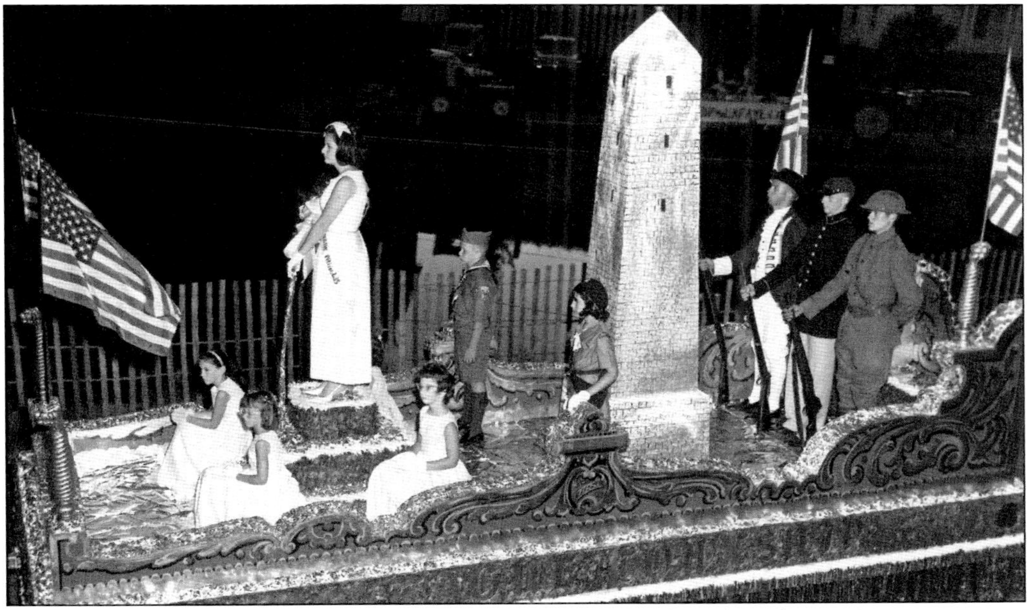

This was Montague Township's prize-winning float that won first place during the tercentenary celebration. It highlighted High Point Monument, which was erected as a veterans' memorial. Riding the float are the tercentenary princess (a Miss Hoffman) and her court, representatives of the Boy Scouts and Girl Scouts, and individuals depicting soldiers from the Revolutionary War, Civil War, and world wars. The parade was at the Sussex County Fairgrounds. (Courtesy of Sussex County Library.)

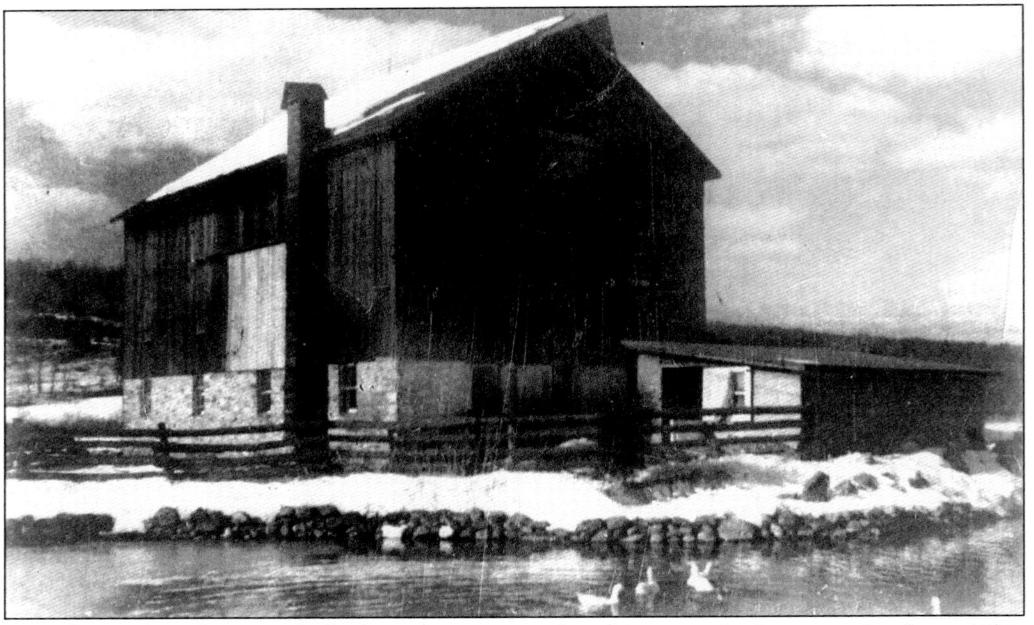

Large barns dotted the roadside throughout town when Montague had more active farms. This one remains on the old Nearpass farm, while many others have collapsed or are in disrepair. In addition, along River Road, there were large chicken coops on the Staudt, the Pratschler, and the Reinhardt farms. (Courtesy of JoAnn VanderWerf Whitesell.)

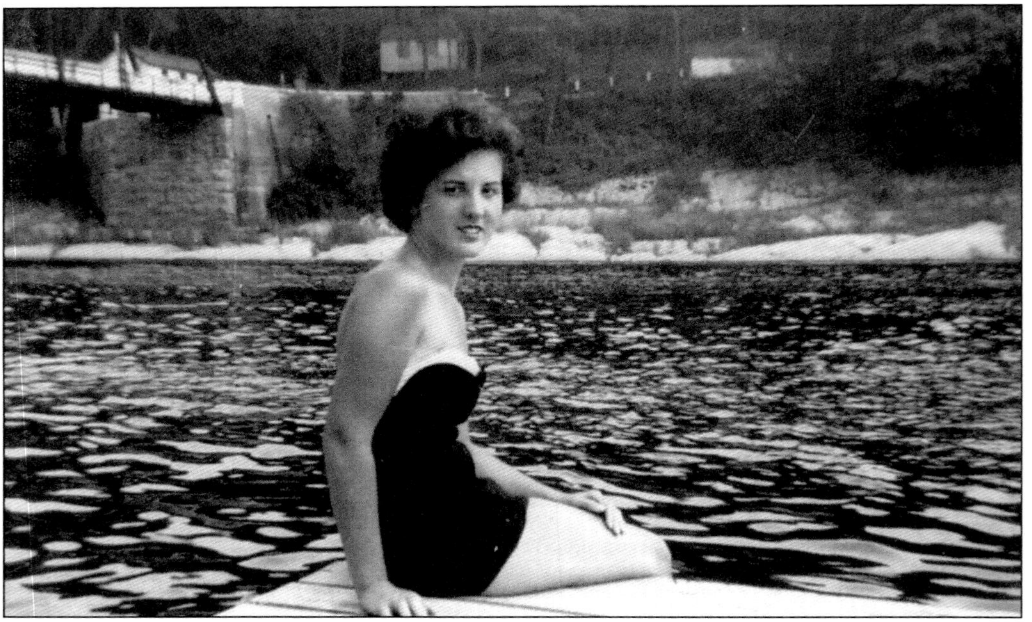

During hot summer days, biking over the bridge to Bob's Beach was a welcome pastime. Visible, up behind Marie Trovato, is the toll keeper's home in Montague. Locals recall the former bridge becoming impassable in winter, whenever trucks slid down the ice-coated roadway with its steep decline on the old New Jersey approach. The remaining abutments are still visible from Milford Beach. (Courtesy of Joseph and Rose Trovato family.)

Five

The Landscape Evolves

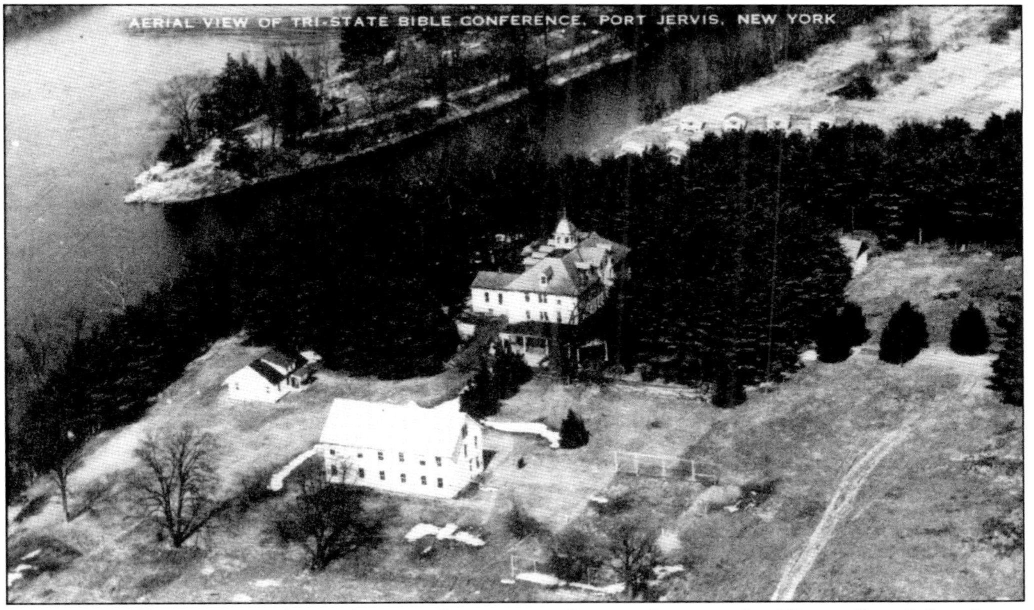

Tri-State Bible Camp and Conference Center, on the northern end of River Road, has been owned and operated by the Fellowship of Fundamental Bible Churches since 1949. The former Pine Cliff property was acquired and modifications made. A former icehouse became a snack bar and the casino, and a former bar and dance hall were refurnished for a chapel. In 1956, a swimming pool was added. Around 1966, a Mr. and Mrs. Hallock funded the construction of a retirement center to be used as residences for the retired missionaries or pastors. (Courtesy of Alicia C. Batko.)

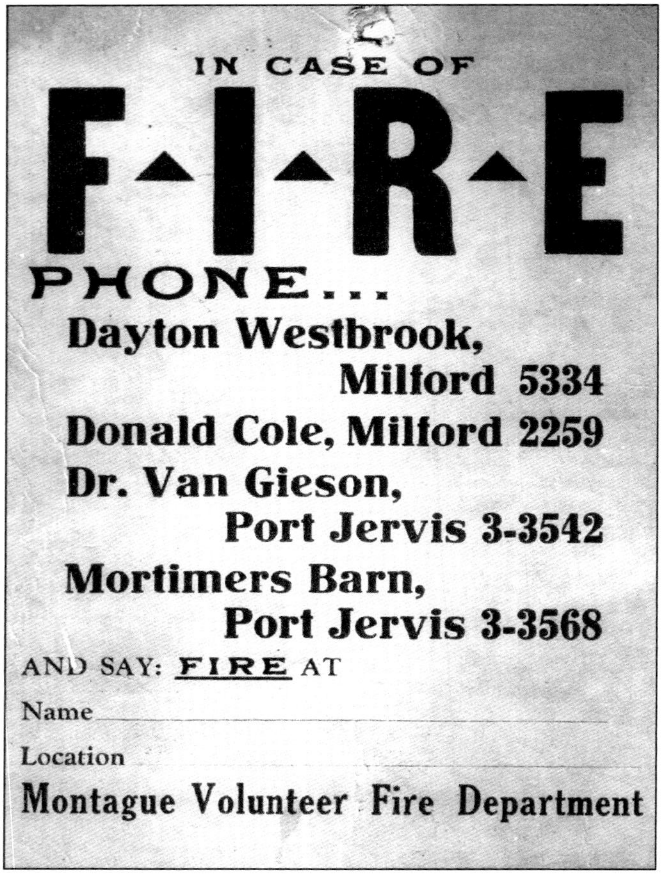

Dr. E. J. VanGieson offered one acre for a firehouse in 1949, if 10 willing volunteers would form a fire company to replace the fire wardens. Twelve men joined up, and each contributed $100. Plans for a firehouse were drawn up by Eston Myers and Joseph Zitone. Timber was hauled from Dayton Westbrook's land by James Carpenter to Robert L. Westbrook's sawmill. Lorenzo Crawn sawed it for the framing, and a well was dug by hand. John L. O'Neil leveled the lot, and all the work was completed on weekends. The founding members were Charles Pratschler, James W. Carpenter, John Ardler, Lloyd Coss, Eston Myers, Donald Cole, Theodore Brace, Robert L. Westbrook, Joseph Zitone, and Irving Aber. (Below, courtesy of Montague Volunteer Fire Company.)

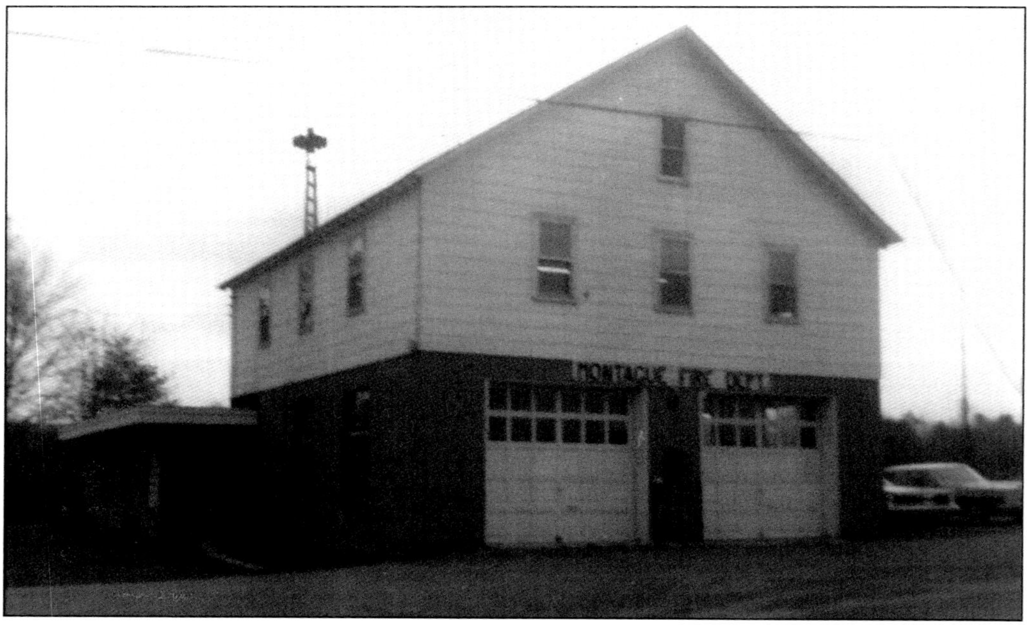

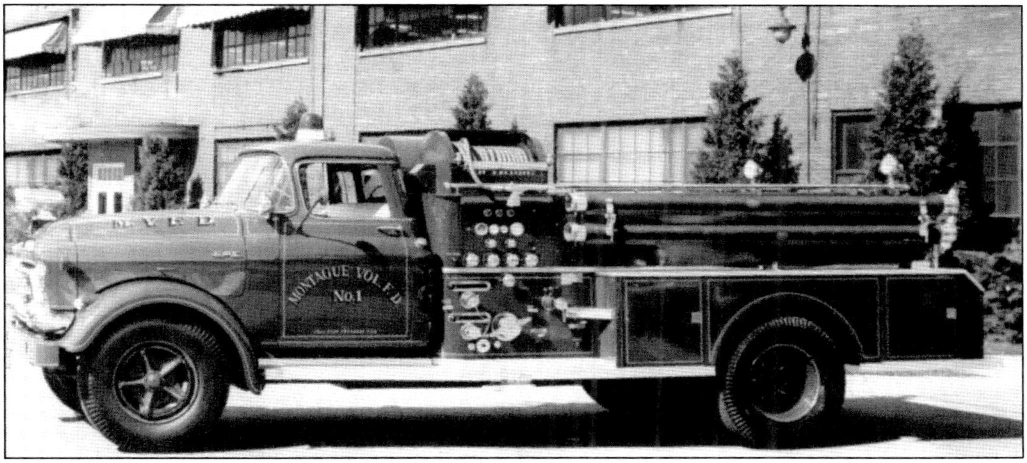

The group first purchased an old pumper for $100 from the doctor's former Bloomfield fire department, and he became the group's first president, alongside Chief John L. O'Neil. This is the first new fire truck they purchased in 1959, equipped with a Bean pumper. Some of the men traveled to Michigan so they could be trained in its operation and drove the truck back to Montague. (Courtesy of Montague Volunteer Fire Company.)

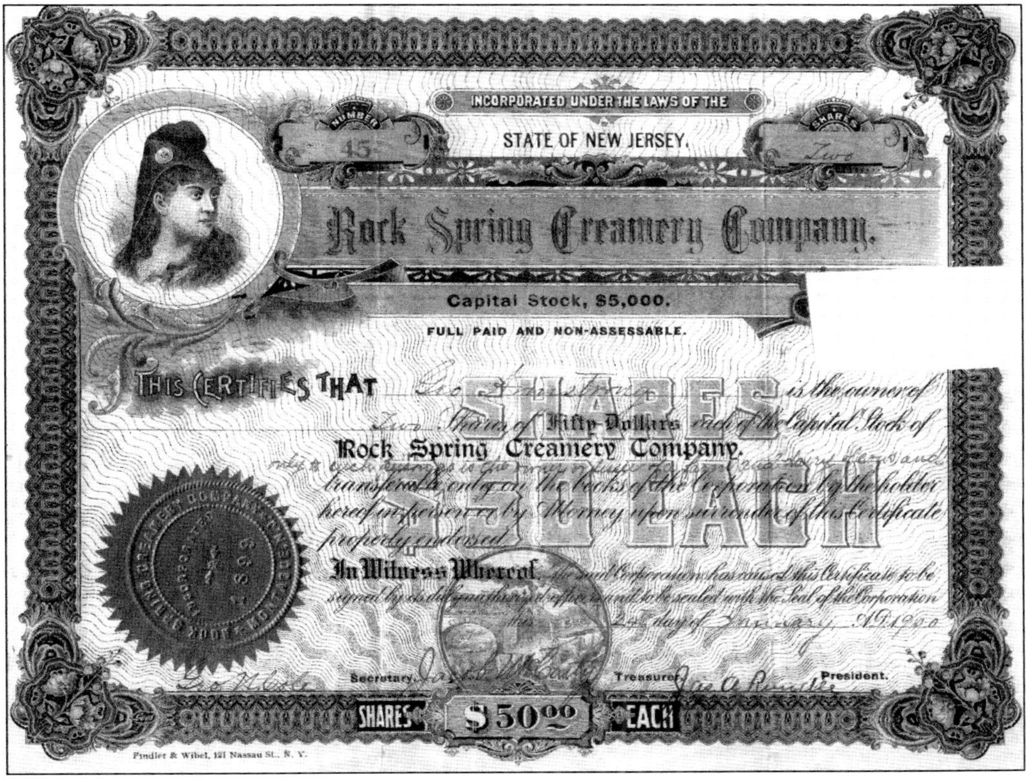

INCORPORATED UNDER THE LAWS OF THE

NUMBER 45 STATE OF NEW JERSEY. SHARES Two

Rock Spring Creamery Company.

Capital Stock, $5,000.

FULL PAID AND NON-ASSESSABLE.

This Certifies That is the owner of Two Shares of Fifty Dollars each of the Capital Stock of Rock Spring Creamery Company. transferable only on the books of the Corporation by the holder hereof in person or by Attorney upon surrender of this Certificate properly endorsed.

In Witness Whereof the said Corporation has caused this Certificate to be signed by its duly authorized officers and to be sealed with the Seal of the Corporation this day of January A.D. 1900

Secretary. Treasurer. President.

SHARES $50.00 EACH

Findler & Wibel, 121 Nassau St., N. Y.

This 1900 stock certificate was issued by the Rock Spring Creamery, which existed on Rubin Hill Road until the structure burned in 1920. There the local dairies had their milk made into butter. Such early businesses and the general stores, blacksmith shops, and other trades have been replaced by malls, delis, and varied small businesses.

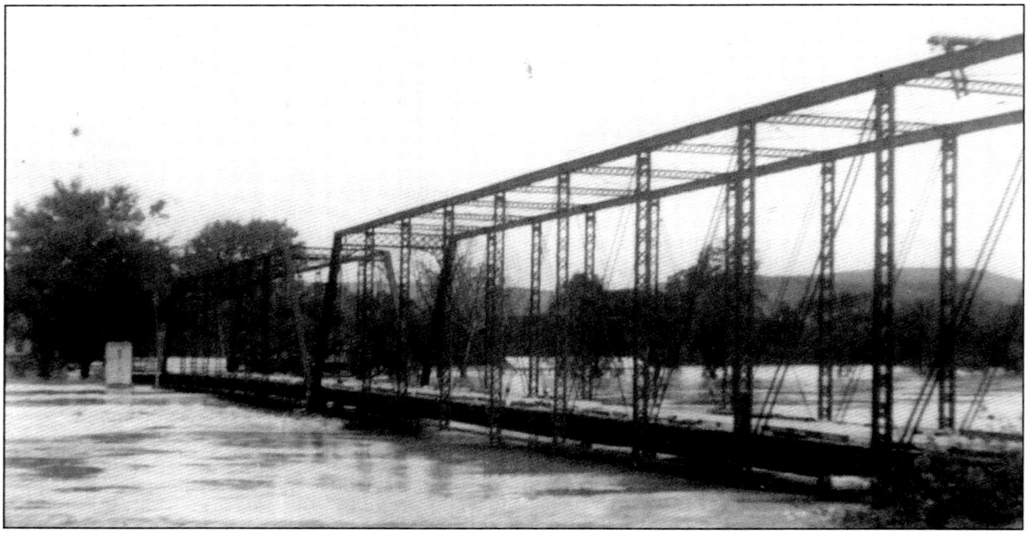

Devastation hit the river valley when Hurricane Diane dumped rain and caused the record-setting flood of 1955. The old bridge's base was touched by the waters that raged all along the Delaware River. The entire beach at Bob's Beach on the Milford, Pennsylvania, side was impacted. The aerial was taken just north of the bridge. Adding to the panic were rumors that the dams impounding the upstream reservoirs were threatened with collapse. It had been some years since the last historic floods of 1903 and 1904. The hurricane brought unexpected amounts of precipitation, which ended the severe drought that had preceded it. It was more typical for ice jams to cause such flooding, and residents were grateful that many lives were spared.

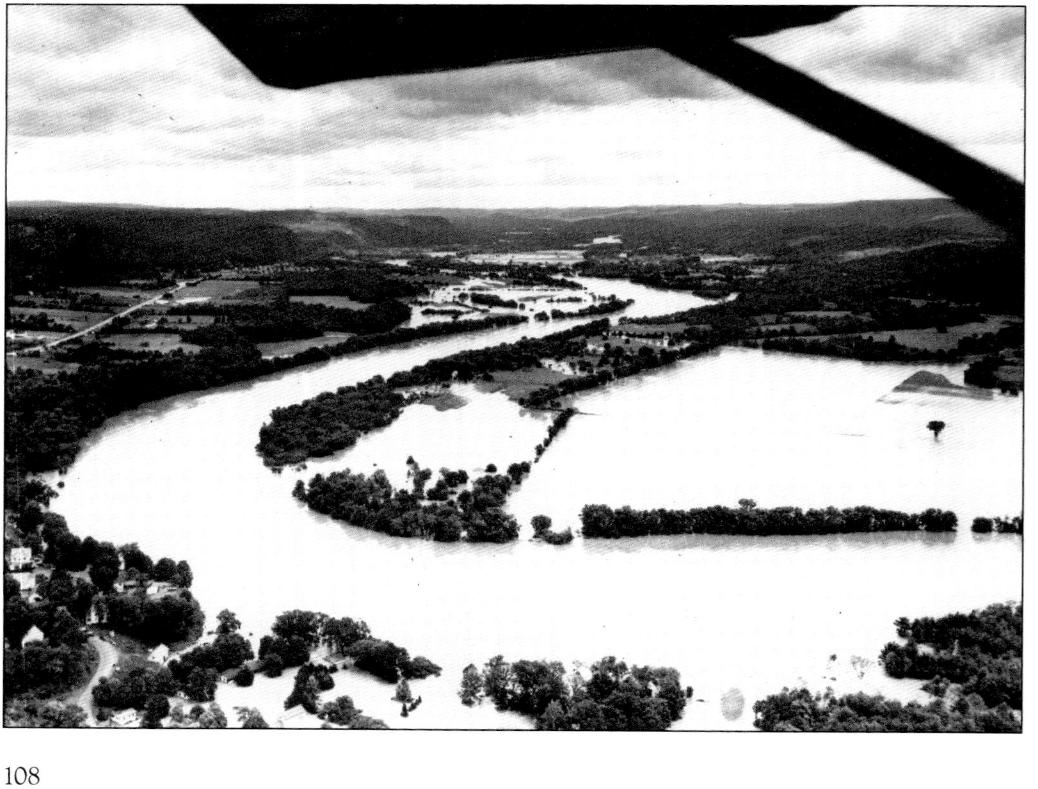

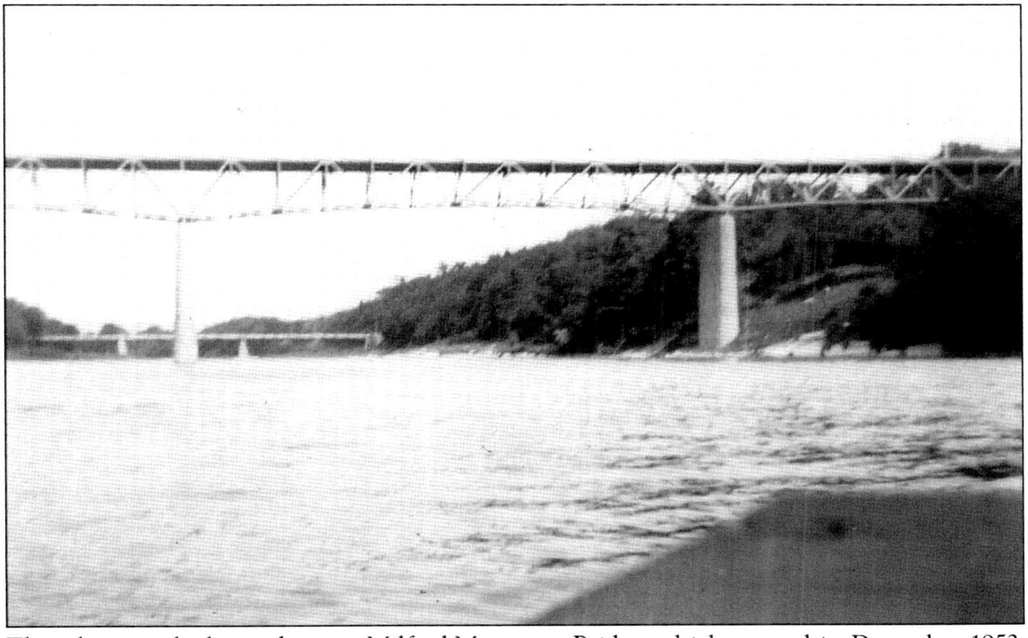

This photograph shows the new Milford-Montague Bridge, which opened in December 1953, with the old one still visible at a distance north of it. The modern bridge was built with a wider roadway and was purposefully constructed higher. That aspect had been specifically planned, in anticipation of the possible damming of the river. (Courtesy of Nicholas Annunziata.)

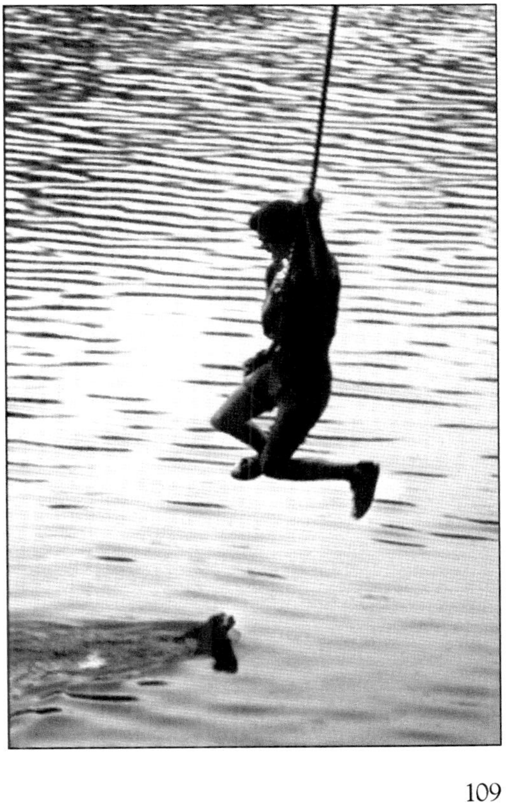

This image captures the sense of freedom that local residents felt when accessing the river. This rope swing is remembered as Hartrim's and had been situated south of the Milford Bridge. Farther down along the river was the Crystal Beach area. It was advertised on the main road nearby by a mechanical billboard that showed swimmers in the process of diving in. (Photograph by Jim Mandeville, courtesy of Tim Mandeville.)

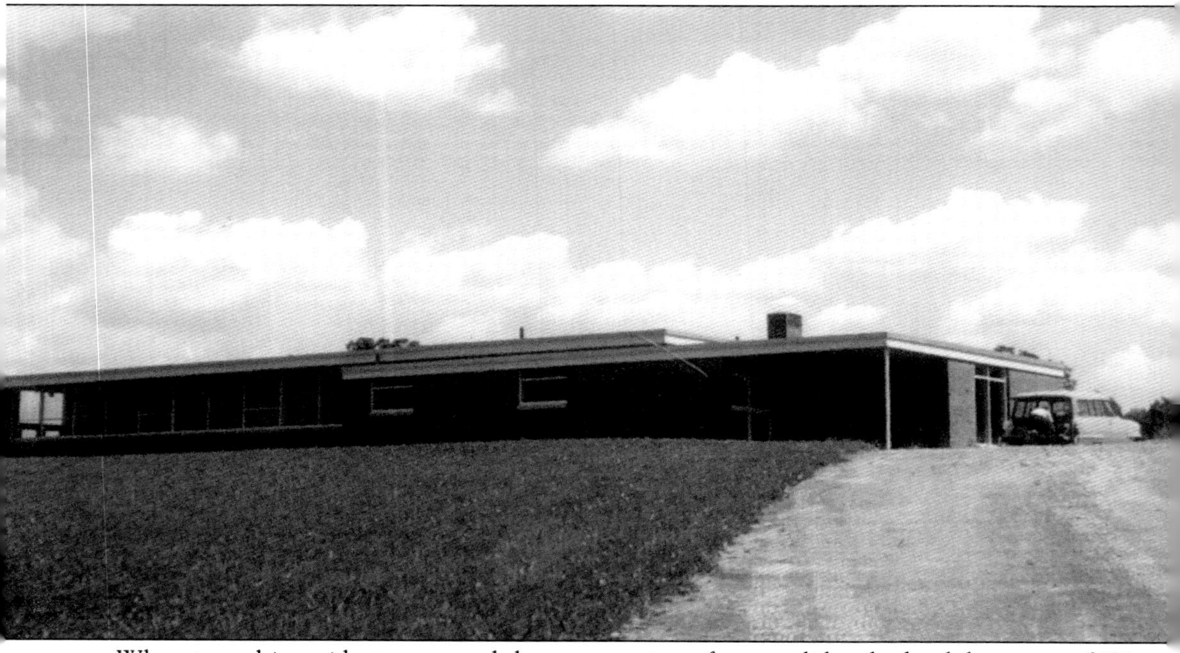

When township residents approved the construction of a consolidated school, by a vote of 171 for and 110 against, the Montague Elementary building was erected in 1955. The principal opposition had come from those who favored sending all the students to Port Jervis, New York. The building was constructed by Joseph Judd and contained only three classrooms, for lower, intermediate, and upper elementary grades. The seventh and eighth grades were sent out of state to attend at Port Jervis Middle School. The structure had a designated capacity of 90. It was soon afterward that the kindergarten and sixth grades would relocate, to be taught at the new firehouse, until rooms were added to handle increasing enrollment. The Grange building was also pressed into service until Charles Mortimer donated funds to add a few rooms and a building referendum passed. The current building reflects further expansions and upgrades, with a large gymnasium, a library, a cafeteria, and a computer classroom added.

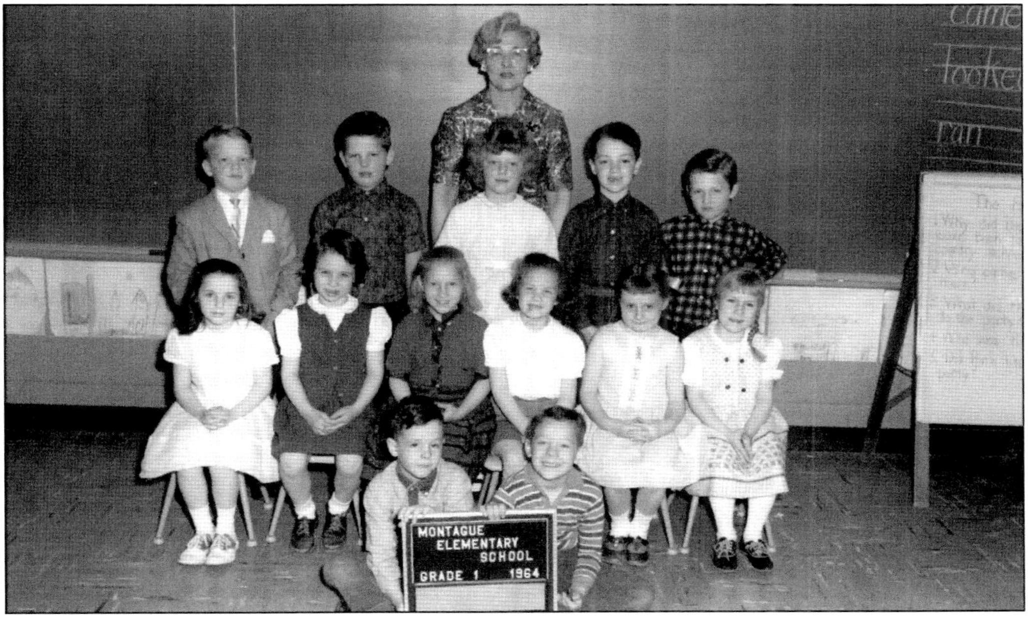

This shows the first-grade class of Montague Elementary in 1964 with its teacher, Cecilia Arnold. The building had already seen a small addition. Seen from left to right are (first row) Warren Wylie and William Dai; (second row) ? Bea, two unidentified, Barbara Rost, Diane Roberts, and Suzanne Miller; (third row) Fred Brenner, unidentified, Christine Grathwohl, Stanley Roberts, and Dale Reim. They had attended kindergarten at the firehouse. (Courtesy of Warren Wylie.)

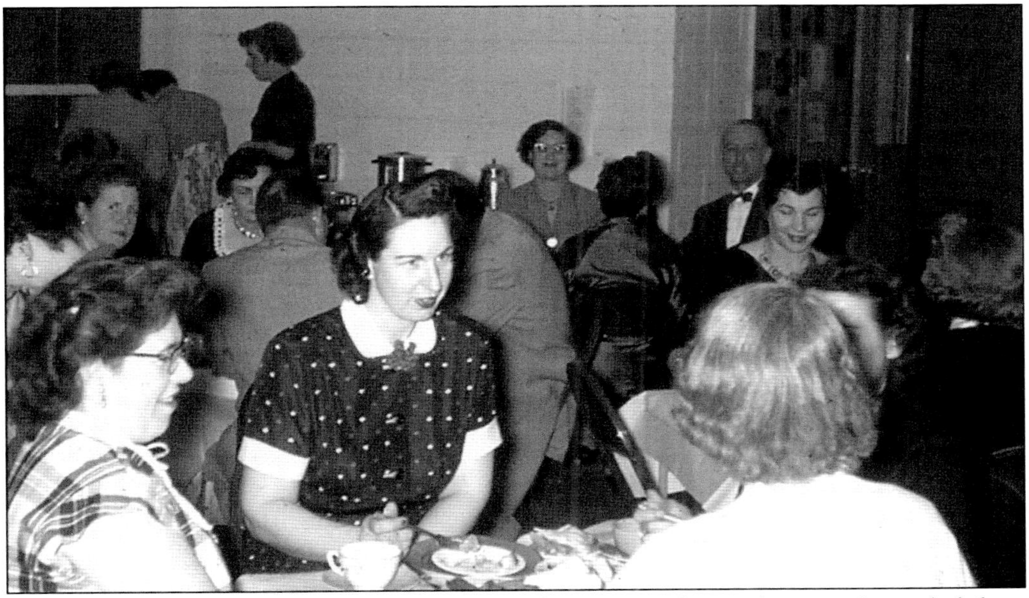

In 1960, Montague boasted a population of around 880. It was during this time that a shift from agricultural use of once-large parcels for a country club and new home building was initiated by developers. The Mother's Club was an active organization, supporting the school and affording new residents an opportunity to meet and socialize. It later became the Parent-Teachers Club and is now a Parent-Teacher Association.

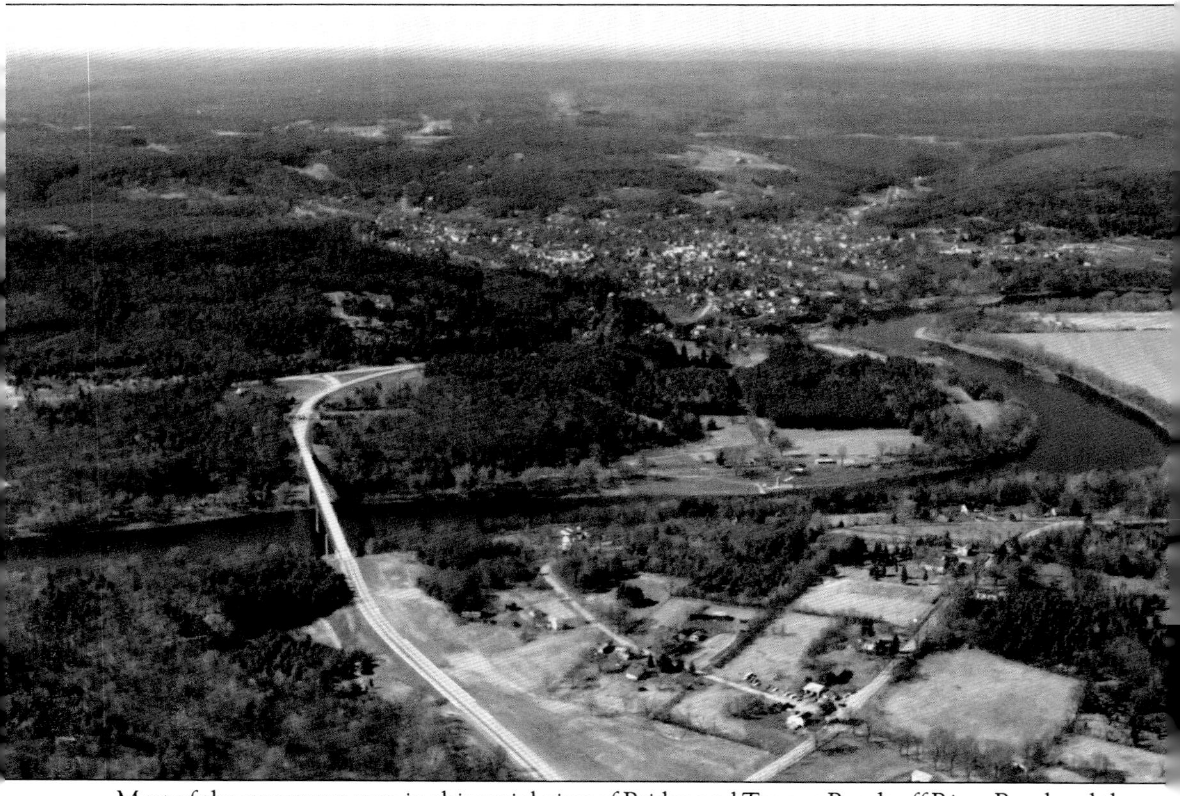

Most of the structures seen in this aerial view of Bridge and Tappan Roads off River Road and the nearby bridge approach were removed when the reservoir project was initiated. Having already lost the Brick House Hotel and with the simultaneous removal or relocation of some structures due to the construction of the new Milford-Montague Bridge in 1953, the loss of this town center dealt a sad blow. The Minisink Reformed Church building was acquired by the Department of the Interior. It and a house and barns on the south side of Rubin Hill Road that were on land included in the acquisitions in this area are all that remain intact from this time and now stand on the government-owned property. (Courtesy of National Park Service/DEWA.)

As the population decreased, the need to use the former Brick House School was eliminated and the town acquired it for use as a township garage from Donald Cole. Its bell now hangs at the Reformed church. The town, at this time, had no central office building and the township clerk, tax clerk, and assessor each worked from their homes. The township would make use of a trailer located on the new elementary school property, where town meetings were then being held, and later rented a small building on the south end of town—used afterward for the Montague Family Restaurant and now as a car dealership. (Right, courtesy of Brian J. Lewis collection.)

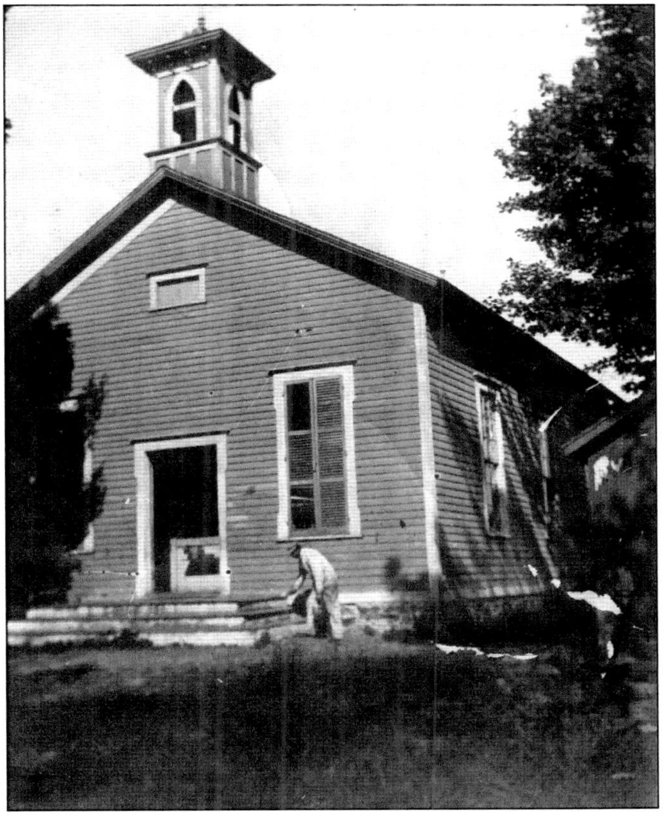

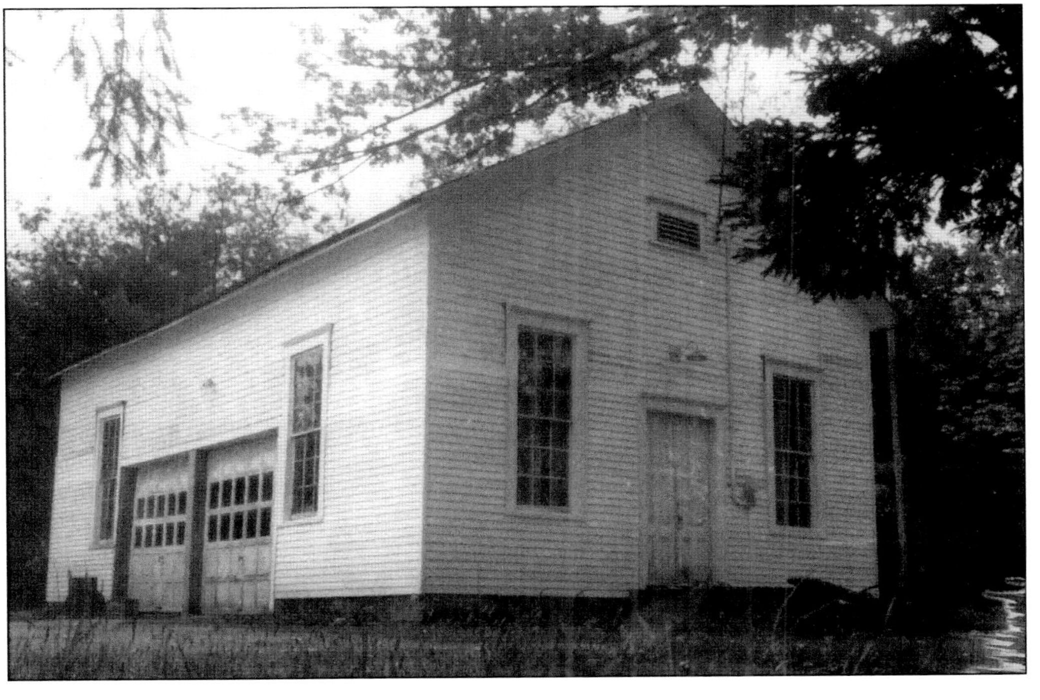

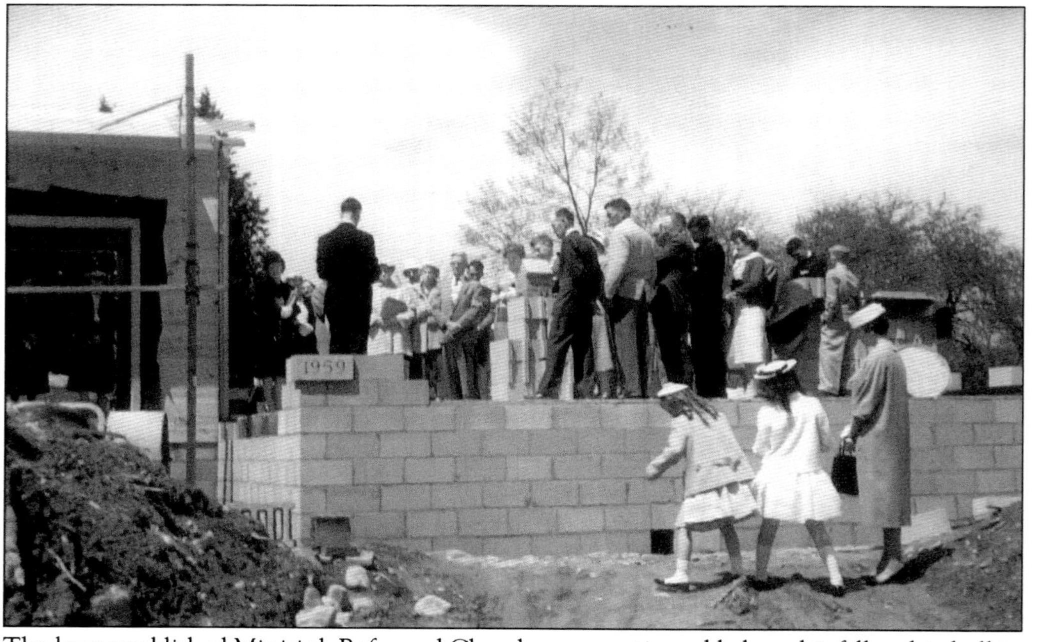

The long-established Minisink Reformed Church congregation added on this fellowship hall in 1959. The addition increased its ability to fully utilize its site. A modern kitchen and meeting hall with bathrooms were included, as well as a nursery where the youngest children of churchgoers could be attended to during services.

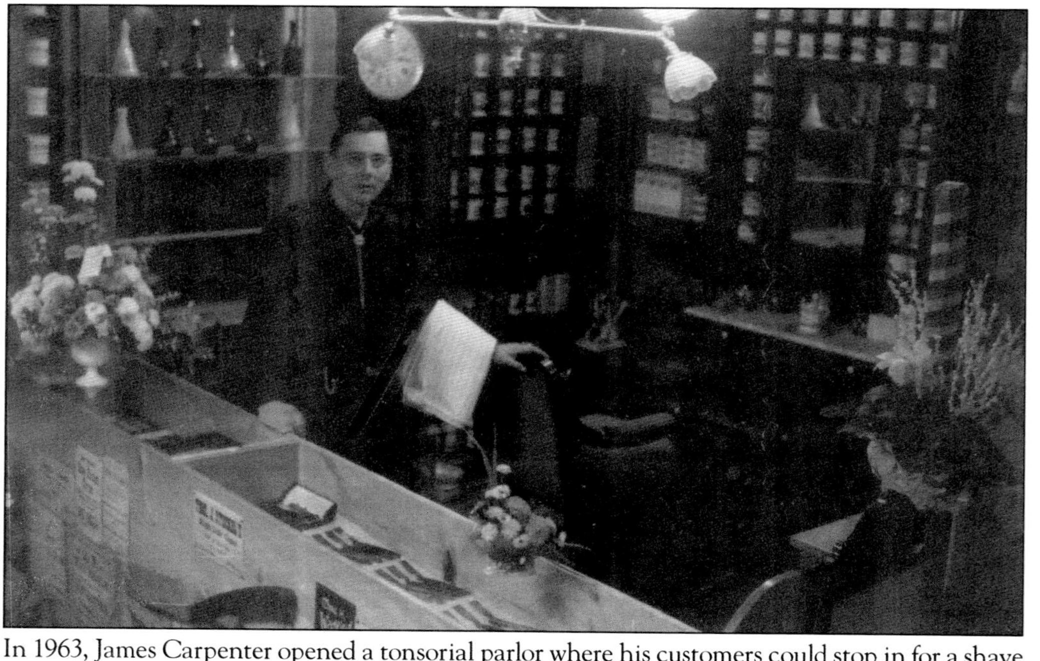

In 1963, James Carpenter opened a tonsorial parlor where his customers could stop in for a shave and a haircut. It combined his love of collecting antiques as he acquired vintage barbershop furnishings to make it look more authentic. This parlor was located on the second floor over his antique shop business. (Courtesy of James and Miriam Carpenter.)

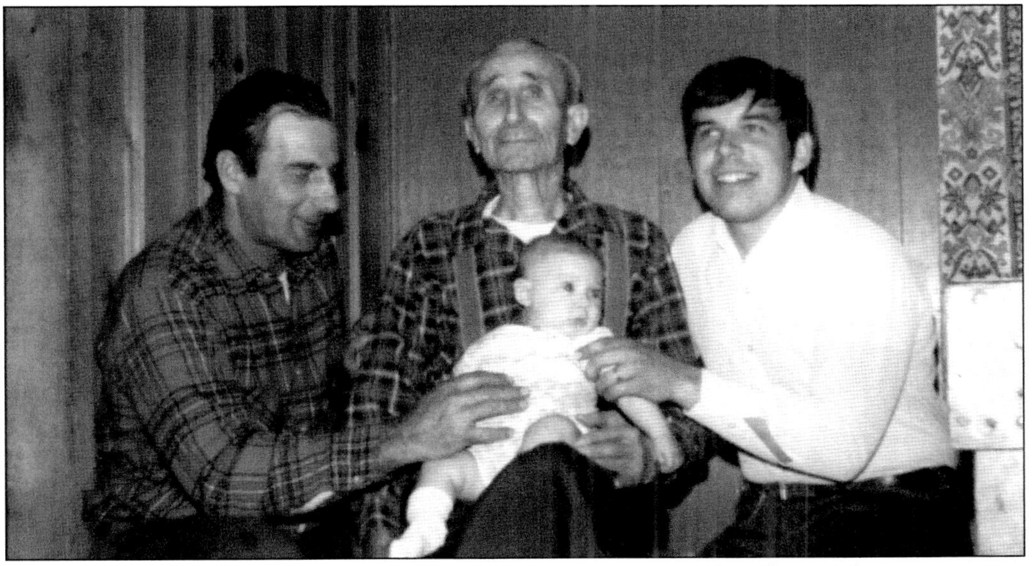

Representing successive generations are the Ayers in this photograph, reflecting four generations. Shown are great-grandson Mark and, from left to right, son Christopher Jr., Christopher Ayers Sr., and grandson Paul. The family members ran a cider mill, and they later opened the Apple Pit located on U.S. Route 206 by Pollara Lane, where their cider and renowned apple pies were sold. (Courtesy of Martha Ayers Aeberli.)

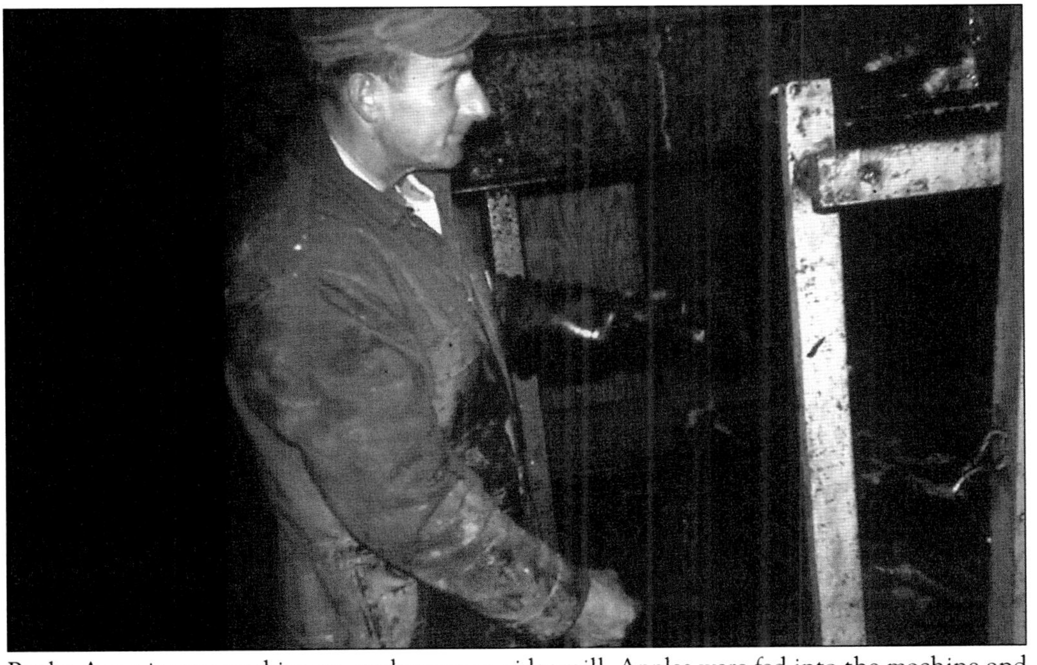

Bucky Ayers is seen working an apple press or cider mill. Apples were fed into the machine and the juice separated from the solids. Leaving the juice unfiltered is what caused it to be referred to as cider. The initial presses where hand cranked, and as time progressed, even this process was mechanized. This is a seasonal occupation, as the fresh local apples were normally only available in the fall.

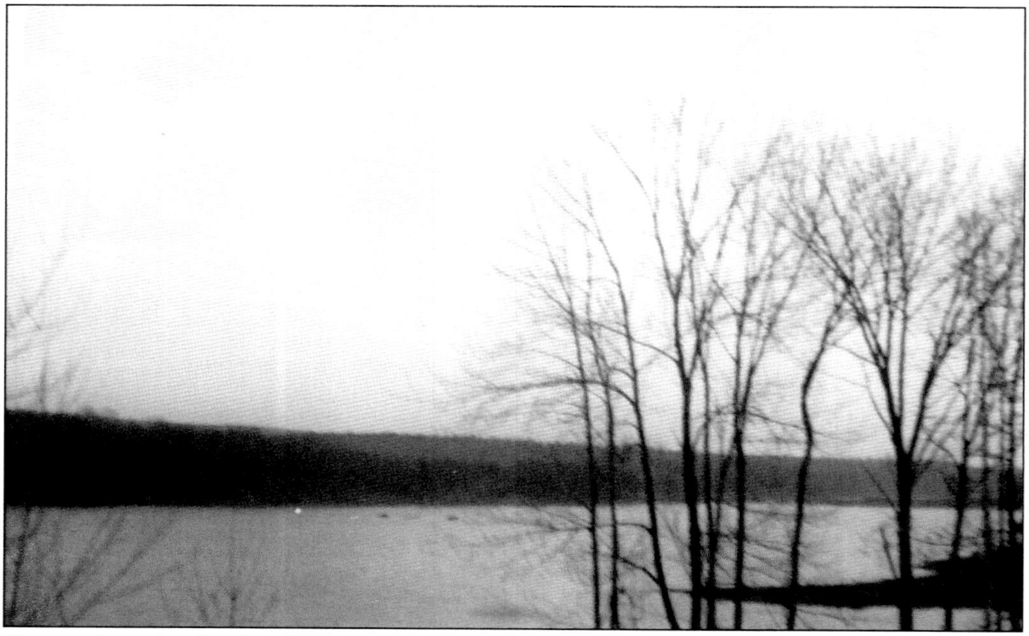

Captured on the Grathwohl farm, this tranquil scene shows the north shore of Holiday Lake, a section of Shimer's Brook that had recently been dammed. Shortly afterward, the area would begin to be transformed in order to create a unique recreational community that would be named after the man-made lake. (Courtesy of Chris Grathwohl Hantman.)

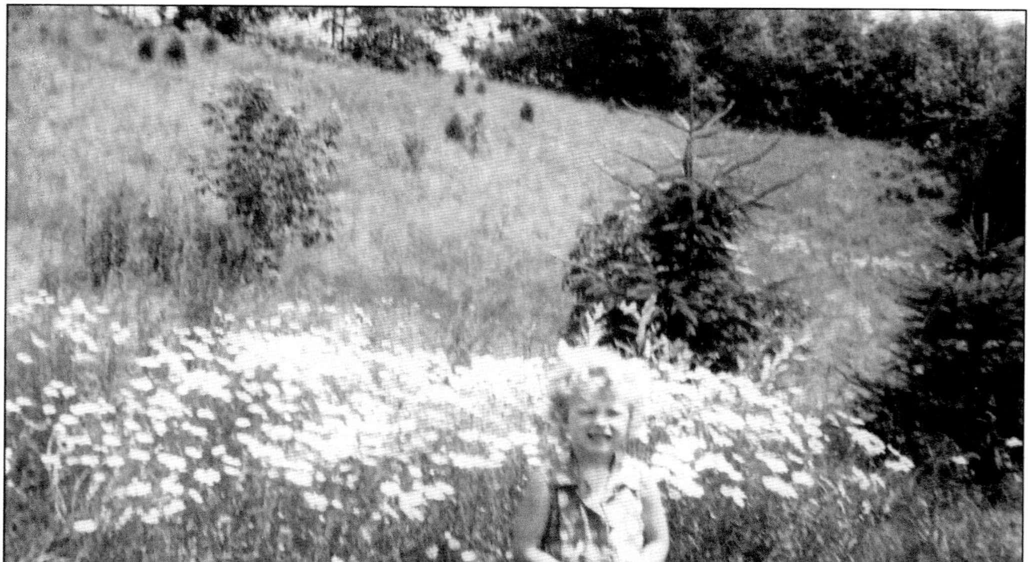

Fields once abounded along Clove Road, like this one by John and Henrietta Grathwohl's home that Chris is seen enjoying. Small farms and cottages had been scattered amid the open spaces where cows or horses grazed and crops were grown. This area would be replaced by early modular structures, single-family homes, and an 18-hole golf course in the late 1960s. (Courtesy of Chris Grathwohl Hantman.)

This brochure's cover advertises Holiday Lake as a recreational community. When it opened, families with school-age children were restricted from taking up permanent residence and the developers focused on attracting professionals and doctors from areas such as Saddle River and Manhattan. It featured many recreational opportunities, including a ski tow, horseback riding, and a premier golf course. (Courtesy of Sussex County Library.)

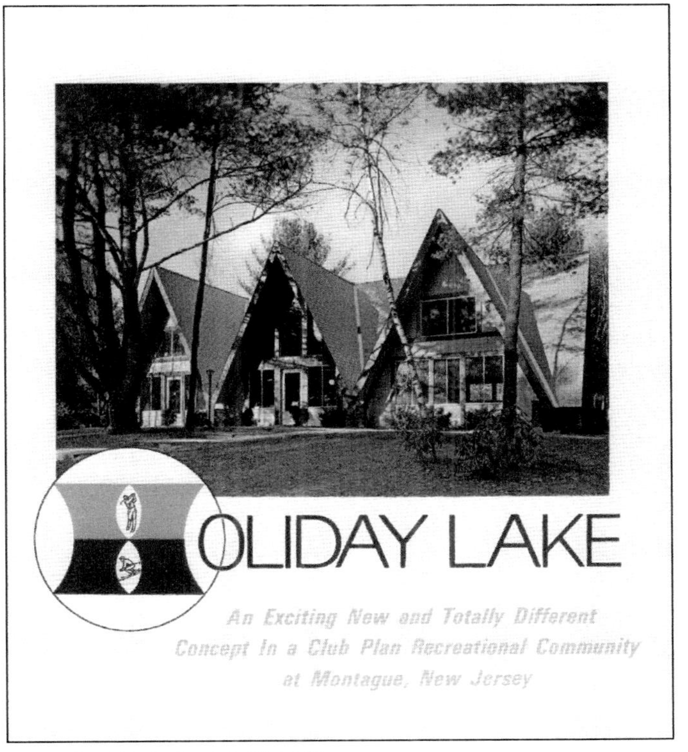

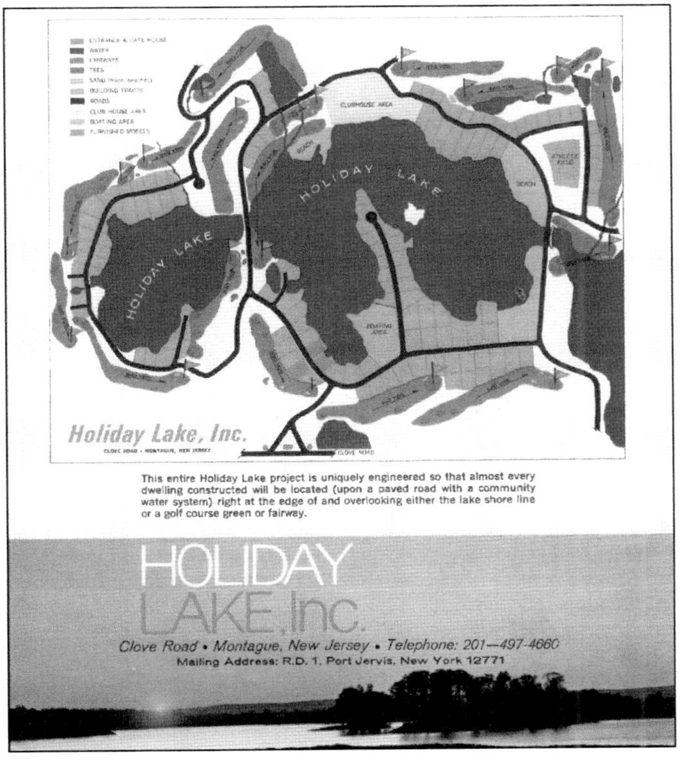

This image shows how the lake community had been planned out. Holiday Lake, Inc., later vastly added to its holdings and owned property scattered throughout the township. In 1979, the name changed to Canyon Ridge, and only the areas around and within the Holiday Lake community would be retained under the property association's control. In 1982, this was again renamed as Highpoint Country Club. (Courtesy of Sussex County Library.)

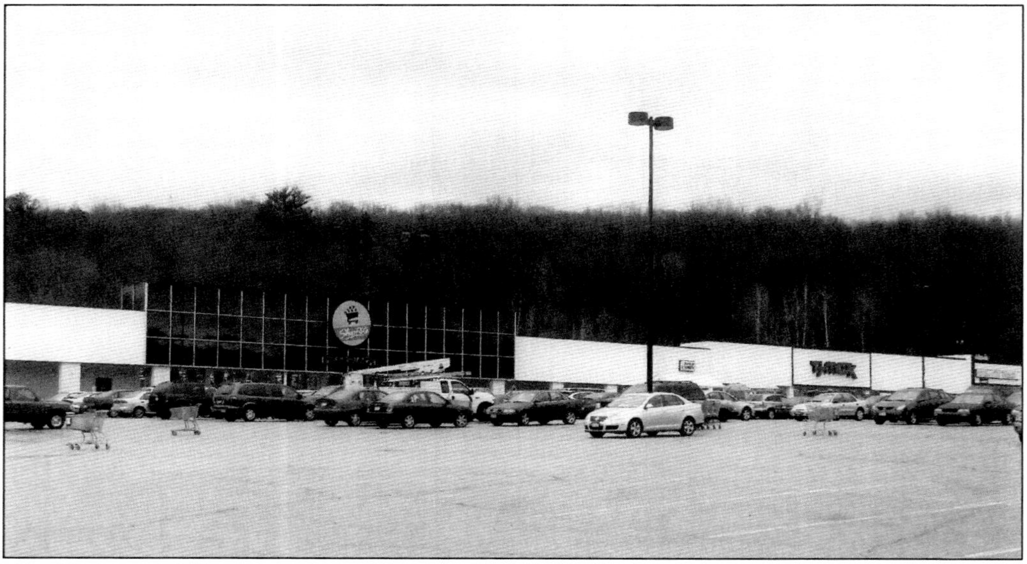

The Tri-State Mall opened in 1968 containing a Jamesway department store and a bank. The Shoprite and other small shops opened in 1969. After the Jamesway chain closed, the Shoprite supermarket relocated to the space used by the department store. It reopened in 1997 featuring a 59,000-square-foot replacement of a 31,000-square-foot store. A variety of businesses now fill the balance of the shopping plaza. (Photograph by Alicia C. Batko.)

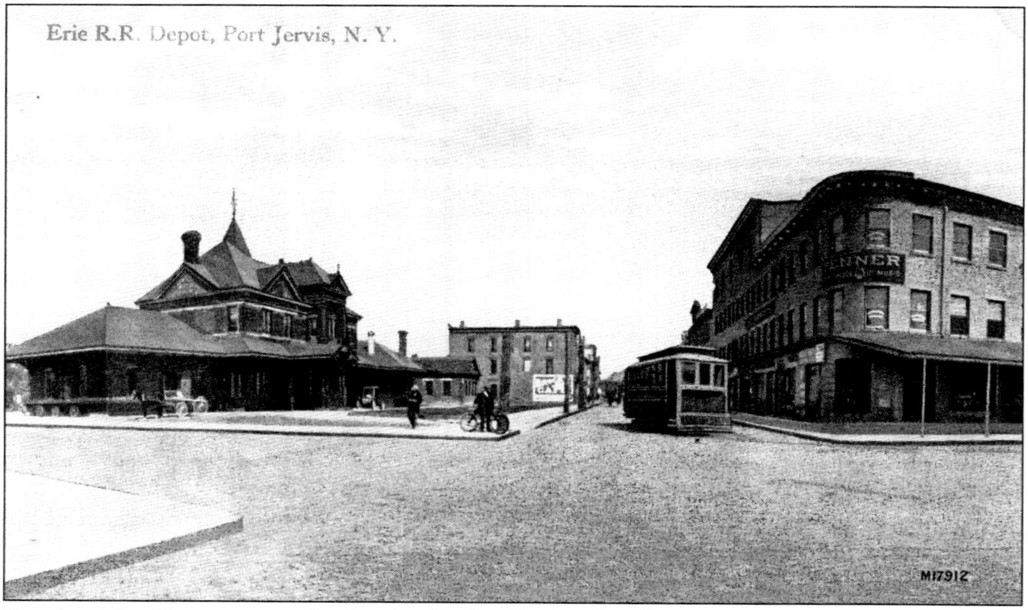

Port Jervis had been a major facility for the Erie Railroad and its successor, the Erie Lackawanna Railway. "Port," as it is still known to this day, was a railroad division point from the late 1800s through the 1970s. With the decline of the railroad and related industries, a ripple effect was felt in the surrounding communities. (Courtesy of Alicia C. Batko.)

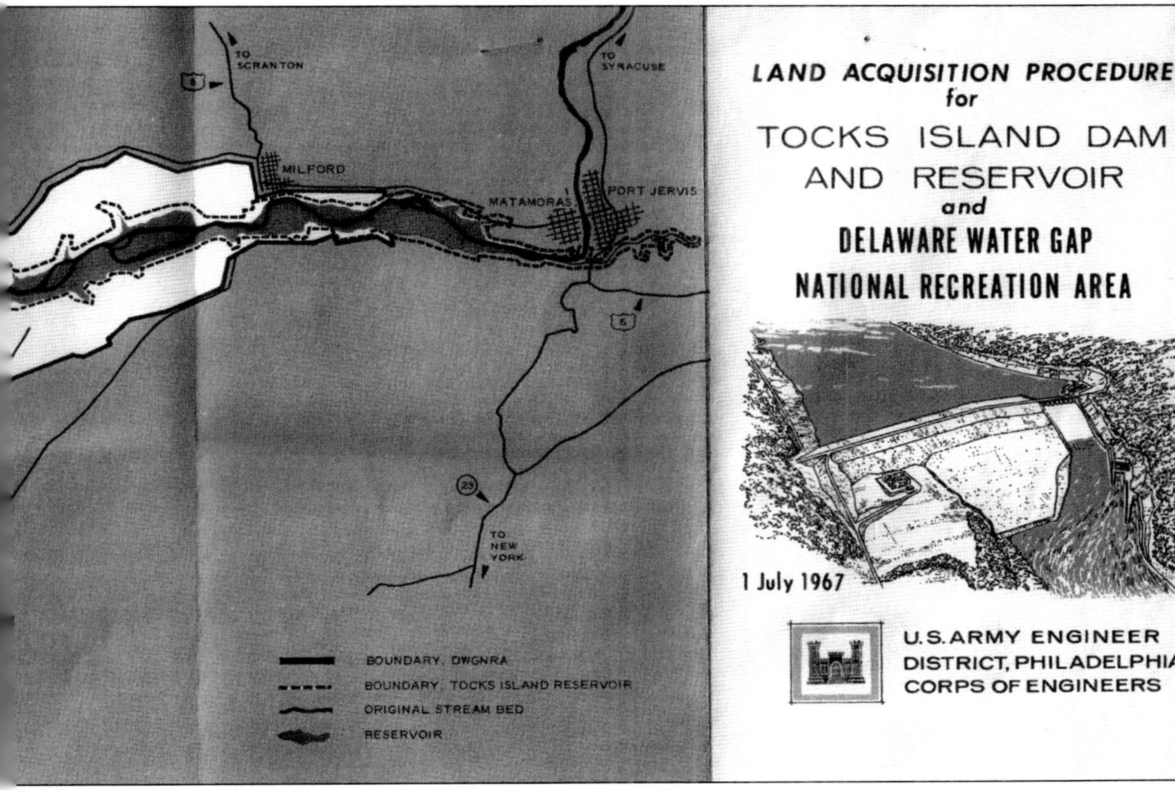

By 1967, a plan was made to acquire private property for public use. Such was the proposal for the creation of the Tocks Island Dam and reservoir project and the concurrent Delaware Water Gap National Recreation Area. A pamphlet was prepared to explain the basic policies of the Department of the Army for such acquisitions through the Army Corps of Engineers. The dotted line reflects the bounds of the anticipated reservoir. The diagram shows the full extent of the project and what had been originally planned. Had the reservoir been created, further acquisitions into Port Jervis would have occurred. (Courtesy of Alicia C. Batko.)

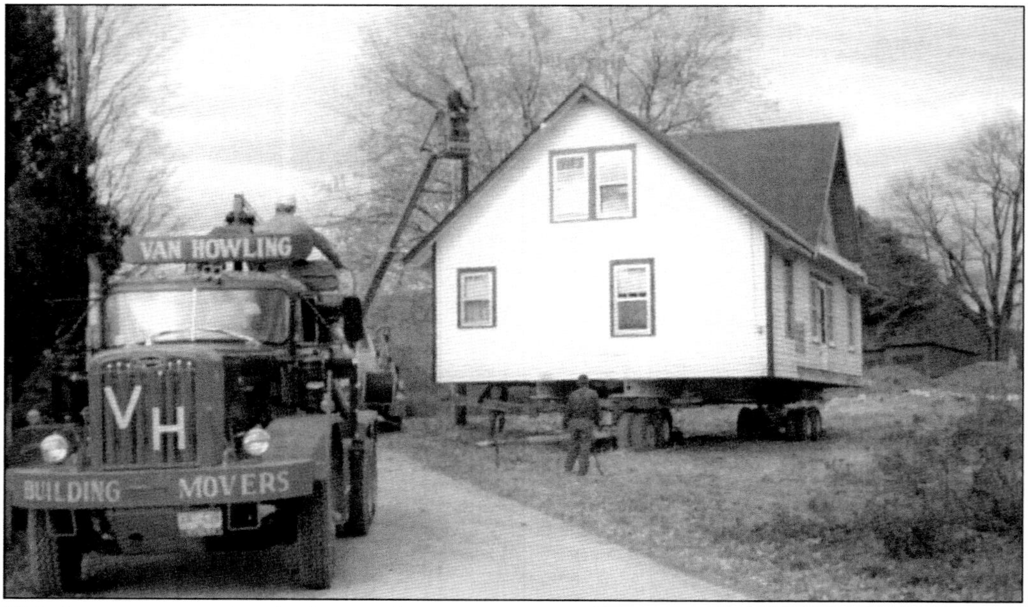

This is one manner in which some homes were spared destruction during the bridge and the Tocks Island Dam projects. This house had been owned by the William Hartrim family and sat on Bridge Road before its move and relocation to Clove Road. The entire frame of the house would be set on a flatbed and escorted to its new foundation, allowing for its survival. (Courtesy of Margorie DeGroat.)

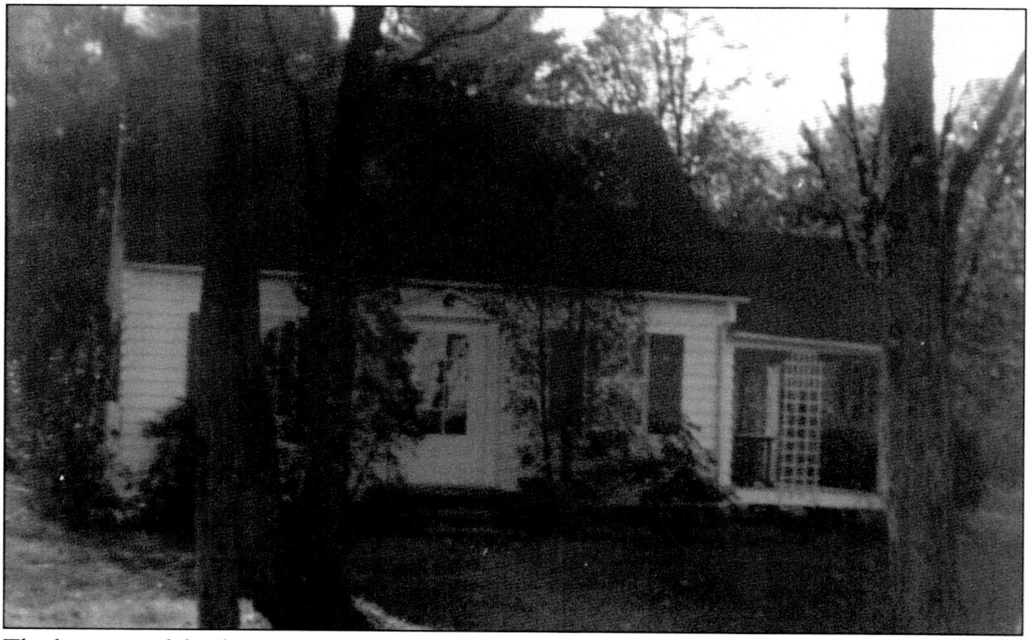

The location of this house is currently better known as the hunters' pull-in near the old Roberts farm. This was just one of the many structures that were saved from planned demolition by being acquired and moved to newer locations. Some recall it as the Thoma or Sauer place, and it now sits on Myrtle Drive.

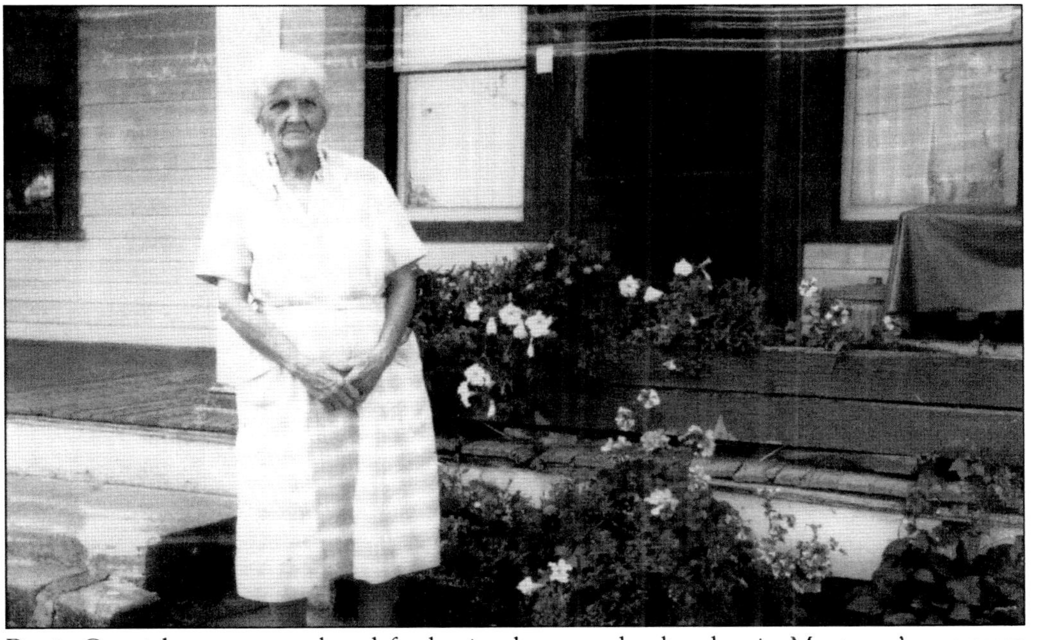

Donie Cortright was remembered for having been a schoolteacher in Montague's one-room schoolhouses. Her home sat at the convergence of Clove Road with State Route 31, later known as U.S. Route 206. Area residents still fondly recall last seeing her sitting on her porch. The building has been converted to residential and professional offices.

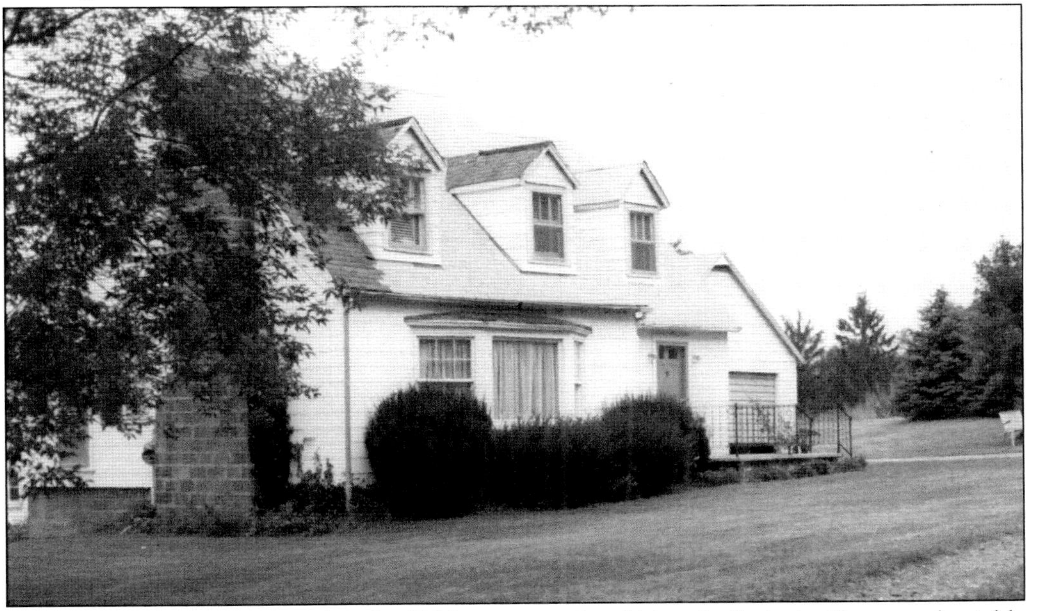

Many a home that was erected in the 1900s was considered historically insignificant and quickly vanished with the destruction and removals that the Army Corps of Engineers initiated for the reservoir project. This home sat to the left of an older stone home owned by John Teller, where a tree nursery business was run. This was William Teller's house and was built about 1946–1947. (Courtesy of Thomas Teller.)

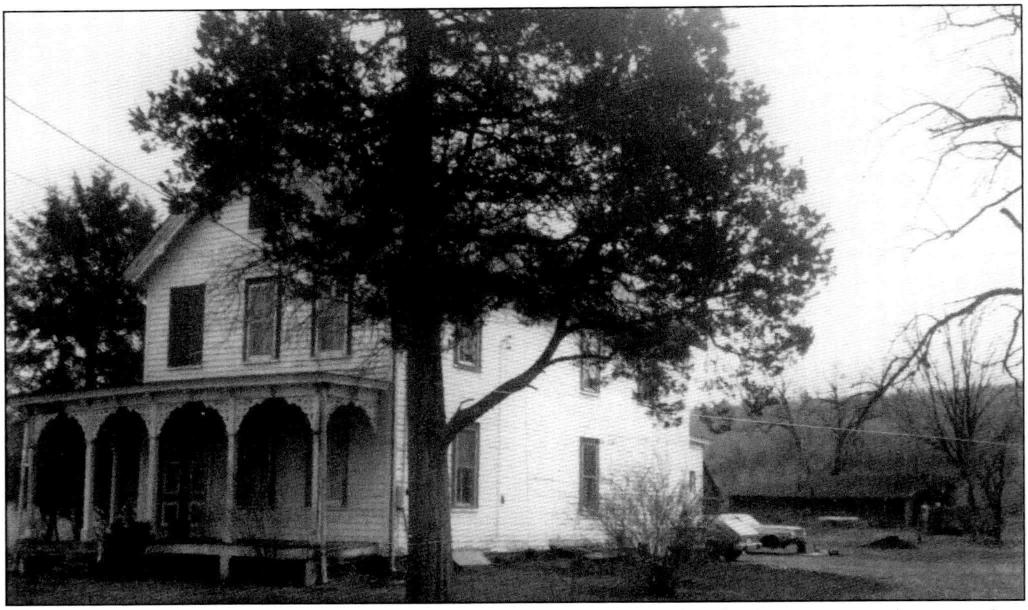

The Cuddeback-Pantis farmhouse would be portrayed in its splendor by a young photographer and that image published in the calendar he created to showcase what Tocks Island threatened. Owen Kanzler and others devoted themselves to capturing the essence of the river valley through photography, before the destruction began. This survived Tocks Island but was bulldozed when the state acquired it under Green Acres.

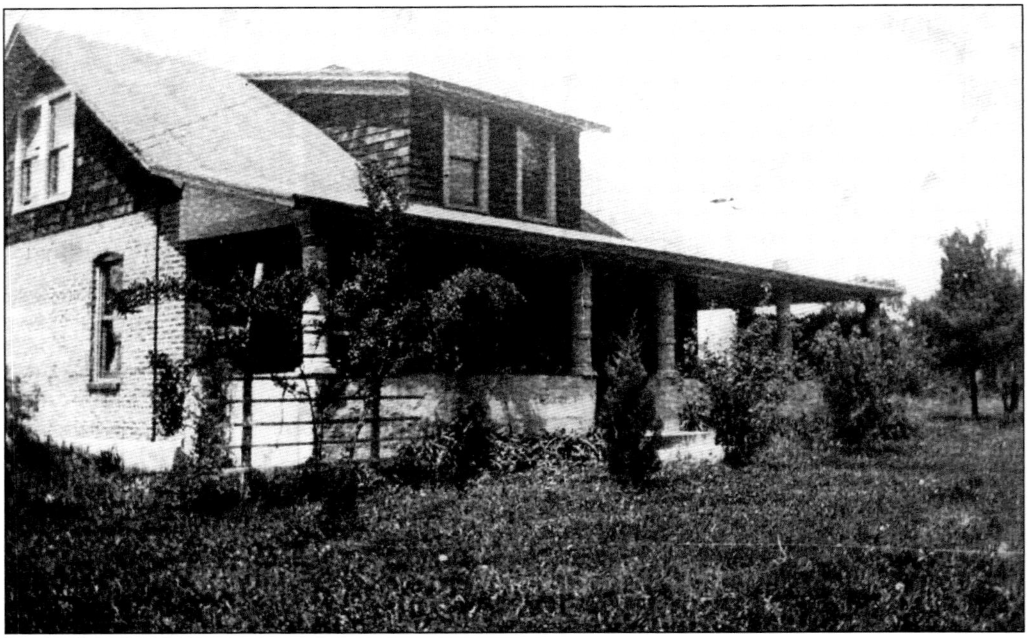

This location was known by the name of Ora Dell Farm when it was purchased by the Brigham family in 1965 from the Welling family. Both previous owners' wives' first names had been Ora, so it is safe to assume the name began with them. The house remains, although modified and modernized over the years. (Courtesy of Harold Brigham and Lori Brigham Mai.)

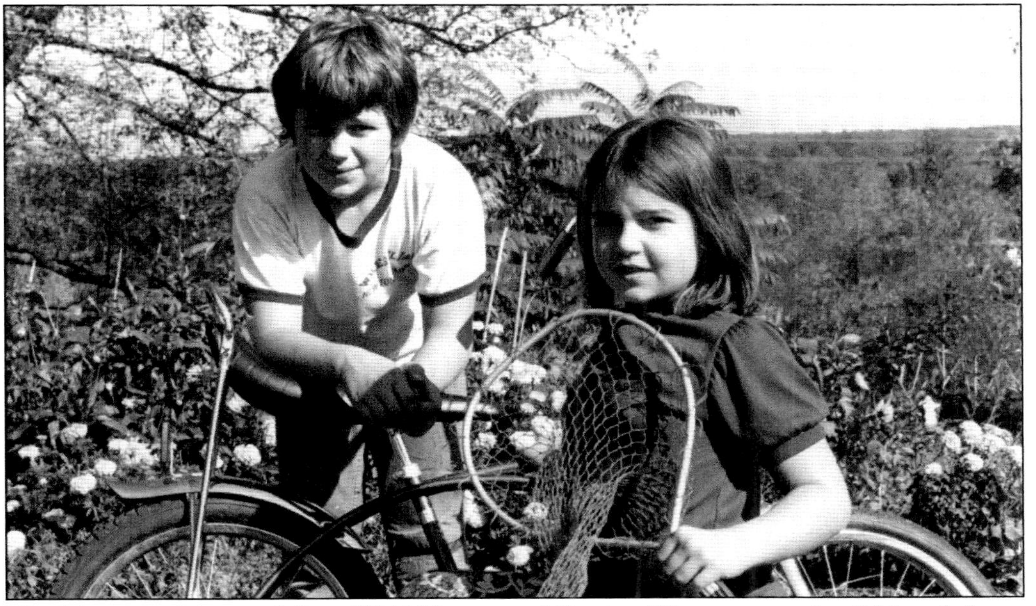

The Montague Memorial Post 10144 Veterans of Foreign Wars sponsored a fishing derby at the Cedar Ridge Campground in the mid-1970s that was followed by its annual picnic. Area youngsters aged 6 to 12 from Frankford, Sandyston, Montague, and Walpack were invited to participate in the contest. Siblings William and Rebecca Thompson show off their prizes of a Spider bike and fishing net. (Courtesy of Christine Thompson.)

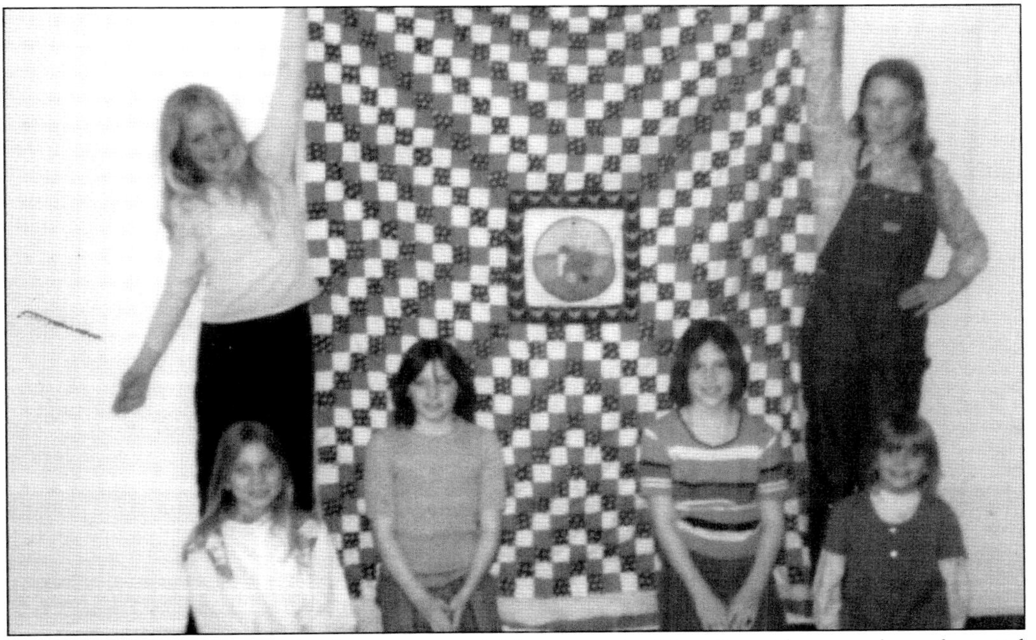

The country's bicentennial celebration in 1976 was marked locally with a number of special projects and observances. Each community group tried to contribute in some way. These Girl Scouts created a quilt. From left to right are (first row) Carol Williams, Donna Dougherty, Shelly Bowman, and Debra Williams; (second row) Kristy Roby and Debra Olszewski.

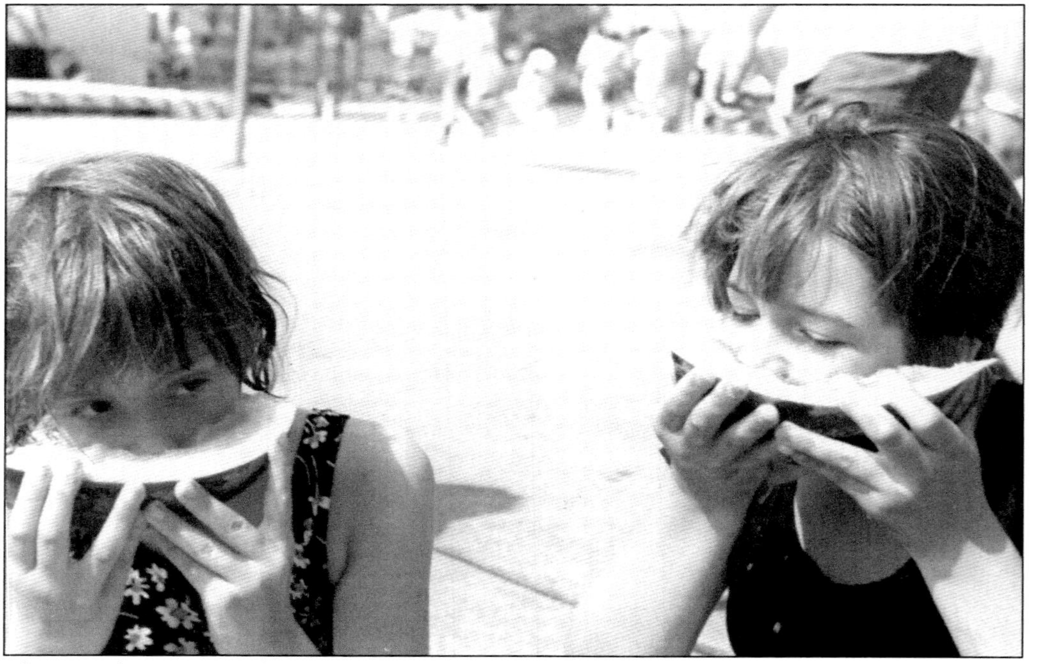

The town has sponsored a Montague Day celebration annually, which is a time for local talent to be enjoyed and for community organizations to come together to participate. It began on the local elementary school grounds with games and contests and families sharing a huge potluck gathering. When the Holiday Lake area evolved, the event was held there in 1976 and included a celebration of the nation's bicentennial. Popular were the watermelon-eating, pie-baking, and frog-jump contests. Square dances were held, and local bands performed. Doing a hobo skit are Rebecca (left) and her mother, Christine Thompson. (Courtesy of Christine Thompson.)

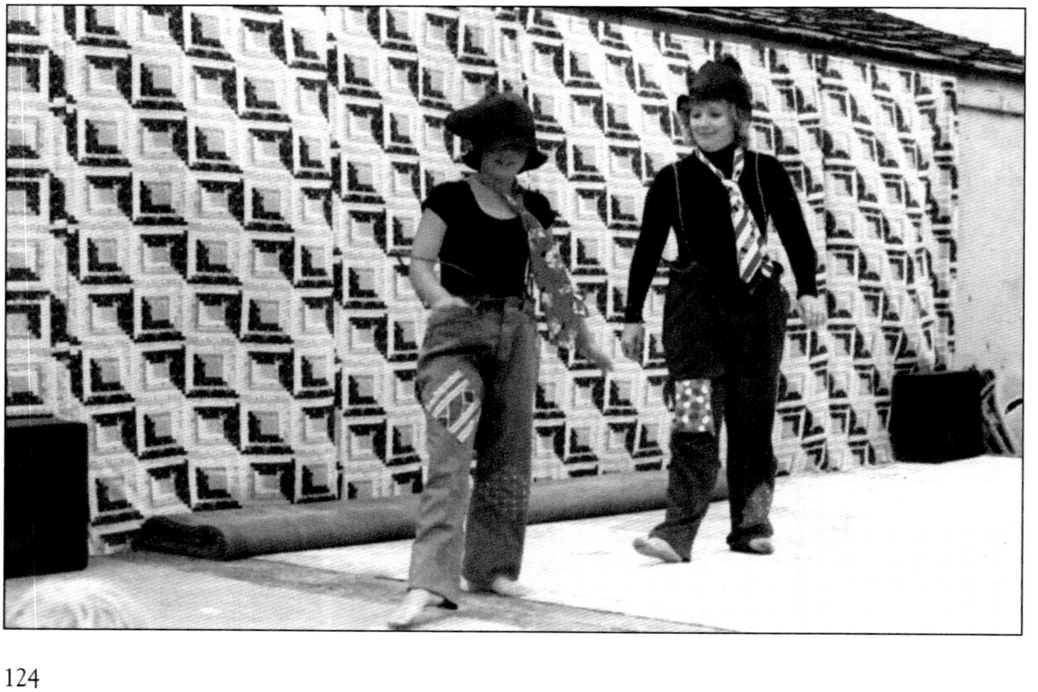

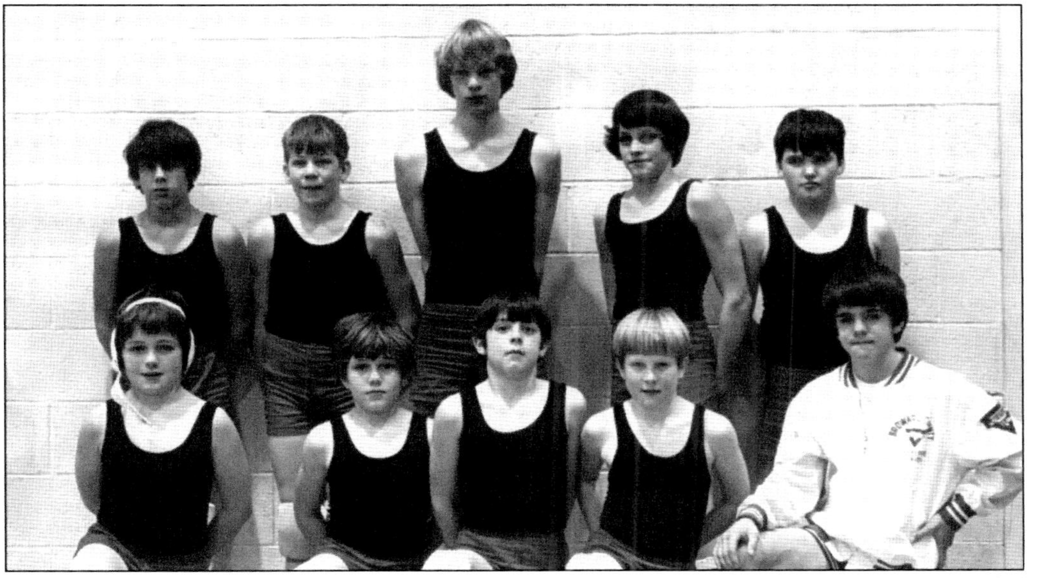

After the school added a gymnasium area, a wrestling team formed. Its first coaches included Louis Savacool and William Thompson. The Banach brothers, who became Olympic champions in 1984, had initially wrestled with Montague's local team. Shown from left to right are (first row) William Thompson, Michael Ellet, James TenHoeve, Arthur Aeberli, and Eric Savacool; (second row) Kevin TenHoeve, Robert Pollara, unidentified, Michael Dougherty, and John DePolito. (Courtesy of Christine Thompson.)

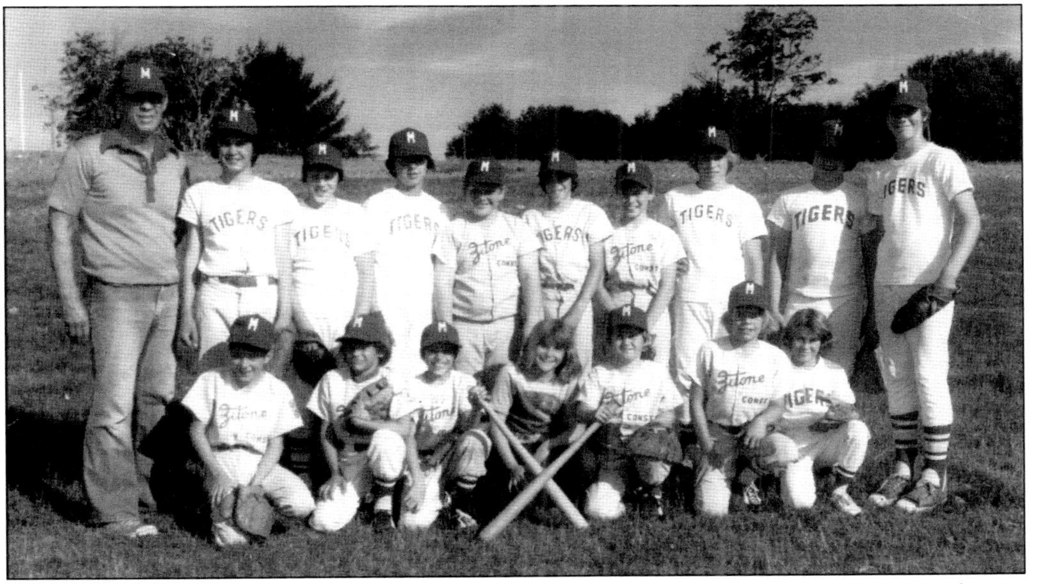

This Tigers Little League team played in its coach's field on the west side of Clove Road, near what later became the Holiday Lake area. Shown from left to right are (first row) Scott Biccum, Ramon Cortez, Christopher Lazar, Reneé Masset, Patrick Duffy, Steven Dutkus, and Catherine Abudasky; (second row) coach Earl Grathwohl, Greg ?, Timothy Conboy, James TenHoeve, George Jones, David Rock, Robert Avenatti, Michael Mann, William Thompson, and Paul Grathwohl. (Courtesy of Christine Thompson.)

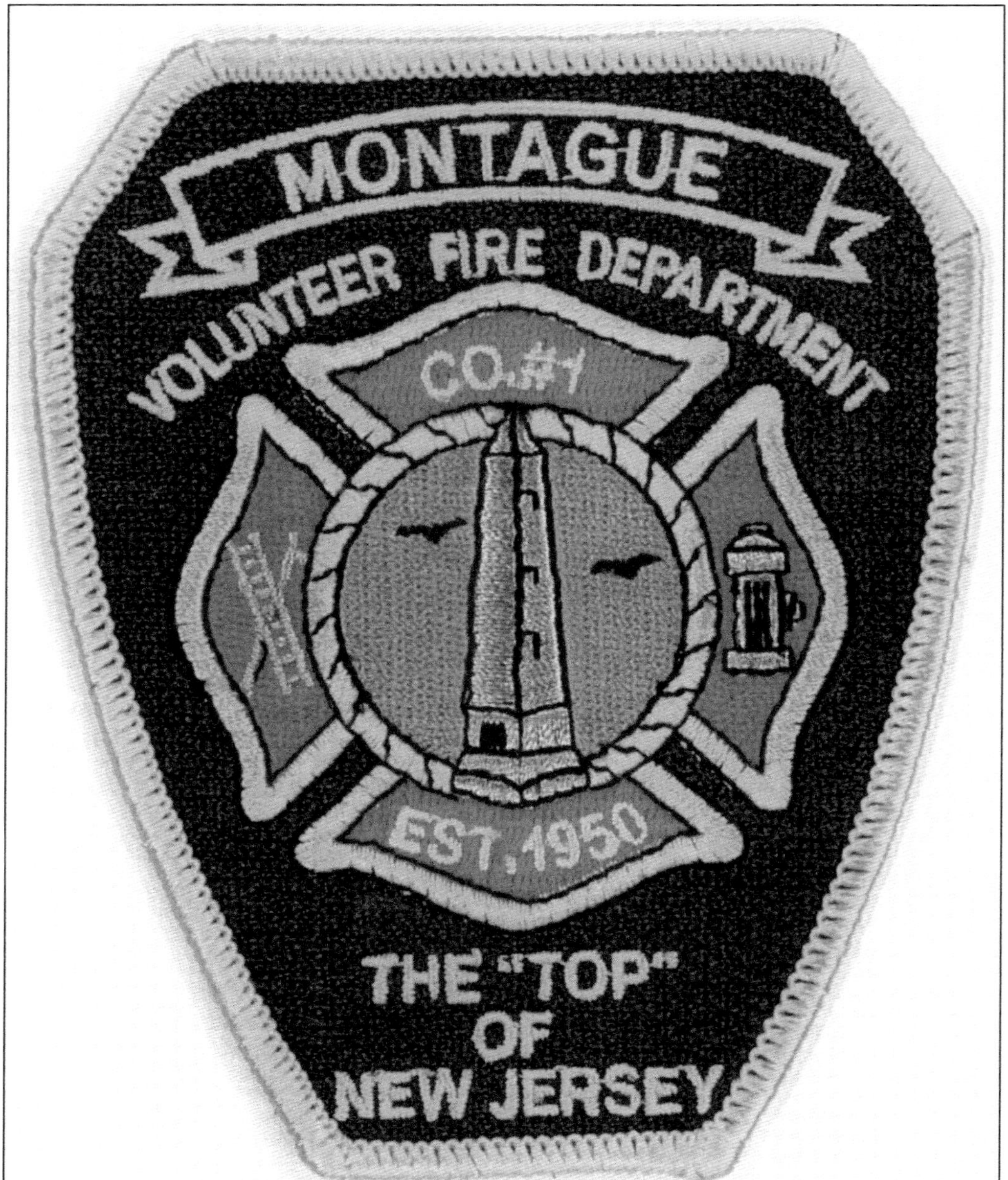

The town's volunteer fire department has grown since its inception, gaining additional fire and rescue vehicles over the years. The volunteers continue to serve the needs of a growing population, with fewer residents available to serve as had the locally employed men who initiated the company in 1950. Montague Township's population sunk to a low of 534 residents in 1920. It has since increased in population significantly, tripling in size from a prior boom period in 1850 when its population count was 1,010. Plans are underway to build an expanded firehouse at a new location. The fire company emblem proudly reflects the township's claim of being at the "Top of New Jersey." (Courtesy of Montague Volunteer Fire Department.)

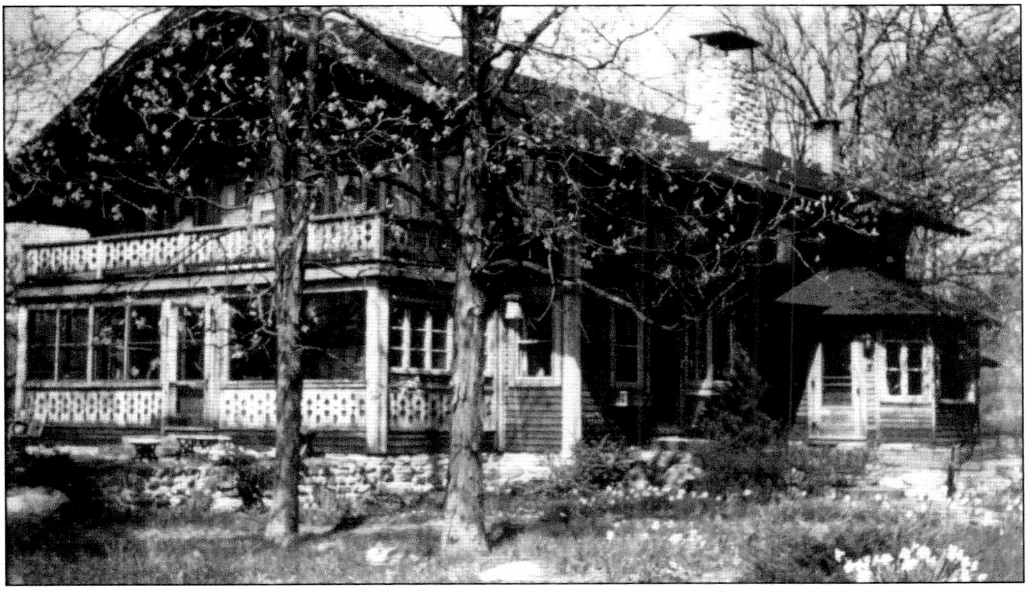

Montague was sought for peaceful retreats, and Karl and Gretchen Keuffel Keller acquired property near High Point Park, building this Swiss chalet–style home. He was an executive of the Keuffel and Esser Company, which played a nationally significant role in the technological development of the United States in the mid-1900s. The property transferred to Fountain House of New Jersey, Inc., where High Point Farm is run. (Courtesy of Lina Scheidegger.)

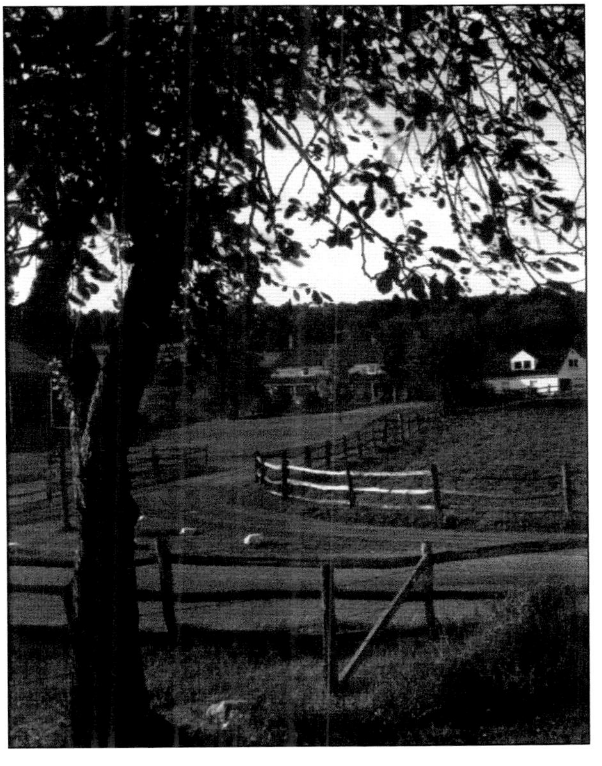

The Westfall Farm has evolved over the years. After modernizing the dairy business in the 1940s, Charles Mortimer donated the award-winning Holstein herd to the Bordentown Reformatory in 1966, when the dairy was no longer viable to maintain. In its place came Morgan horses that also won coveted ribbons. Now protected under farmland preservation, the winery still maintains the farm's blue-ribbon status. (Courtesy of Duke and Loren Mortimer.)